SKILLS FOR LIFELONG LEARNING

UNIVERSITY OF PHOENIX

Pearson
Custom
Publishing

Cover art: "Color Conscience III," by Christina Lanzl

Printed in the United States of America

10 9 8 7 6 5

Please visit our website at www.pearsoncustom.com

ISBN 0–536–02128–7

BA 990627

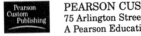

PEARSON CUSTOM PUBLISHING
75 Arlington Street, Boston, MA 02116
A Pearson Education Company

Copyright Acknowledgments

Contributors

The University gratefully acknowledges the contribution of the following persons to the completion of this course of study:

- Cheryl Dorenbush, MA, faculty member
- Kenneth B. Hunt, PhD, JD, faculty member
- Ernest Price, MA, MPA, faculty member
- Virginia Mayer Chan, PhD, faculty member
- Ken White, PhD, MEd, faculty member

Table of Contents

Excerpts from Peak Learning
Ronald Gross

VI. Improving Your Learning, Reading, and Memory Skills

VII. Developing Your Critical and Creative Thinking

VIII. Developing Your Optimal Learning Environment

Excerpts from Overview of the Internet
Virginia Mayer Chan

Excerpts from Business and Professional Communication
Wallace Schmidt and Greg Gardner

Excerpts from Organizational Communication: An Introduction to Communication and Human Relation Strategies
Ken W. White

◆ ◆ ◆ ◆ ◆ ◆ ◆ ◆ ◆

Excerpts from

Peak Learning

*A Master Course in Learning
How to Learn*

Ronald Gross

◆ ◆ ◆ ◆ ◆ ◆ ◆ ◆ ◆

I.
Peak Learning—Skills for Today and Tomorrow ◆◆◆◆

What is a peak learner? It is someone who has learned how to learn in the fullest sense of the word. Although this label may be unfamiliar, chances are you already know peak learners. In fact, you've probably been one yourself from time to time. For example, think about those occasions when your mind has quickly soaked up information about a new subject that fascinated you—whether new recipes or batting averages—seemingly without effort. Or when you got a sudden flash of insight about how to solve a difficult problem that had been stumping you. These were moments of Peak Learning.

O! this learning, what a thing it is.
WILLIAM SHAKESPEARE

Perhaps you can also think of people you know who constantly are getting excited and involved in some new interest and running to tell you the latest new information they've found out about it. While they are in that first flush of enthusiasm, the excitement and delight they find in their new discoveries seems contagious. They too are peak learners.

At work, you probably know colleagues—or competitors—who miraculously seem to stay on top of new developments. They can sift through stacks of memos, newsletters, advertisements, correspondence, magazines, and books to find just the nuggets of fact they need. Their capacity to handle that flood of information and ideas gives them a decided edge. They too are peak learners.

Learning has a different *feel* for these people. It isn't just a matter of going back to school to sit in a classroom and listen to a teacher. It has little to do with tests or grades. Instead, this type of learning springs from within them: it is self-education. Whether sparked by joy or driven by need, it expresses who they want to become, what they want to be able to do or to know about.

Peak learners have a number of distinctive characteristics. First, they feel best about themselves when they are learning something new. They are unusually open to and interested in new experiences, ideas, and information, whether they be sampling a new cuisine, listening to a scientist describe her work, or reading an article on corporate mergers. Typically, they do not think of learning as some special activity; for them, learning is just part of the way in which they habitually live. They take pride in meeting their daily challenges, from a newspaper's cross-word puzzle to mastering a new computer program.

Learning can be defined as the process of remembering what you are interested in.
RICHARD SAUL WURMAN

Another characteristic of peak learners is that they are keenly aware of how much they don't know, but that doesn't bother them! As they wander along the shoreline of wonder—the boundary between what they know and the vast sea of things they could know—they feel exhilarated by the prospect of constantly learning new things. They know that there are always things to know more about, to appreciate more deeply, or to learn to do. Because they are not afraid of their own ignorance, such learners aren't afraid to ask dumb questions or admit they don't understand something the first time it's explained. Instead of pretending to understand, they keep asking until they do. They then take action to use their new information quickly, to draw connections between what they already knew and what they have just learned. Peak learners look for similarities and differences, make analogies, and try to find out what something is *like* in order to understand it.

Peak learners have learned enormously from important life experiences and in other ways outside the usual channels of study. They seek a wide range of helpful resources for learning, rather than giving up if their usual sources of information run dry on a particular topic.

Confidence in one's ability to learn and to understand is another key characteristic of peak learners. They know that anything that one human being truly understands can be understood equally well by others willing to follow the right steps. They know how to judge sources of information shrewdly and how to narrow down any gap in an explanation. These learners have a repertoire of simple but powerful tools for processing information, tools that help to select the information they need, to store it in memory, and to use it.

Finally, peak learners believe that investing time in their own personal growth is the best investment they can make in the future, occupational or personal. They begin to learn new things now in order to prepare for the life they want to be leading in five years.

These and other characteristics are what define a peak learner—somcone who has made learning a part of his or her lifestyle.

Our lives today call on each of us to become a peak learner. When you think of the people you most admire, or of yourself at your best, it is easy to recognize that this sort of learning is a major part of the *good life*. At work or in our personal lives, practically anything we want will involve some kind of learning above and beyond the knowledge and skills we got in school.

Anyone who stops learning is old, whether at twenty or eighty. Anyone who keeps learning stays young. The greatest thing in life is to keep your mind young.

HENRY FORD

Why Be a Peak Learner?

We are the first generation of human beings born into a world that will change *drastically* during the course of our lives. As the noted anthropologist Margaret Mead pointed out, only two hundred years ago people knew that the world they grew up in would be about the same when they died. A few things might change, but the basic texture and quality of their lives would remain constant throughout their life span. Things simply changed more slowly. When she pointed this out some thirty years ago, Mead could already see that modern men and women no longer had that assurance.

In 1970, in fact, Alvin Toffler introduced the term *future shock* to describe a pervasive reaction he saw developing: People seemed to be overwhelmed by accelerating change. In every field, knowledge was doubling every decade or so. Doctors and engineers found that the information they had struggled to master in their professional training had a *half-life* of about fifteen years—after that, half of it was no longer true or relevant. New discoveries seemed to be made every week, and they resulted in newer ways of doing things or new kinds of gadgets almost every day.

Today, the pace has not let up. At this very moment, it is already trite to talk about an information explosion. As computers have become ever more capable of generating quantities of new information, we human beings have been increasingly challenged to keep learning and to remain up-to-date. Continual growth has become a requirement of contemporary living. We must be able to master new facts, new skills, and even new attitudes and beliefs.

At work, for example, most Americans will change fields three or four times in their careers—to say nothing of even more frequent changes of *jobs*. All of these changes require substantial learning. Indeed, in today's world, *learning a living* is an integral part of earning a living for most people in professional, managerial, and other high-level jobs. Change is so rapid in the business world that virtually every day presents new challenges and opportunities to learn.

The illiterate of the year 2000 will not be the individual who cannot read and write, but the one who cannot learn, unlearn, and relearn.

ALAN TOFFLER

In our personal affairs as well, the mobility and fluidity of social life means we have to be more adaptable, better able to learn quickly. Just consider how many of these areas you needed to learn about in the last year in response to needs of your own, your family, friends, or your company:

◆ Health and medical developments, including new knowledge about diet, exercise, and stress or new treatments for specific illnesses.

◆ Economic developments affecting your business or profession, such as new tax regulations, investment opportunities or dangers, or financial innovations in your field.

◆ Technological developments that have an impact on your career and personal life, including new machines, appliances, materials, and methods of information transfer.

◆ Social developments around the country and in your own community that have an effect on your lifestyle or that concern you as a citizen, such as housing trends, employment policies, or legislative proposals.

◆ Changes in your personal or business relationships that require you to learn more about the causes and consequences of your own behavior or that of others.

In short, learning in our time has become a stern necessity. "Under the conditions of modern life," warned the philosopher Alfred North Whitehead fifty years ago, "the rule is absolute: The race that neglects trained intelligence is doomed." Today we must update Whitehead's warning. Under today's conditions of future shock, *this* rule is absolute: The individual who neglects self-development is doomed.

Leading experts in our emerging world of ever more rapid change agree that *learning throughout life* is now a key to personal success. "In the new information society where the only constant is change," says John Naisbitt, author of *Megatrends*, "we can no longer expect to get an education and be done with it. There is no one education, no one skill, that lasts a lifetime now. Like it or not, the information society has turned all of us into lifelong learners." And Alvin Toffler agrees that "in the world of the future, the new illiterate will be the person who has not learned how to learn."

The Learning Tradition

It is surprising to realize that school-learning is a relatively recent invention. One of the earliest roots of Western culture was the Greek city-state of Athens, home to Plato and Socrates and to a vital kind of learning that went far beyond classrooms or grades. Instead, citizens discussed important questions in their open-air market, or *agora*, at the baths or the gym, or over a late, post-theater dinner. Learning was inextricably a part of life, work, and leisure; it drew on every resource of the community: its arts, crafts, professions, history, and laws. "Not I, but the city teaches," declared Socrates.

Belief in a similar kind of learning was a key part of the thinking of the founding fathers of the United States. Their republic could work only if the people could make their own appraisals of their needs and wants. The national ideal was intellectual self-reliance and personal responsibility for self-development.

Liberty cannot be preserved without a general knowledge among the people.... Let us dare to read, think, speak, and write.

JOHN ADAMS

Our country's political system is based on the belief that each of us can function, in however modest a degree, as free-thinking, independent centers of understanding, judgment, and action. We have encouraged free speech and a free press because we think the best way to find the truth is for the full range of ideas and information to be debated openly by citizens.

"Jefferson was a great believer in schooling," points out educational historian Lawrence Cremin, "but it never occurred to him that schooling would be the chief educational influence on the young. Schooling might provide technical skills and basic knowledge, but it was the press and participation in politics that really educated the citizenry." Thus, the early leaders of the United States did not, as we so often do, make the mistake of confusing schooling with education, nor the still worse mistake of judging people by their diplomas.

We can find many exemplars of this potent tradition of self-education from Ben Franklin and Abraham Lincoln through Thomas Edison and Henry Ford to Malcolm X and Eric Hoffer in our own day.

Now that tradition is under siege. While the sheer mass of information grows beyond the capacity of many, we also find our beliefs in independent thinking and self-education threatened by the conformist pressures of our ever-present, ever-distracting media—what cogent critic of television Neil Postman calls the "and now ... this" mentality. Our consideration of vital public issues is reduced to the two-minute TV news story and the fifteen-second sound bite.

Another serious threat grows from our mistaken belief that credentials are trustworthy guides to competence. More and more professions try to protect the reputation of their practitioners by creating licensing requirements. And, inevitably, they produce more and more professionals whose major qualification is that they could pass the licensing examination.

As critic and novelist Philip Wylie put it shortly before he died, "If there are any Americans with an education sufficient for useful criticism and constructive proposals, one fact about them will be sure: They will be self-educated.... They will be people who learned how to learn and to want to learn—people who did not stop learning when they received

---

LACHES: *Did you never observe that some persons, who have had no teachers, are more skillful than those who have, in some things?*

SOCRATES: Yes ... but you would not be very willing to trust them if they only professed to be masters of their art, unless they could show some proof of their skill or excellence in one or more works.

PLATO

---

their degree or degrees—people who developed a means of evaluation of all knowledge in order to determine what they had to understand for useful thought—people who, then, knew what they did not know and learned what was necessary."

Peak learners are those people. They are increasing in numbers and becoming recognized in the very nick of time. Their abilities to make learning a continuing part of their living may offer our best chance of survival as a culture, a species, a planet.

Breaking Through to Peak Learning

By now I hope I've given you a good idea of what Peak Learning is about, why it is important, and how it restores a part of the Western cultural tradition we've neglected. My guess is that at this point you're intrigued by the idea of becoming more of a peak learner, but that you have some reservations about the process.

That's entirely natural. In the workshops I give, about 85 percent of the participants feel the same way. That's why we always start off with some ghost busting. We puncture the major fears and anxieties about learning that still haunt most of us from our days in school. We'll deal with these in detail later, but let me just tick them off here to assure you that they will not interfere with your learning when you use Peak Learning methods.

Anxiety about learning. Throughout school and college days, we were constantly being told to learn things—but never told *how.* "Learn the vocabulary words in this chapter for a quiz on Friday" was a typical assignment. And then? Either we sat down and tried to stare at the list of words until, somehow, we found a way to store them in our heads until the quiz, or we didn't find a way and so became fearful and frustrated, because we didn't know what to do when we sat down to learn. But once you really learn *how* to learn, that anxiety will disappear. Peak Learning is relaxing and enjoyable because you have specific strategies you can select to master facts, concepts, and principles.

Anxiety about time. Typically, the people who come to my workshops have fully packed schedules, both personal and professional. They can't really afford to *take time out* to study. But Peak Learning methods are concurrent with your other activities. Your learning is part of your personal planning and decision-making, part of your professional and personal reading, part of your social contacts and leisure, part of your work and your family time.

Negative myths about learning. School experience has left many of us with a negative attitude toward learning, a nagging sense that learning is boring, tedious, lonely, or unrelated to our real interests. It has been

---

Cultivate your faith in yourself as a learner. Research shows that adults are better learners than children, if they have the patience to be beginners.

MARILYN FERGUSON

---

easy to think that learning must be passive, involving sitting and listening to a teacher or struggling to absorb material from a book. None of this is true with Peak Learning, which is first and foremost learning what you are most interested in and excited by. Furthermore, Peak Learning is fundamentally *active*. Not only do you choose what to learn, you also choose how you learn it from a range of techniques most appropriate to your personal learning style.

I'll come back to each of these difficulties and others later. For now, rest assured that Peak Learning is not only something desirable, a way to develop a greater appreciation of life, but also something possible for anyone who wants to try it.

The Principles of Peak Learning

The principles of Peak Learning are based on some fundamental truths about learning and growth—many still considered heretical by educators—that can liberate you from over-reliance on schooling and strengthen you for the adventure of self-development. Some of these truths are:

- ◆ Adults who take command of their own learning often master more things, and master them better, than those who rely on being

taught. They tend to have greater zest in the learning process, retain more of what they have learned, and make better use of it in their lives.

◆ Adults learn in different ways than children. We have a different sense of ourselves, of our time, and of what's worth learning and why.

◆ No one can learn *for* you, any more than someone can eat for you. *To learn* is an active verb; your education is something you must tailor to yourself, not something you can get ready-made.

◆ No particular way of learning is in itself superior to another. How you learn depends on your temperament, circumstances, needs, tastes, or ambitions. Success in learning depends not on the subject itself or the conditions (how, where, and when) of learning, but basically on the learner's engagement—her or his fascination with the subject.

There are six fundamental principles that define the Peak Learning system. All of the specific techniques and strategies you will learn in this book are derived from them.

1. *You can learn how to learn.* As you will see in Chapter II, Peak Learning is not based on wishful thinking or pious hopes but on sound scientific discoveries. Twin revolutions in the study of the human brain and the psychology of learning have overturned the long-held myths that learning is an inborn talent and that

people become too old to learn. We now know that the brain is organized in many complex ways, that it is an active, processing organ influenced by our bodies and emotions, and that, with the right stimulation, it continues to grow throughout our lives! We have learned that traditional theories of learning, derived from inaccurate early models of the brain, can be replaced with more effective approaches that enlist our total human capacity in the cause of our learning.

2. *You are already a superb learner on occasion, and you can build on that natural skill to make the rest of your learning easy, enjoyable, and productive.* Chapter III discusses many of the blocks to learning we've inherited from school days and shows how they can be removed. You'll see that some of our earliest and most enjoyable learning came before our potential was blocked, a state that is called Flow Learning. I'll explain the nature of this state and provide several different methods for getting back into that state of easy, effortless, enraptured learning. Chapter IV will build upon these techniques, offering two other strategies to enhance your learning confidence.

3. *You have your own personal learning style, which you can identify, take advantage of, and strengthen to become an even more accomplished learner.* While most of our previous education relied on a single style of learning for everyone, we now know that everyone has his or her own unique combination of skills, talents, and preferences for getting and using information. Chapter V covers several ways to help you identify your own best approach. You'll learn how to discover the right mixture of facts, feelings, guidance, independence, and resources to help you learn in the way that is most natural for you.

4. *You learn best when you are most active mentally (and sometimes physically), making your own decisions about what, how, where, and when to learn and using strategies that activate your mind.* Chapter VI covers the best of the current strategies and techniques for active learning. These specific, practical approaches help you learn by putting you in control, giving you a full range of resources to steer your learning in the most rewarding directions, and speed you on your way.

5. *You can design your optimal learning environment, one that makes your learning more comfortable and hence more effective.* It's easy to be brainwashed into believing that learning happens only if you're squirming uncomfortably in a classroom, lecture hall, or library. In fact, the opposite is true. The more you can create a room or area where you can be alert, comfortable, and productive, the better your learning will be. Electronic brain

gyms that offer refreshing workouts for your nervous system are just emerging from the laboratory, and a vast range of computer-assisted learning resources are at your disposal.

6. *You learn most enjoyably by choosing from a rich array of media, methods, and experiences.* This is especially easy today, as the treasures of the human mind and spirit are available to all of us in unprecedented measure. Inexpensive paperbacks enable each of us to build a finer library than emperors could command two hundred years ago. Fine reproduction and printing provides an entree into what André Malraux calls "the museum without walls," so that you can see more magnificent art in one afternoon in the library than Goethe could view on the grand tour of European cities in the nineteenth century. Crafts, skills, and technologies that once were accessible only through lengthy apprenticeships are now available through self-study or expert instruction. The greatest teachers, scholars, and scientists of the age can be brought into our living rooms via video and audio cassettes.

Every man who rises above the common level has received two educations: the first from his teachers; the second, more personal and important, from himself.

EDWARD GIBBON

In short, modern technology has made new means of learning available to everyone, everywhere, at every point in one's life. It puts at your disposal just what you want, just when you need it. You can bring the most inspiring authorities in any field into your home, your car, or your vacation retreat or communicate with them via phone, computer, or mail. You can suit your own style by learning not just via books and teachers, but through simulations, games, and action projects.

Making Peak Learning Work for You

The key to becoming a peak learner is to develop your own *program*—a clear, systematic set of learning techniques. Most of us have no such program. We've managed to pick up a more or less random collection of learning tricks over the years: some principles of speed reading, some tricks to improve memorization, and perhaps a few pointers on taking good notes.

These separate skills have only limited usefulness. What good does it do, for example, to take great notes on the wrong book or spend four hours studying when you could derive much more information in only two hours? If we don't have the skills to use what we learn effectively, the greatest training program in the world won't provide much lasting value.

The key to greater success is to go beyond individual techniques. A good metaphor for this process is *orchestration*, used by Charles Garfield in his book, *Peak Performance: Mental Training Techniques of*

Anyone who can read and write can keep some form of New Diary—a personal book in which creativity, play, and self-therapy interweave, foster, and complement each other.

TRISTINE RAINER

---

the World's Greatest Athletes. In Garfield's words, the point of the orchestration idea is that "individual skills are enormously enhanced when they are blended together as a whole."

That's what this book will enable you to do. In learning techniques, as in so much of life, the whole is greater than the sum of its parts. Peak Learning is most successful when you harness the best skills you already have, complement them with the new techniques you'll learn here, and use them together to become all you are capable of being.

Your Learning Log

As you embark on your personal adventure of learning how to learn, the first strategy is to keep track of your progress right from the start in a learning log. Beginning such a log now is taking a major step in getting the most out of this book.

First, your log will be the place to do the exercises that appear throughout these pages. For example, you will be creating *mind maps*, conducting *instant replays* of significant experiences, *idea breeding* to create your own new concepts, posing penetrating questions that will guide your inquiry in new fields, and using dozens of other new techniques. By completing these activities in a learning log, you will multiply the benefits from each one.

Second, there is a tremendous benefit to your learning that arises out of writing. A learning log is vital because writing is itself one of the most powerful learning processes. "Writing is how we think our way into a subject and make it our own," says William Zinser in his inspiring book, *Writing to Learn:* "Writing enables us to find out what we know—and what we don't know—about whatever we're trying to learn ... writing and learning [are] the same process."

The most important benefit of your log will be the picture you will be building of *yourself* as a learner. The log will display, visually, the methods and techniques that you find most congenial. It will reveal, especially in review, the kinds of learning activities you enjoy and can use to greatest advantage in your personal learning goals.

In short, your learning log becomes a visual record of your mind's activity in learning. Its special *benefits* (different from the benefits of the typical diary or personal journal) are:

- ◆ You will create your own vivid portrayal of the ideas in the fields that are meaningful to you.

- ◆ You will develop a flexible playground for indulging your personal learning style by translating and transforming your subject into the medium and mode you prefer. You can write, draw, or doodle in your log to help yourself remember and explore new ideas.

- ◆ You will build creatively on what you are learning with your own insights and discover connections among the things you are learning that would not have emerged in any other way.

- ◆ You will be able to easily access the most important materials you have collected for subsequent reflection or further development.

- ◆ You will have a gratifying record of how much you've done and how your skills of learning are developing, which may prove useful at some point in showing others what and how you've learned.

- ◆ You will have a record for review that will be pleasurable and powerful because it is formed by your own interests.

Reading maketh a full man; conference a ready man; and writing an exact man.
FRANCIS BACON

Learning logs of this kind are behind most great learners. History brims with examples: Leonardo da Vinci's notebooks are coveted by collectors worldwide; Benjamin Franklin's journals have inspired generations of autodidacts; Thomas Edison's logs are so numerous that they fill a warehouse in New Jersey; Buckminster Fuller created miles of notebooks.

Yet most of us are unaware of the essential role of logs in the learning process. When we see the finished products of accomplished learners, whether they are artists, entrepreneurs, or politicians, it's easy to forget the years of previous learning. The finished product, whether a symphony or a treaty, seems to our uneducated eyes to appear full blown, the result of a single, clear, complete inspiration.

Creativity is often portrayed as a lightning flash, exploding mysteriously out of nowhere. However, a less dramatic but more useful model is the beehive. Honeybees tirelessly buzz about, visiting this flower and that, tasting each one. These thousands of intimate visits ultimately result in a mass of sweet honey, a concentration of the nectar of countless flowers. The products of human genius, likewise, are the result of the dedicated pursuit of small gains.

As consumers of ideas, we generally see only Edison's "one percent of inspiration," the tiniest tip of the iceberg. The remaining 99 percent, the trial and error, the blind alleys, disjointed observations, and dream musings, lie hidden from view. As a peak learner, you work on that invisible 99 percent in your journal.

Creating Your Learning Log

***Use a three-ring binder*.** This allows you to add items, remove them, and change the order of the pages. It gives you total creative control.

Every man is his own Pygmalion, and spends his life fashioning himself. And, in fashioning himself, for good or ill, he fashions the human race and its future.

I.F. STONE

***Buy some kind of note pad you can carry everywhere*.** You must develop the habit of jotting down thoughts as they occur to you. Forget about "making a mental note"—write it down. Our memories simply aren't built to move spontaneous thoughts into long-term memory. You'll lose 90 percent of your best ideas if you don't make some note of them the moment they occur. If you want to start out simply, you can carry a piece of 8-1/2" x 11" paper folded to quarter-size, which provides enough space for the spontaneous thoughts you're likely to have during one day. A 5-1/2" x 3-1/4" leather slip-holder holds five or six slips that size.

Whenever you make a note pad entry, transfer the thought to your journal that same day or shortly thereafter. This gives you a chance to permanently record your thoughts in your journal and to reexamine your initial ideas.

We all note such items continually. However, they have little impact because we don't record them, review them, reflect on them, and respond to them. Your journal provides the medium. It is a culture-bed for these seeds of interest that would otherwise be swept away by the breezes of onrushing circumstances.

Recording your thoughts on paper is essential if you wish to be able to work with them in the future. Newly forming ideas, no matter how vivid they may seem at the moment, are extremely vulnerable to being forgotten. Other activities demand your attention and pull you away from your work for a minute, an hour, a day, or a week. That shimmering idea is like a seed: If it is not tended, it will turn to dust and blow away.

***Use a double-entry system*.** Paste into your log passages from your reading (or visual images, musical notation, incidents recalled, and so on) on the left side of your log's double spread, and formulate your own response (even if it's only one word or image) on the facing page.

Start your log now even though you may not yet be engaged in a specific learning project. You can even use the log to discover some things you'd like to learn right away. Dr. Ari Kiev, author of *A Strategy for Daily Living*, suggests a method: "Start by clipping and pasting newspaper articles that interest you for the next thirty days. At the end of that time, see if there is a trend suggestive of a deep-seated interest or natural inclination. Keep alert each day to the slightest indications of special skills or talents, even when they seem silly or unimportant to you. Take note of the remarks of friends and relatives when they say that something is typical of you." In time, your learning logs will become valuable and treasured items marking your journey to Peak Learning.

You learn as much by writing as you do by reading.
ERIC HOFFER

II.
Science Confirms It—You Are a Superb Learner! ◆◆◆◆

There have been many theories of learning, but within the last few decades something revolutionary has started to happen. Thanks mainly to startling new information in two areas of research— how our brains work and the psychology of thinking—our theories about what learning is and how it works have profoundly changed. New answers are emerging to questions like:

I thank the Lord for the brain He put in my head. Occasionally, I love to just stand to one side and watch how it works.

RICHARD BOLLES

◆ Can we keep learning throughout our lives?

◆ Are there different learning styles for different people?

◆ How do we learn anything?

Why is brain research so important? Over the last fifty years, several new tools and research techniques have given us a window into the brain that's beyond anything we've ever dreamed. Brain studies now engage brilliant theorists and researchers from a broad range of fields such as anthropology, artificial intelligence, linguistics, neurophysiology, and psychology. Today's high-tech instruments and computer-processed experimental data offer scientists an unprecedented view of the brain at work.

This section will explode some physiological myths about learning, outmoded theories that have told us that our learning was more limited than it really is. It will briefly survey some of the surprisingly complex ways in which our brain is organized. Simply and directly, you will start to see how this new information leads to new conclusions about how we think and learn from experience.

The chapter will then turn to the realms of psychology to examine how older kinds of learning theories have changed. In recent years, new theories of learning have been created that give us a solid foundation for the learning techniques you will practice in later chapters.

"Can't you give me brains?" asked the Scarecrow.

"You don't need them," answered the Wizard. "You are learning something every day."

"That may be true," said the Scarecrow, "but I shall be very unhappy unless you give me brains."

The false Wizard looked at him carefully. "Well," he said, with a sigh, "I'm not much of a magician, as I said; but if you will come to me tomorrow morning, I will stuff your head with brains. I cannot tell you how to use them, however; you must find that out for yourself."

"Oh, thank you—thank you!" cried the Scarecrow. "I'll find a way to use them, never fear!"

L. FRANK BAUM

The New Brain

Make both your hands into fists and put them together with your thumbs on top. This will give you a good rough model of the size and shape of your brain. Your forearms represent the spinal cord, the nerve highway that continues down the back and carries information between the brain and the body.

The brain is a double lump of pinkish-gray jelly weighing about three pounds. It is made up of billions of *neurons,* specialized brain cells that function like electrochemical circuits and connect with other neurons in all directions. The place where extensions of two neurons, called *dendrites,* almost meet is called a *synapse.* That's where a tiny electrical signal, generated in one brain cell, releases special chemicals that cross the gap to another neuron.

Don't let these terms throw you. The key point is simply that the never-ending dance of signals from neuron to neuron is the essential feature of the living brain. Moreover, the neurons in our brains are intricately connected in vast networks, suggesting that learning and memory are incredibly complex.

Our exciting tour of brain-research results begins by looking at the most visible feature of the brain—its two halves.

The Two-Sided Brain

A breakthrough in our understanding of the brain occurred in the late 1960s and early 1970s when Professor Roger Sperry and associates at the California Institute of Technology launched a series of bold experiments. They explored a phenomenon observed since ancient times but that never had been rigorously investigated until Sperry's work.

Hippocrates, the Greek founder of medicine, had noted that soldiers struck on the left side of the head by a sword would suffer speech impairment, whereas those struck on the right side did not. From this he concluded that the two sides of the brain must function differently. Nineteenth-century doctors made similar observations, resulting in the identification of more specific functional areas, such as the two speech centers named after Paul Broca and Carl Wernicke, both found on the left side of the brain. But no one was able to explore this phenomenon experimentally until Sperry and his team conducted split-brain research on epileptics who had turned to a surgical solution for relief from their seizures. Sperry's team of surgeons had separated the two hemispheres of their brains.

What's in the brain that ink may character?

WILLIAM SHAKESPEARE

In general, the left hemisphere is more important for language and certain motor skills. On the average, the right side of the brain does better with certain kinds of spatial functioning ... that don't depend on verbal descriptions.

DR. RICHARD RESTAK

Think back on our two-fisted brain model for a moment. Down the middle, where your fingernails touched, the brain has a massive nerve fiber called the *corpus callosum* that connects the two halves. The two hemispheres communicate by sending signals through the corpus callosum. By disconnecting the corpus callosum in epileptic patients, Sperry was able to study the functions of the two brain hemispheres separately.

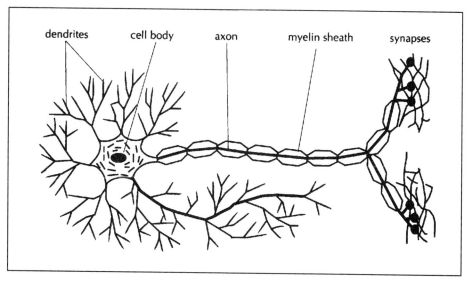

Simplified diagram of typical neuron. Electrical charges are received from other cells by the dendrites.

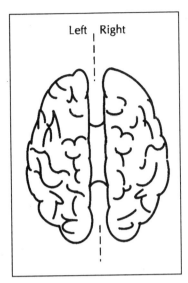

Left | Right

Left and right hemispheres of brain connected by the *corpus callosum*.

Feeding information to just one side enabled him to observe what each half of the brain could and could not do.

In a typical experiment, a patient would put his right hand behind his back. He would then be handed a familiar object and asked to name it. Since the right side of the body is controlled by the left side of the brain, which is the naming, language-using side, it could interpret the experience verbally. The patient had no problem naming the object. However, when another, equally familiar object was placed in the patient's left hand, the mute right brain could not come up with a word for it. Since the hemispheres could not communicate via the corpus callosum, the right brain could not obtain help from the speech centers located in the left hemisphere. The right brain could often draw a picture of the object, or point to a similar object, but was essentially speechless.

Of course, Sperry's experiments included more complex procedures than this. But in sum, they provided a vivid new picture of our dual brains—a picture so significant that Sperry received a Nobel Prize for this work in 1981.

In the past decade, right-left brain experimentation and theory have made rapid progress. As one book on the subject, *Left Brain, Right Brain* by Sally Springer and Georg Deutsch, notes:

> Interest in this topic increased dramatically after the split-brain operations of the 1960s and led to an explosion of research seeking to characterize the differences and to explore their implications for human behavior. Considerable attention has also been directed to seeing whether these differences may be related to diverse phenomena such as learning disabilities, psychiatric illness, and variations in cognitive styles among cultures.

Since Sperry's time, we have begun to view each brain hemisphere as having distinctive areas of strength as follows.

Left	*Right*
analytic	holistic
verbal	pictorial
sequential	simultaneous
temporal	spatial

Sperry welcomed this broad and diverse follow-through on his findings. Summing up the significance of his discoveries, he wrote:

The main theme to emerge ... is that there appear to be two modes of thinking, verbal and nonverbal, represented rather separately in left and right hemispheres respectively, and that our educational system, as well as science in general, tends to neglect the nonverbal form of intellect. What it comes down to is that modern society discriminates against the right hemisphere.

I would go without shirt or show ... sooner than lose for a minute the two separate sides of my head.

RUDYARD KIPLING

Think about Sperry's conclusions for a moment. We've known for thousands of years that most people favor one hand over the other for most tasks, although a minority are ambidextrous, meaning they can use either hand equally. This preference for one side or the other is called *dominance* by scientists.

Although there are many theories about why dominance evolved in our brains, the important point is this: there are actual, physical differences, sensory and motor-nerve connections, in the side of the brain that control the dominant hand. Such differences may be similar to what happens when we train certain muscles for sports. If we naturally use and train one side of the brain more than the other, the functions of that side might grow stronger. Hence, dominance may imply that we have preferred styles of *thinking* too, not just preferred hands for pitching a ball or writing. In the light of Sperry's results, that would mean some people might prefer—and be better at—one particular style of learning rather than another. As a relatively crude example, one person might wander through a museum simply staring at paintings without being concerned about artists' names or periods, while another might prefer to follow the catalog listing or view the paintings in order, from the earliest to the most recent. Neither approach is right or wrong; both can involve learning.

Here is our first major breakthrough based on brain research: learning is *not* a single process. People may be better learners when they use the kind of thinking controlled by their dominant brain hemisphere. I will return to this idea in the next chapter, which considers psychological blocks to learning.

The Triune Brain

Another different functional division in brain areas proposed by Dr. Paul MacLean, a senior research scientist at the National Institute for Mental Health's Laboratory for Brain Evolution and Behavior, also points to the complexity of our brains. Based on his studies of the evolutionary development of nervous systems in many species, including man, Dr. MacLean proposed a vertical, three-point distinction in brain areas.

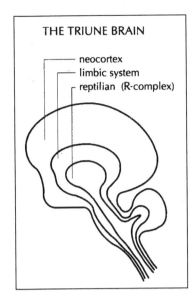

THE TRIUNE BRAIN

neocortex
limbic system
reptilian (R-complex)

The R-Complex. According to MacLean, as our human brains evolved they added new lobes and functions onto an original basic brain similar to one that developed in reptiles. This oldest area is still present in our heads. It includes a number of parts—the brain stem, basal ganglia, reticular activating system, and midbrain—in the lowest part of the brain, closest to the spinal cord. This root brain, which MacLean calls the R-complex, deals with instinctive behavior, including self-preservation, claiming territory and status, and fighting and mating.

The Limbic System. A newer, second section of the brain evolved after millions of years, as mammals developed from reptiles. This part of the brain, the limbic system, literally wraps around the reptilian brain area. Its functions, Dr. MacLean believes, are closely related to emotional behaviors, such as play and rearing young, to the sense of self, and to memory. It also controls the autonomic nervous system, which regulates many bodily functions—including sweating, blood flow, digestion, and dilation of the eyes' pupils—that go on continually, without our conscious knowledge.

Dr. MacLean points out how great a role the limbic system plays in sense perception and memory, something that makes this area vitally important for learning. The limbic system monitors all our sensory input, converts it into appropriate modes for processing, and directs it to the appropriate memory-storage system. Neurochemicals in the limbic system also affect our ability to transfer memory from short-term to long-term storage. Unless this transfer takes place, we literally lose what we have learned within 30 seconds, which is the time it remains in short-term memory.

It is this new development [of the neocortex] that makes possible the insight required to plan for the needs of others as well as the self, and to use our knowledge to alleviate suffering everywhere. In creating for the first time a creature with a concern for all living things, nature accomplished a one-hundred-eighty-degree turnabout from what had previously been a reptile-eat-reptile and dog-eat-dog world.

DR. PAUL MACLEAN

The second major breakthrough from the new brain research is the discovery that memory and emotion are related to structures and processes in our brains that are deeply interconnected and that this cannot help but have a significant effect on learning. While the interconnections are not yet fully understood, most learning experts agree that feelings play far stronger roles in our learning than the purely rational, logical processes we were confined to in school. Many of the methods you will learn in this book enlist emotions to help learning.

The Neocortex. The third part of the brain, according to MacLean, is the distinctively primate and human neocortex, the latest neurological roll of the evolutionary dice. It lies at the top of our brain, on both sides, surrounding the limbic system. Research has shown that this part of the brain is where most of our mental activity happens. Spatial and mathematical thinking, dreaming and remembering, and processing and decoding sensory information all function through this area.

The neocortex is where many sorts of specialized functions take place, such as understanding language and imagining a mental picture of things. These are obviously essential to learning, and so we'd expect any injury to have a serious effect. Yet almost miraculously, we often find that, with training, another area of the neocortex can substitute for a damaged area, taking over its functions.

The competition of organisms for survival in the external world mirrors a competition in the inner world among neurons to fashion the circuits that will be the most effective in the external world.

GORDON M. SHEPHARD
Professor of Neuroscience, Yale University

The theory of the triune brain implies that emotion, memory, and the state of our bodies may be linked through the middle section of our brains, the limbic system, in ways that crucially affect learning. Our ability to remember information for future use may depend more on our feelings at the time than we had realized. Also, rather than one smoothly functioning brain, we really have an often contentious committee, whose members are constantly striving for domination. Linkages between the newest part of our brain and its older relatives can play hopscotch with our learning. This might influence how easily we can keep cool under a threat, for example, or remain clear-thinking when faced with strong emotion.

The Ever-Growing Brain

We used to believe that the brain developed to a certain age and then stopped and began to die. This made it easy to believe that learning was the province of the young and that, as we grew older, we began to lose our knowledge. Sperry and MacLean showed that our brains were more complex than that. Our next bit of brain research explains why.

For much of human history we imagined that the brain was a passive receiver of sensations from the outside world, the famed *tabula rasa,* or blank slate. But two trends of current research have erased that image and substituted a far more interesting one.

First, the brain is now pictured as constantly growing. "The structure and abilities of the cerebral cortex can be changed throughout life by enriching sensory environments," declares Professor Marion Diamond of the University of California at Berkeley. The implications of this newer, truer picture is that we actually can become smarter as we grow older, if we provide our brains with the right encouragement and environment in which to "do its thing."

One of the profound miracles of the human brain is our capacity for memory.

JEAN HOUSTON

Diamond has provided astounding evidence of the potential for brain growth in her laboratory at Berkeley, where she has continued a line of experimentation on rats that was started twenty years ago by Mark Rosenzweig. Her basic experiment was to place each of three comparable rats (often siblings) in one of three environments: standard, enriched, and impoverished. The standard cages contained the basic necessities of life: food, water, and adequate space. The enriched environments were larger cages with several rats, into which different toys, including objects to play with and treadmills, were introduced each day. In the impoverished situations there was little stimulation, and movement was restricted by a small cage size resembling solitary confinement in a prison.

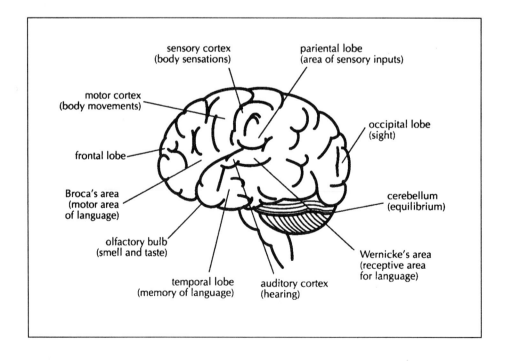

sensory cortex (body sensations)

pariental lobe (area of sensory inputs)

motor cortex (body movements)

occipital lobe (sight)

frontal lobe

Broca's area (motor area of language)

cerebellum (equilibrium)

olfactory bulb (smell and taste)

Wernicke's area (receptive area for language)

temporal lobe (memory of language)

auditory cortex (hearing)

Diamond found that the enriched environment caused an actual increase in the weight of the rat's brain—about 10 percent—even in young adult rats whose growth *should* have stopped! Her findings astounded fellow biologists, especially hard-liners who had insisted, at first, that external conditions could not significantly influence the built-in development pattern of a rat's brain except in cases of major physical damage.

In recent years, Diamond and her associates have been so encouraged that they tried this experiment with rats equivalent in age to human beings in their sixties and seventies. Again, each of the old rats' brains grew by 10 percent when they lived with younger rats in an enriched environment.

As Robert Ornstein, a fellow brain scientist, has commented on Diamond's findings: "Specific changes in the brain took place in the dendrites [the parts of neurons that connect at synapses] of each nerve cell, which thickened with stimulating experiences. It is as if the forest of nerve cells became literally enriched, and the density of the branches increased."

Mental skills get rusty from disuse. Learning of any kind cleans off rust, and restores the gears to fuller functioning.

DENNIS THOMPSON

The crucial lesson here is that despite our traditional beliefs about old dogs learning new tricks and our increasing apprehensions as we grow older about premature senility whenever something slips our minds, our brains can continue to grow throughout our lives. For that to happen, however, we need to create for ourselves the human equivalent of Diamond's enriched environment. For us, of course, that goes way beyond toys and treadmills; our enriched environment must include constant stimulation from new ideas and understanding and from all the other challenges and opportunities offered by the best that humankind has thought, felt, and done.

A second new view of the ever-growing brain is that it is constantly active. In a complex, ongoing process, our brains organize sensory data into experience and experience into information. When we see something new, our brains take the effects of light on our eyes and construct the edges of the object. Discovering an author's views in a new book may lead us to reevaluate her earlier works. Thus, because our brains are constantly reorganizing our ideas and experiences, we are the source of our own learning.

The evidence for this comes from the world of artificial intelligence, commonly called AI. Neural networks are a recent field of AI research that uses computers to model how connections between brain cells operate. While it is not necessary to get into technical details, it is important to understand how this illuminates the way we learn.

A neural network is a computer simulation of a miniature brain, having anywhere from a dozen to a thousand or more artificial neurons. The computer is programmed so that each imitation neuron can, like the real ones in your brain, send signals to many of the others. Some fairly simple rules that mimic how real neurons alter their communication pathways on the basis of input are also programmed into the machine.

If the brain is a computer, then it is the only one that runs on glucose, generates ten watts of electricity, and is manufactured by unskilled labor.

DAVID LEWIS

Once this mock brain is turned on, it's on its own. The experimenters feed it stimuli—words, pictures, even odors—and the mock neurons, following the simple rules of processing, begin reorganizing themselves on the basis of the input. For example, frequently used neuron connections will grow stronger, and new stimuli are more likely to be processed by the existing pathway. The artificial brain begins to build its own order.

NETTALK, invented by Professor Terrence Sejnowski of Johns Hopkins University, is a good example of a neural network. It can be trained to pronounce English words. At first, NETTALK operates almost randomly, much as a baby produces its first babble of sounds and talk. As it guesses at how to pronounce different words, rules ensure that a correct guess is reinforced, so that the associated connections between stimulated neurons become stronger with use.

After half a day of such training, NETTALK's pronunciation becomes clearer and clearer. Eventually it can recognize some one thousand words and, after a week, twenty thousand! NETTALK isn't given any rules for pronunciation, just as a baby isn't taught such rules. It invents them afresh, based on its experience. Only after the fact can the researchers go in and find out how the system has organized itself.

"It turned out to be very sensible," Sejnowski told a reporter recently. "The vowels are represented differently from the consonants. Things that should be similar are clustered together."

Neural-network theory gives us a powerful new image of how the brain works when we are learning. The image is not that of the conventional classroom or student situation, in which tightly focused concentration absorbs a single piece of information. Rather, the image is that of a combination of a New England town meeting and a Turkish bazaar. Incoming information sparks literally thousands of neurons that shout, whisper, or mumble in ways in which lots of new data fit into patterns the brain has processed before.

This complex, ongoing, multi-neuron conversation has recently been described by M.I.T. professor, Marvin Minsky in his book, *Society of Mind.* Reasoning backwards from computer programs to brains, he suggests that we are a more complicated committee than even that suggested by Sperry's two divisions or MacLean's three. There may be a myriad of small processes operating semi-autonomously at any moment, with our attention darting among them.

The Brain and Learning

What do these findings add up to? The brain is much more than a passive lump sitting in our heads like a dumb switchboard system; it is as active an organ as our muscles. It processes the raw information sent by our senses and literally constructs the world we experience day by day.

What has been discussed so far about the brain suggests some important implications for how we go about learning. These were briefly summarized; now they can be described in more detail.

As the brain is part of the body, every brain shares its body's chemical and emotional environment, which influences learning. The physiological conditions of learning such as light, temperature, bodily posture, state of wakefulness, and hunger—affect how well your brain works. Your brain even goes through time cycles of attentiveness and fatigue, some of which are unique to you.

The limbic system routinely checks out your physiological state whenever you call upon the brain to perform. You need to be in condition and warmed up for mental workouts just as much as for physical ones.

Brains can continue to grow throughout life. Your brain can continue to learn and grow for the rest of your life, barring trauma or grave illness Aging per se does not undermine learning capacity; *attitudes* and *lifestyle* do that. "Use it or lose it" applies to your brain as much as to other parts of your body.

Brains are active, constructing organs. Your brain is constantly processing sensations and thoughts in myriad ways. "Normal brains are built to be challenged," says Dr. Jerre Levy of the University of Chicago. "They operate at optimal levels only when cognitive processing requirements are of sufficient complexity." To put it more bluntly, you can bore your brain to the point of sickness. Professor August de la Pena of the University of Texas has documented the deleterious effects of under-stimulation in his *Psychobiology of Cancer.* He found that information underload can trigger disease.

Your brain responds positively to being challenged by a rich environment and, as Dr. Diamond showed, can even continue to grow new cells and connections. It operates best when properly stimulated by interesting, complex materials, as long as it has methods for processing them effectively.

The brain has a large repertoire of functions and powers. In addition to being a magnificent biological computer, your brain is a source of rich and complex emotions, intuitions, creativity, and wisdom. It can operate in both an analytic/linear mode and a holistic/pattern-making mode. It can respond to information and situations with logic or feeling, rote instinct, blind emotion, or creative insight—or all of them at once.

But most of us become entrenched in only one or, at most, two kinds of thinking (rational versus emotional, for example). We grind away in our accustomed ways with less and less return on the energy expended. If we merely changed to an alternative mode of thinking, we'd regain our energy and enthusiasm. Learning is most effective when we use the full range of our powers, not just the ones we use most.

Your brain is as individual as you are. Each brain is unique in physiological development, and it has distinctive preferences in how it functions. Some have to do with which side of our brain gets used most (dominance), or with the environmental conditions for learning; some with the way in which what we're learning is presented or organized; and others with the people factors in the situation. But most of us have never had the opportunity to arrange our learning to accommodate our personal preferences. When we are able to do that, learning takes on a completely different psychological flavor. Rather than being something imposed on the brain, against the grain as it were, learning occurs with ease and pleasure.

So much for the *hardware* side of learning, that is, how the brain works. What about the *software*, the process of learning itself? What is learning? To answer that question we must look beyond the physical nature of the brain, beyond even our as yet still limited understanding of its function. We must make a leap into the realm of the mind. This will take us to cognitive psychology and new theories of *how* we learn.

The experimental subject, whether animal or man, becomes a better subject after repeated experiments.... He also, in some way, learns to learn. He not only solves the problems set him by the experimenter; but more than this, he becomes more and more skilled in the solving of problems.

GREGORY BATESON

What Is Learning?

For all our shiny new knowledge about the brain, the mind remains a mystery. How we, as humans, experience our world and change our actions as a result of that experience is far from understood. An excellent overview of the field of learning comes from Robert M. Smith's *Learning How to Learn: Applied Theory for Adults.*

> Learning has been variously described as a transformation that occurs in the brain; problem solving; an internal process that leads to behav-

ioral change; the construction and exchange of personally relevant and viable meanings; a retained change in disposition or capability that is not simply ascribable to growth; and a process of changing insights, outlooks, expectations or thought patterns.

Noting that the above uses of the term *learning* can refer to a product, a process, or a function, Smith summarizes as follows.

Learning, then, is an activity of one who learns. It may be intentional or random; it may involve acquiring new information or skills, new attitudes, understandings or values. It usually is accompanied by change in behavior and goes on throughout life. It is often thought of as both processes and outcomes. Education can be defined as "the organized, systematic effort to foster learning, to establish the conditions and to provide the activities through which learning can occur."

Now that we have a better definition of learning, we can ask how learning occurs. Malcolm Knowles in his book, *The Adult Learner, A Neglected Species,* lists more than fifty originators of learning theories from 1885 to 1980. Of these, I will focus on two different styles, or approaches to learning theory, a classification created in 1970 by two developmental psychologists, Reese and Overton. They grouped learning theories according to whether the theories assume a *mechanistic* model of the world or an *organic* one.

If men were the automatons that behaviorists claim they are, the behaviorist psychologists could not have invented the amazing nonsense called "behaviorist psychology." So they are wrong from scratch—as clever and as wrong as phlogiston chemists.

ROBERT A. HEINLEIN

Mechanistic Learning Theories

A mechanistic worldview takes the machine as the basic metaphor for learning. From this perspective, complex events can ultimately be reduced to predictable and measurable interactions among the components, resembling the way the parts of your car engine work together to turn the wheels and get you where you need to be.

According to this approach, the model learner is reactive, passive, a blank slate responding to outside forces. Learning theories based on this model typically emphasize quantitatively measurable results, such as test scores. They try to explain complex learned behaviors by showing how they are built out of simple, more primitive ones.

These theories view learning as neurological *stimulus and response* and the process of *conditioning*. For example, when a doctor tests your nervous system by tapping your knee with his hammer, he's providing a stimulus; when your foot kicks up, it's in a reflex response. What is going on in this simple experience is that the hammer has stimulated a nerve that runs to the spinal column. Even without traveling up to the brain, the neurological circuit that is activated sends an automatic reflex reaction down through other nerves that makes the leg muscles kick out. The same sort of principle applies when you smell a delicious dinner cooking and start to salivate.

The Russian psychologist Ivan Pavlov discovered that if he regularly rang a bell whenever he fed a dog in his laboratory, eventually the dog would start to respond as if food were present whenever the bell rang. Pavlov called this process the creation of a *conditioned reflex*, a neurological response developed by associating a new stimulus, the bell, with a previous reflex, salivation in the presence of food.

The American psychologist B.F. Skinner, building on Pavlov's discovery, decided that behavior is completely determined by its consequences. He believed that rewarded behavior is more likely to be repeated and punished behavior is more likely to be stopped. Skinner suggests that if an environment can be completely controlled, any organism's behavior can be modified, or conditioned, by an appropriate pattern of rewards and punishments—and that this is essentially what learning is.

This process may seem quite similar to the standard types of schooling most of us were subjected to growing up. Correct answers on tests were rewarded; mistakes were punished with poor grades. Our development as learners was measured by how well we could produce the desired behaviors on command.

However, as we have seen, our brains are far more active and complicated than was previously supposed. The new brain research results cast strong doubts on the blank-slate model. If the brain is actively constructing its own experience, learning is a more complex process than simply rewarding good behavior and punishing bad. Mechanistic learning theories do not seem to hold up against the recently discovered potential of our brains.

Organic Learning Theories

The other side of the standard learning-classification system involves a different basic metaphor in which the world is seen as an interconnected, developing organism. From this perspective, the model learner is an active creator of new patterns and meanings. Theories of learning derived from this view focus on processes, organizing principles, and *qualitative* change. Complex learned behaviors may emerge unpredictably, like a flash of intuitive insight.

Organic theories of learning stress that it is more than simply associating a given stimulus with a desired response. Instead, the learner actively organizes experience according to both physiological processes (such as the way our brain organizes color, light, and shade into the objects we see) and psychological processes relating to motivation, needs, and personal meaning.

Humanistic psychologists such as Abraham Maslow and Carl Rogers developed theories about these inner, psychological needs that drive the learning process. For both of these men, the primary issue was not a passive reaction to outside events leading to modification of behavior, but rather a process of *self-actualization,* of self-initiated development of a person's skills and potentials to lead to a fulfilling life of challenge and growth.

If the brain-mind is an open system, then it is also intimate with what lies outside it.

BOB SAMPLES

Rogers formulated a set of hypotheses that defined a new kind of student-centered learning. These included emphasizing that one cannot be taught anything directly and that teachers can only facilitate another person's learning; that significant learning happens only with those things perceived as maintaining or enhancing the structure of the self, (i.e., punishment does not lead to learning); that experience seen as inconsistent with the self can be learned only if a person feels sufficiently safe and unthreatened to relax his or her boundaries; and that the most effective learning experience is one in which a learner feels the least threat and is helped to make the greatest number of distinctions about the experience.

A more recent development in this type of learning theory is suggested by Bob Samples in his book, *Openmind/Wholemind.* Drawing on the works of neurophysiologist Karl Pribram, physicist David Bohm, and chemist Ilya Prigogine, Samples has distilled a radically new model of the brain-mind as an open, holistic system interacting in a multitude of ways with the surrounding environment. I'd like to paraphrase some of his assumptions about how such a system could work because these points are relevant to the understanding of lifelong learning.

◆ Each part of the brain-mind system experiences everything that other parts experience. The brain-mind system should be seen as a unified whole.

◆ Every part of the brain-mind system *knows* everything other parts *know.* We can find out what we know in many different ways.

◆ We can expand the range of what we pay attention to in our own brain-mind systems. We can choose to use more types of connections among our experiences.

◆ The more types of brain-mind connections we pay attention to, the more we expand our consciousness and increase the flexibility and fluency of our mental functioning.

- ◆ The more ways of mental functioning we honor and appreciate, the more ways we have to express ourselves and, equally, more ways to learn are available to us.

- ◆ We can't avoid using our whole brain-mind system. Our response to life both shapes and is shaped by all that we are and what we may become.

This has been a brief look at two different kinds of learning theory. The older, more traditional, mechanistic theories generally assume a passive learner and are close to what we may have experienced in our childhood schooling—learning governed by the reward-and-punishment system of grades and scores. The newer, organic learning theories, in agreement with recent brain research, assume an active, *empowered* learner participating fully in the creation of his or her own learning.

Strange that I was not told that the brain can hold in a tiny ivory cell God's heaven and hell.
OSCAR WILDE

Now it's time to go back and connect these results with the earlier conclusions about the structure of the brain. Only then will it become clear how brain theory and learning theory will affect how we understand the process of lifelong learning.

Learning Theory and Lifelong Learning

The best summary of the changes needed in theories of learning was developed at an unprecedented international conference, The Education Summit, held in Washington, D.C. in 1988, at which I delivered the keynote address. Researchers who produced the new findings listed above came together with innovative educators who have gone farthest in applying those findings in school and college classrooms. The conference was based on the principle that intelligence is not a static structure, but an open, dynamic system that can continue to develop throughout life, and that it therefore is possible for everyone at every age and ability to learn.

Here is the way in which these leading experts saw education needing to change to take full account of what we now know about the brain:

Traditional Learning Emphasizes	*Modern Learning Emphasizes*
Memorization and repetition	Excitement and love of learning
Linear and concrete intellectual development	Total human capacity in ethical, intellectual, and physical development
Conformity	
Individual/competitive efforts	Diversity and personal esteem
Static and rigid processes	Cooperative/collaborative efforts

Traditional Learning Emphasizes	*Modern Learning Emphasizes*
Content learning	Thinking, creativity, and
Teachers as information providers	intuition
Departmentalized learning	Process learning of quality
Cultural uniformity	content
Isolated teaching environments	Teachers as learning facilitators
Technology as an isolated tool	Interdisciplinary learning
Restricted use of facilities	Cultural differences and
Parental involvement	commonalities
Autonomy of the community	Collaborative teaching
The industrial age	environments
	Technology as an integral tool
	Flexible use of facilities
	Extensive parental partnerships
	Community partnerships
	An information/learning society

The following chapters will demonstrate just how the shifts in emphasis of modern learning lead to a distinctive style and approach for adults wishing to reawaken a lost love of learning. You will come to understand why we must develop our personal learning programs around a flexible, exciting, holistic model of learning rather than using techniques developed for children and that may have helped us to lose our natural learning skills.

III.
Entering the Flow State
to Overcome Your
Learning Fears ◆◆◆◆

As was seen in the last chapter, recent brain research suggests that emotions and learning are strongly related. Feelings can determine how hard or easy it is to pay attention, or how well we can transfer information from short-term to long-term memory. Of course, we know this from personal experience: if we hated Latin, for example, studying for Miss Trout's test was sheer torture.

> *There is a learner within you, able and confident, waiting to function freely, usefully, and joyfully.*
> MARILYN FERGUSON

What we may not remember is that the opposite was also true: if we felt good about a subject, learning seemed almost effortless. We could become so absorbed that we never noticed time passing or the effort of studying. This and the following chapter will examine this relationship more closely. We want to understand how some kinds of feelings block the ability to enjoy learning or even to learn at all. More important, we want to understand the feelings that encourage learning and make it a joy and delight because those are the feelings that can help make us peak learners.

The two key issues here are that your *feelings are important in learning* and that you *can* change your feelings. While the first may seem obvious from our example above, what you may not realize is that feelings you developed during school, years ago, can block your learning today! That's why it's important to take some time to examine those early anxieties in order to understand what they mean, where they come from, and how to deal with them.

The second point, however, is the real kicker. If our feelings are locked in, beyond any hope of our changing them, then we're stuck and nothing can help. But that is simply not true. As we go through life, our feelings are continually evolving, based on our experience. We know that feelings can change, whether from discovering that we can develop a taste for something we once disliked or from realizing that someone we once thought was ideal has a few flaws.

Now, granted, choosing to change how we *feel* can be more difficult than changing our minds about other things. The reasons for this are complex. Simply put, feelings are *deeper* than thoughts, connected in complex ways to a wider range of experiences. We can think of emotions as extremely fast, subconscious evaluations of a situation. They happen so quickly we generally do not recognize where they come from. The result is that when we decide to change our feelings, we have to go through a process of retraining. We need to learn how to notice a feeling, name it, connect it to other experiences, recognize how our current situation differs from past ones, and decide to try a different and new approach, despite what the feeling tells us. If we can do this enough, we will discover that our feeling about the situation has changed.

You can begin that retraining process right now by examining the sources of negative feelings about learning and taking the first steps to dispel them. This chapter will explore why people have such fears, what they are, where they come from, and what to do about them.

Conquering the Fear of Learning

Chapter 1 discussed anxieties and negative myths about learning: the fear of not knowing *how* to learn and the feeling that learning is boring, difficult, passive, lonely, and unrelated to your real interests. Such fears and others like them are not new in human history.

The Greek philosopher Plato told a famous story comparing the human condition to life in a darkened cave, where people spend their time staring at flickering shadows on the wall caused by dim reflections of sunlight. (The image has an eerie similarity to the picture of today's couch-potato television addicts.) When a wise man suggests that people leave the cave and see the outside world in the full light of the sun, they refuse, afraid to leave the familiar shadows. They resist the opportunity to learn—to see and understand something new.

Let me assert my firm belief that the only thing we have to fear is fear itself.

FRANKLIN DELANO ROOSEVELT

I believe a basic point this story makes is that many people are afraid, not just of the opportunity to learn, but of their own power to

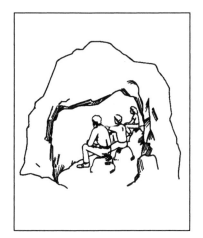

learn. They fear the responsibility such power entails, the need to face possible conflicts between one's own ideas and what others would prefer that one believe. After all, how many times have you seen a student get away with disagreeing with the teacher—especially if the student happened to be right? Most people would rather not rock the boat.

Another point here is the fear of change. As we grow up, we are taught by parents, peers, and teachers to believe in certain things. In many ways, these teachings define who we are, our relationship to the world around us, our community, our allies, and our enemies. Learning new ideas has the potential to change our comfortable picture of things, to force us to re-evaluate who and what we are. For many people this is too disturbing to think about, so they stop learning.

Both these fears—of our own power to learn and of changing ourselves with new ideas—can lead to resistance to learning. Most of us can remember classmates in school who were always making trouble and being sent down to the principal's office—some were even pretty smart, when they wanted to be. But their unwillingness to play the game of passive students led them to break out and ignore any of the benefits of learning as well.

All of us have, to some degree, this blend of fear, discomfort, and resistance to learning. To become peak learners, however, we have to meet these fears, understand them, and work our way past them. Because you have taken the trouble to read this far in the book, you are already well on the road to dealing with these basic fears of learning.

We are not troubled by things, but by the opinions which we have of things.

EPICTETUS

But these two areas are at the deepest level of our fears of learning. There are other negative feelings, closer to the surface, that grow out of those. Unfortunately, these more visible fears often arise directly from our experiences in school—the place where we're supposed to learn to love learning. Such negative feelings are produced because, in many cases, old theories of education were based on mistaken beliefs about how learning works. The result was to make learning more difficult—and much less pleasant—for most of us. When we experience problems with learning anything, when we feel blocked, bored, overwhelmed, or fearful, we are experiencing the effects of these past mistakes and our own reactions to them.

This is where you can start the process of retraining your negative feelings about learning into the joy and delight you can feel about Peak Learning. You will begin with an exercise, and then go on to consider some of the typical fears of learning produced by our school experience and the mistaken beliefs about how we learn that contributed to our fears. So brace yourselves: you're going to take a guided tour of the dark side of learning.

Those Slow-Learning Blues

In the following exercise—the only negative one I will ask you to do— you will recapture the kind of experience that led to any present apprehensions you may have about learning. I simply want you to recall a typical day at school. When you recall such a day, it will evoke the feelings and sensations that you learned along with your subjects. These feelings shaped your current attitude toward learning—your self-confidence or lack thereof. Only by feeling once again what your attitudes were can you begin to transcend them.

Record your feelings and reactions in your learning log, in whatever form you like. You might jot down key words and feelings, draw a picture, or describe an incident you recall.

1. Sit in a chair, close your eyes, and relax. Picture yourself in a typical classroom from your school days or in a recent class if you are currently in school. Feel yourself settling into the chair you remember from that class. Really try to feel your body in that chair. Picture the desk and the markings on it, too.

2. Now picture the teacher doing what you recall, probably talking to the class. Recall one specific moment that stands out in your memory. Does this teacher belittle you, another student, or the whole class for your ignorance or other supposed deficiencies? Recall what words are used.

> *Groucho Marx recalled a conversation with his mother, when she learned he'd been cutting school: "Don't you want to get an education?" she asked. Groucho replied: "Not if I have to go to school to get it!"*

3. Now consider these questions: How do you feel? Are you interested? Scared? Timid? Does the information you are being asked to learn relate to your life? Can you see how you'll use this information in the future? Do you feel smart? Energetic? Creative? Dead from the neck up? How about the passage of time? Does it seem to be going slowly or quickly?

How do you think the other students feel? Do you feel the support of the group, or do you feel alone despite the presence of the other students?

What would you rather be doing? How would you feel if you were doing that? Would you be learning anything if you were?

Do you feel that the experience you have recalled has been designed with your needs or feelings in mind? With the other students'? With anyone's?

How does this experience make you feel about learning itself?

◆ ◆ ◆ ◆

What Do People Fear About Learning?

When I present this exercise in my seminars, I ask people to discuss the things they felt. We do this so that everyone can understand exactly how the typical fears and anxieties produced by our schooling contribute to problems with learning. The effects of such feelings are dangerous in all stages of the learning process. When you *start* to learn anything new, they undermine your confidence in being able to understand and master the subject. During the learning process, they sap the energy you need, so that you bog down or lose momentum, becoming frustrated and despondent. And even *after* you have learned something, these feelings make it harder to remember or apply what you've learned, forcing you to start all over again—or give up.

Here are two typical examples my students produced of how their negative feelings blocked their ability to learn. Perhaps you will recognize some of your own anxieties from the exercise:

Self-education is, I firmly believe, the only kind of education there is. The only function of a school is to make self-education easier; failing that, it does nothing.

ISAAC ASIMOV

Dorothy K. had math anxiety. During the exercise, she recalled a feeling she often had during her school days: that she was unable to follow what was going on and feared she would never be able to catch up. The result was a vicious cycle. As each new math problem came up in class, she was still thinking about the last one and whether she had really *got* it. That was enough to distract her from the current problem. After the exercise, she realized that her attitude had become a self-fulfilling prophecy.

Arnold M. recalled an art class that had gone to a nearby park to do sketches of nature. All his life, he remembered, he had been told he had no talent in drawing. As a result, he felt uncomfortable with his new sketch pad and set of charcoals. This past conditioning was so strong that, even though he had tried to draw repeatedly in later life, he remained self-conscious about handling his artistic tools. He was unable to stop feeling that he would probably be unsatisfied with whatever he produced. He recalled how he was unable to draw anything the first three times he went out on his own.

From discussing hundreds of cases like these with my students, I've identified six major fears we commonly have about learning. Once you realize where they come from, these fears can lose much of their power over you because merely describing feelings in words gives us a handle on them and reduces our anxiety. We'll cover each of the six and then go on to discuss the mistaken beliefs about how we learn that contribute to these fears.

Fear 1: I don't understand what I'm learning. We've all had that sinking sensation in the stomach upon realizing that we've lost our way in following a subject. Sometimes this feeling arises because a speaker or author uses words we don't understand. Other times, we understand all the words but can't seem to figure out what the point is supposed to be. At a lecture or in a seminar this can be even worse. People around us seem to be getting it. We can look and even sound like we are too, but deep down we know we're faking it. We feel lost, helpless, embarrassed, and unwilling to admit we don't know what's going on.

Some people never learn anything, for this reason, because they understand everything too soon.

ALEXANDER POPE

This universal experience often stems from the way we were taught in school. The pace and style of presenting information was determined by the teacher. If our own way of grasping things was different, little accommodation was made. Moreover, we were expected to master the same body of material as the other students in the class. It didn't matter what was really interesting to us, what parts we'd enjoy pursuing in depth, or what we didn't care much about. Finally, we seldom had the opportunity to process the material in our own ways, by applying it to our own interests or concerns, or by making our own unique connections to other things we knew.

None of this needs to apply to the way we can learn now. As adults, we can and should be learning in our own ways, at our own pace, according to our own personal priorities. Only when we give ourselves permission to do that will the feelings of helplessness disappear—and, if they arise, we will have techniques to deal with them productively.

Fear 2: I'm not a person who can learn this subject. No matter how good a student you were in school, there is *something* you think you can't learn. For many people this is math; for others it may be foreign languages, the arts, athletics, salesmanship, or woodworking.

The reason we feel this way relates once more to the idea of our personal learning style. As has been seen, each of us has a unique brain. The combination of that brain and our experience of life produce certain talents, usually abilities we start to exercise at a young age.

Those areas are where we each have our personal head start. In the same way, there may be things that are harder for us to learn because they did not come easily to us or we didn't start to practice them early in our lives.

Because our schooling tends to make only minimal concessions to different styles of learning or even differences in the subject matter, we often feel that learning in some areas is too difficult for us to ever accomplish. However, as peak learners we can call the shots. If one style of learning doesn't work for us in some subject, we can switch to other ways to pick up the information we need. If memorizing vocabulary lists and grammar bores us to tears, we can learn Japanese or Spanish by going to immersion classes where everyone uses the new language to socialize. If math textbooks make our eyes glaze, we can try an interactive computer program that will show us each step only when we're ready for it.

Learning is not a task or a problem—it is a way to be in the world. Man learns as he pursues goals and projects that have meaning for him.
                                                        SIDNEY JOURARD

Fear 3: I don't know how to learn this effectively. As was mentioned in Chapter I, the typical pattern in school learning is the assignment to "go and learn this" with never a hint as to how you're supposed to go about it. There is little that can more effectively kill enjoyment than a challenge that comes with little direction, with no place to start.

It is as if you set out to meet some friends on a hike. They've told you where they'll be camping and where to park your car. You get out and look at the forest in dismay: Which trail should you take? What landmarks should you look for? But once you know how, its easy and fun. You look for the white triangle painted on trees until you get to the stream, follow the current until you reach a tree with a yellow circle, and follow that marked trail to the campsite.

Peak Learning techniques will give you the trail signs you need to learn what you want to learn—and to have fun along the way. Once you have several options to try out in various learning situations, you need never feel lost with no place to start. And, as a peak learner, you will realize that anything one person learned can be learned by anyone else willing to put in the work.

Fear 4: I won't remember what I'm learning. Most of us can remember frantically cramming facts, dates, names, and so forth on the night before an exam. We got through the test and relaxed. The next day, however, we were lucky to remember half of what we tried so hard to learn.

Here again, school has given us a skewed picture of how learning should work. For school courses, we were tested periodically on how well we could regurgitate masses of information and we were graded on a curve that compared our retention to that of others. In that system, the fact that most students had forgotten as much as 90 percent of the information within a week of the test was irrelevant. What a waste of time and effort!

But in real life—which is what Peak Learning is about—you have the choice to retain as much or as little as you like, based on what you need, find relevant, or enjoy using. Once you have an overview of any subject, enough of a grasp of it to find your way around, it's far easier to go back and look up specific facts or brush up on whole areas if necessary later on. There's simply no *need* to retain everything in your head. No one is comparing how much you remember with what others remember. It is up to you to decide how much of what you're learning is merely nice to know about and which small parts are interesting, enjoyable, and useful enough to hold on to, think about, and build on.

Fear 5: I feel ashamed that I don't know something. Whenever we try to learn something, we have to start by *admitting we don't know it yet.* Often, that means we need some help to get started—even if it is only a book recommendation.

Learning is the very essence of humility, learning from everything and everybody. There is no hierarchy in learning. Authority denies learning and a follower will never learn.

J. KRISHNAMURTI

But ever since we first sat in a classroom and the teacher called on us for an answer we didn't know, we've been taught that admitting we don't know something is shameful. Most school situations assume that the teacher knows what is worth knowing and our job as students is to get it from him or her. If we didn't get what the teacher knew, we were punished for not knowing. Now, when we try to become *learners*, we revive all the resentment about being controlled, evaluated, and put on the spot as *students*.

But things are different for us now as adults. Unlike the constraints and obligations in other parts of our lives, as learners we have the perfect freedom to explore whatever we wish, when and how we want to. No one is going to ridicule us because we don't know something we're supposed to—the only evaluation that counts is our own.

To continue the hiking analogy I used earlier, as learners we can blaze our own trails, choose any path we wish, and camp wherever we like. As powerful and self-directed peak learners, we can realize that anything we don't know is an exciting trail we've never been on. We can choose which trail to walk along and explore the new horizons we reach.

Fear 6: There's too much to learn. Here again, school experience gives us a mistaken assumption. In school, learning is organized around courses, a defined body of knowledge. It is as if we had to eat an entire cow, even if we wanted only a quick hamburger. So we are left with the belief that to learn something means mastering every detail covered in the thick, heavy textbook. That image helps to kill any joy or interest we might find in the subject. We feel overwhelmed, tired before we begin, and decide to put things off until we are able to tackle them again.

But, again, the real world is totally different. There are no subjects, no courses, no fixed body of knowledge that is required. (When was the last time you saw a fence around a rock saying "Igneous Geology Required"?)

Instead, learning is an ongoing process in which you first identify the things that intrigue you, then find out about them to whatever degree you want. Next, you process that knowledge and build on it, fitting it in where it is useful for your purposes. You then make a decision about what's truly useful and worth keeping, while noting where you can find out the rest when and if you need it. Finally, you start the same cycle over again.

What matters is how much you've done and what you're doing with it, not someone else's idea of how much there is to learn about something. Day by day, month by month, your learning continues to grow in the directions you want, at whatever speed you set. At any moment, you are free to pass by something complex but irrelevant or to spend days on something simple but useful to you.

Remember that all of us have to contend with these fears when we decide to return to learning on our own terms. In order to change and grow and become able to use more of our potential, we have to let go of the parts of ourselves that get in our own way. The price we must pay for a happier, more fulfilling, and more rewarding life is stepping out of our caves and leaving behind the darkness and the pale, flickering shadows.

The Myths of Learning

For most of us, our years in school and college have also loaded us with beliefs about the process of learning that do not apply now that we are adults. During all those terms and semesters, you were absorbing a kind of mythology of learning. Whatever subject you thought you were studying, you were also being taught a subliminal curriculum that shaped your view of *how* you learn. For example, your learning was usually for someone else: for your parents, your teachers, or the school. *They* decided what was worth learning, how it could best be learned, and whether you'd learned enough of it.

Here, again, as was the case with our fears about ourselves as learners, we can dispel much of the power of these myths simply by dragging them out of the dark corners of our mind and submitting them to the light of reason. The following section will run them down quickly by first stating each myth in its boldest form, then examining where it comes from, and finally formulating the truth of the matter.

There is no limit to the process of learning to learn. Indeed, once human beings have been bitten by the excitement of finding new ways to structure knowledge, they will never again fear being bored.

ROBERT THEOBALD

Myth 1: Learning is a boring, unenjoyable activity. Being bored while learning stems from our being compelled to learn things we don't care about in an uncongenial environment without regard to our own needs and style.

Moreover, you were very likely too smart for the pace of learning that typically occurs in school and college, where classwork is often a lockstep dictated by the syllabus, the textbook, and the lowest-common-denominator pace of the group as a whole. "We descend to meet," wrote Emerson, meaning we slow down our natural rate of learning when we are in a group situation. Trying to slow down your brain makes learning tedious.

But learning is really one of the most natural and absorbing experiences you can engage in. Learning can move with the speed of thought, which outstrips any existing computer. Even when you are learning the rudiments of a subject by conventional studying (which can usually be avoided in favor of better strategies), your learning can be exhilarating once your are doing things with the information you acquire.

The Truth: Learning can be one of the most absorbing, compelling activities you can engage in—when it is the shortest path to what you want and need to know.

The best lesson anyone can learn from business school is an awareness of what it can't teach you—all the ins and outs of everyday business life. Those ins and outs are largely a self-learning process.

MARK MCCORMACK

Myth 2: Learning deals only with the subjects and skills taught in school. The formal school curriculum is only a sliver of what's worth knowing. Properly designed, a personal education program gives you the tools with which to take your learning into your own hands. Once you have graduated or left school, your curriculum is entirely for you to determine.

The most successful people choose their own highly personal trajectory once they are on their own. Some throw themselves deeply into one field, skill, or area; others explore several realms. In many cases these subjects were not part of any school or college curriculum, and quite often they are literally created by the learners themselves as they move along.

The Truth: The best subjects and skills for you to learn depend entirely on what you want to make of yourself and your life. This is true because each of us has a unique range of interests.

Myth 3: We must be passive and receptive to "absorb" knowledge. This is an old-fashioned image of education best described as "pouring information into an empty vessel." It doesn't apply to adult learning. In the last chapter it was noted that the brain is an active, constructing organ. Learning by doing is a far more accurate picture than the one that views it to be passive and book-based. As an adult learner, you will increasingly discover the learning aspects of any actions you take.

A good way to understand this is to think of an inventor. He or she wants to build a gadget to do something and may try many different combinations of components to get the right result. With each trial, the person has to evaluate how close he or she has come. Each new trial *creates knowledge,* and it is knowledge that can't be passively absorbed from a textbook because no one has built this gadget before. So each action of testing the gadget brings new knowledge, new learning. This is no less true if you're not an inventor.

The Truth: True learning is an active process of examining information, evaluating it for some purpose, and going on to the next action. You will get a direct feel for this with techniques described later in this book.

Myth 4: To learn, you must put yourself under the tutelage of a teacher. Education in most schools and colleges is based on the teacher as the driving, controlling force. The teacher decides the scope of the subject, the approach, the pace, the breakpoints, and the style. The teacher is the one who says whether or not you've learned satisfactorily and what to do about it if you haven't.

> A [teacher] is like a fire. If you get too close, you get burned. If you stay too far away, you don't get enough heat. A sensible moderation is recommended.
> FROM A TIBETAN PROVERB

Of course, a good teacher can be a wonderful resource for your learning. But you will get the most value from teachers by using them at the right time and for the right purpose. For most of your learning, you will find other resources more convenient and effective: a tape cassette in your car during commuting time, a conference brimming with exciting experts in a new field, or a video or computer program that you can play as the mood strikes you—late at night, early in the morning, or on weekends. Generally, you will find that a live teacher is best used either as a last resort (when there's no other way to start a subject) or as a capstone (to provide a peak experience based on your other learning).

The Truth: As an adult, you are in charge of your learning. Teachers are one important resource for your use, but they should be on tap, not on top. It's *your* learning, not theirs.

Myth 5: Learning has to be systematic, logical, and planned. This myth derives from our having observed that our classes always had a curriculum or syllabus—a complete plan for learning a subject. This course of action was already preset when we entered the picture, and our job was to get through it. The syllabus dictated what needed to be covered, in what order, using what materials, and how we'd be tested. Since every course and, indeed, most lectures and laboratory sessions had their own plan, we naturally came to assume that whenever something was to be learned, the first thing to do was to plan out the learning in advance, in detail.

But research has now revealed that this is not the way learning takes place naturally (i.e., outside of a classroom). In the everyday world, and in the lives of the best learners, such as writers, artists, teachers, and higher-level business and professional people, learning progresses organically. When interviewed about their learning, people readily recall that much of it was spontaneous, even serendipitous.

In short, any subject has a myriad of entry points and a multitude of

---

I am a stubborn little autodidact. My own way, or none at all.

PAUL GOODMAN

---

ways you can work your way through it. Each adult learner's path is a unique one, based on which directions and topics are most appealing and useful to the individual.

The Truth: Good learning balances reasonable planning with flexibility. Adult learning is sensitive to your changing interests and to the opportunities available.

Myth 6: Learning needs to be thorough, or it's not worth doing. In school, the criterion of success is to get a score of 100 or an A—meaning that you have learned virtually everything that the teacher presented in the course. But what if that's not your objective? Suppose that you found that just two topics in the entire course were of passionate interest to you and you spent most of your study time pursuing them, applying them, and building on them. You might actually have carried your study to the point where you had some original findings or thoughts of your own on those two topics. But, of course, you would fail the final.

The idea of *covering the subject* was invented by teachers and those who supervise teachers as a way of measuring whether or not they were doing a complete job. It rarely has relevance for the individual adult learner. Moreover, in many subjects and skills, you can learn 80 percent of what you want or need to know in the first twenty hours of study.

The Truth: One of your most useful decisions about any learning project is simply that of how much of the subject you want and need to learn—a decision that often is best made after you have started, not before.

Flow Learning—The Myth-Buster

This section will explore the alternatives to the fears and myths of learning. It starts by examining a distinctive state of mind and feeling in which learning is effortless and delightful. This state has been studied intensively by psychologists for the past fifteen years. They have interviewed and tested students, blue-collar workers, professionals, and the elderly. The findings all agree: when our brains are working in this distinctive state of mind, we can overcome our fears about learning.

This state is called flow, and it is vital to our personal happiness. The term was coined by the pioneer researcher in the field, Mihaly Csikszentmihalyi (pronounced Chick-SENT-me-hi, though he prefers to be called Mike), head of the Department of Behavioral Sciences at the University of Chicago and author of *Flow: The Psychology of Optimal Experiences.*

"What do we mean by being happy?" Professor Csikszentmihalyi asks. "Is it just pleasure and the absence of pain? These are rewarding conditions, indispensable to maintain psychic processes on an even keel. But happiness also depends on something else: the feeling that one is growing, improving. That process is, by definition, a process of learning, broadly defined. One might conclude that learning is necessary for happiness, that learning is the pursuit of happiness."

Flow is the state in which learning and happiness are most completely merged. An article in the *New York Times Magazine* described it as "a state of concentration that amounts to absolute absorption in an activity. In this state, action flows effortlessly from thought and you feel strong, alert, and unselfconscious. Flow is that marvelous feeling that you are in command of the present and performing at the peak of your ability ... research suggests that flow may be a common aspect of human experience."

Flow happens in every activity. In sports, it's that moment of reaching the zone where your ability and performance excel. In music, it takes place when you know your instrument and the piece so well that you just do it, as if you have *become* the instrument and the music. In dancing, painting, surgery, and even writing, there's a sense of control, a profound focus on what you're doing that leaves no room to worry about what anyone will think of your work. There are a number of features that characterize the Flow state:

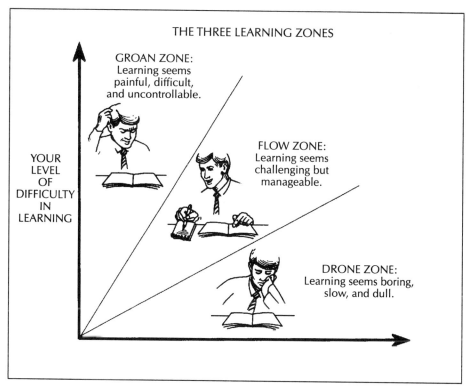

YOUR ABILITY—Skills, Attitudes, Strategies

Flow can occur when perceived challenges match perceived skills. Perhaps the most crucial feature is the delicate balance between what you *perceive* to be the challenges in the situation you face and how you *perceive* your own abilities to meet those challenges. Perception is important here because, as has been seen, the mind *actively constructs* the situations it faces. Any activity can be turned into a flow experience if viewed in the right way.

> *Humans can balance on strange surfaces. Even on unpredictable ones. It's called "getting in tune." Great musicians know it. Surfers ... knew it. Some waves throw you, but you're prepared for that. You climb back up and go at it once more.*
>
> FRANK HERBERT

The first step in recognizing the conditions for flow is to *have something to do,* an opportunity for action, a challenge. The next step is to recognize that you have some skills you can use to decide what to do next. The balance between these two will start the ball rolling for flow.

Let's try to make this issue of balance clearer by comparing it to experiences in which there is an *imbalance* between challenge and skills. Imagine you had to take a beginners' course in what you currently do for a living. Your skills and experience are already far beyond what is being taught. Sitting through endless explanations of things you already know would be agonizing torture, immensely boring. That sort of experience takes place in the Drone Zone.

Alternatively, suppose you attended a graduate seminar in something you know nothing about, quantum physics, for example. The

---

The ancient Greeks knew that learning comes from playing. Their concept for education (paideia) is almost identical to their concept for play (paidia).

ROGER VON OECH

---

speaker goes on and on, but you sit there, comprehending about one word in a hundred, hopelessly over your head. You are now in the Groan Zone.

Flow happens in the region between Groan and Drone. It happens when you need to use all you can bring to the situation—and to stretch yourself just a little bit more. *For flow to occur, the balance between what the situation demands and your skills must result in an advance, an increase in what you can do.* This gives us our first crucial characteristic for flow learning.

Flow states involve a sense of control in the situation. With that perceived balance comes another characteristic of the flow experience: a sense of control. Imagine sitting down to play a game of chess for the first time. You have some idea of how the pieces are supposed to move, but as the game develops, it may be hard to figure out what you should do next. Yet as you play more, and learn more, you start to recognize certain kinds of situations that repeat. You don't fall for the same traps again. You have a better idea of what to do, and so you have an increased sense of control instead of feeling as if you're helplessly floundering.

Flow happens in situations in which one has clearly defined goals and feedback. Games provide a good model for describing other features of the flow experience. According to Csikszentmihalyi, it is important in learning to have a clear sense of the goals in a situation and clear feedback about the results of your actions. This knowledge of what you're aiming for and what difference your actions make encourages you to concentrate on what is relevant to the situation, to become immersed in it.

In flow experiences, intense concentration on what is relevant develops the ability to merge unselfconscious action with awareness and to alter the experience of time. Think of kids who get involved in computer games, even the arcade shoot-'em-ups. What needs to be done to find the treasure or destroy the alien invaders is totally clear in each moment. And so it becomes easy to lose track of time, forget your hunger, and even ignore pain until you stop playing.

Thus in a clearly defined situation in which challenge is balanced by

---

Transformed perception could be called ordinary *magic.... It is ordinary because it is hidden from us by nothing other than our reluctance to see it, by habitual beliefs. It is* magic *because such transformation of perception happens suddenly, without cause or condition, even though the training may be long, requiring great practice and energy.*

JEREMY HAYWARD

---

skill and there is a sense of control, it becomes possible to focus concentration intensely on the relevant cues, to merge action and awareness in a way that drops any self-consciousness and may even change how the passage of time is experienced. This feature is our next essential in the flow experience.

Flow experiences arise from intrinsic motivation, not from concern with external rewards or goals. Csikszentmihalyi has found that this feature is as important as the balance of skills and challenge. It is also the most important part of flow for us as peak learners.

As we saw before in discussing learning fears and learning myths, feeding back information for the sake of a good grade can rob learning of its joy and make it torture. Sure, you can be pleased by a good grade, but it is not likely to make the process of cramming for exams any more pleasant.

On the other hand, if you're jamming on a guitar with friends or perfecting your jump shot on a basketball court, what makes those things fun, according to Csikszentmihalyi, is that you're doing them for their own sake. You may wind up with a good riff for a song or the ability to sink a basket from mid-court, but while you're getting there you are just having fun. That is, the experience of learning is enjoyable in itself, not for what you will eventually get out of it.

Csikszentmihalyi believes that people who use flow actually use *less* mental energy than those who are struggling to concentrate because they're bored or anxious. He sees the flow experience as something that's a built-in part of being human, of having a mind that processes information. In his view, new challenges are enjoyable because they prepare human beings to be involved with their environment and to succeed. For Csikszentmihalyi, the joys of learning are as natural as the pleasures of sex, and both serve evolutionary goals for the human species.

Learning in the Flow State

How does it feel to learn in a flow state? What would you experience if you could put yourself into this frame of mind whenever you chose? Here is how several clients and participants in my workshops have described it.

Helen, learning real-estate salesmanship

Flow learning was like scooping up sand at the seashore as a kid, and plopping it into place on a sand castle. Sure, there was an infinite amount to learn, an infinite amount of sand around. But I knew what I was after in those books, what I needed to build my castle, and just how to reach in for each handful and put it where I needed it.

Alice, learning pre-med organic chemistry

For me, the key was realizing that learning is a *feeling* thing as well as an intellectual process. Taking just ten minutes to enjoy and evoke my strong feelings about the subject, before each bout of studying, seemed to give me more energy and staying power. Also, keeping one favorite piece of music going whenever I turned to this subject helped evoke those feelings.

Jack, learning Spanish

After two previous unsuccessful attempts to learn Spanish in a class-room setting, I finally found a way that felt easy and safe to me: audio tapes that gave me confidence that I was making progress, and an im-mersion experience, where I simply talked Spanish at a party with other learners. The sense of being caught up in the social interactions, sometimes comically, as we all groped for words and grammar, left me too absorbed to worry about whether I was forgetting previous lessons while learning the next one.

Charles, learning astronomy

Nothing relaxes me more after a day's work in computer programming than to see things the average person will never see. It's a first-hand, direct experience of the universe. When the seeing is good, I find I often lose track of the hours I'm spending staring up at stars and plan-ets. The experience becomes an end in itself.

Fred, learning to play a computer game

At first, there's some mild frustration in figuring out what you have to do to get the game to respond. But in a very short time I find I've mas-tered the basics, and when I get caught up in the game itself I feel a tremendous urge to go further, surpass my past limits in the face of tougher challenges.

Susan, studying Chinese cooking

There is a sense of freedom and pleasure that I really enjoy about it. It almost feels as if I go into some kind of trance, deciding on ingredients and seasonings, mixing, stir-frying, or whatever. And then I can taste the results and decide what needs to be different next time.

Damn braces. Bless relaxes.
WILLIAM BLAKE

Getting to Flow: Some First Steps

To approach the flow state, you can begin with two preliminary exercises: Relaxation and Activating Your Inner Learner. In the next chapter you'll discover several other Peak Learning techniques for getting more flow into your learning.

Relaxation

Relaxation techniques have been around probably since the first cave dwellers got nervous about where they were going to find their next meal. A wave of attention on relaxation crested in the 1960s, when Transcendental Meditation got much media attention. Some people were put off by the religious trappings and Eastern flavor, but Harvard Medical School's Dr. Herbert Benson investigated TM scientifically and found that there really were measurable differences in improved performance as a result of using generic relaxation techniques. He wrote two books on the subject: *The Relaxation Response* and *Your Maximum Mind.* (Another good source is Lawrence LeShan's simple and straightforward *How to Meditate.*)

The benefits of relaxation involve the ability to get out of your own way. By regularly practicing relaxation exercises, such as the one below, you can cultivate the habit of letting go of daily stresses and strains and *reset* your mind for a new task.

Mike Csikszentmihalyi has noted the usefulness of ritual in preparation for a task, as a way to focus attention and help to create a situation in which the total immersion in flow can happen. But don't think you need to burn incense and chant spells in order to learn: ritual here means only a set of steps you take for the purpose of clearing your mind in order to enhance your concentration. Surgeons, for example, may develop a particular way of washing their hands and putting on gowns that they repeat for every operation they perform. The consistency of the practice simply helps them to peel away mental distractions and prepare them to concentrate fully on their work.

A personal relaxation ritual can work the same way. Rather than sitting down to learn something and being distracted by whether you remembered to lock the car or by remembering something you left off your grocery list, spend a few minutes relaxing before starting your learning. The relaxation exercise lets you become calm, clears away mental clutter and static, and prepares you to devote full attention to making sense of what you have chosen to study.

There are many fine exercises for relaxation available today in books and on audio tapes. If you already have one that you like, continue using it. If this sort of exercise is new to you, take a short break right now and try this easy introductory exercise taken from Dr. Benson's research. When you're ready, you can go on to the technique of imagining you're *already* a better learner than you think.

◆ ◆ ◆ ◆

Learning Relaxation

1. Select a focus word or short phrase that's firmly rooted in your personal belief system. For example, a Christian person might choose the opening words of Psalm 23, "The Lord is my shepherd"; a Jewish person, *Shalom;* a non religious individual, a neutral word like *one* or *peace.*

2. Sit quietly in a comfortable position.

3. Close your eyes.

4. Relax your muscles; bend your head slightly.

5. Breathe slowly and naturally, and repeat your focus words or phrase as you exhale.

(repeat focus word on exhale)

> *The concept of contacting the inner guide ... means going inward, quieting ourselves, opening to help, and asking for that help.*
>
> O. CARL SIMONTON

6. Assume a passive attitude. Don't worry about how well you're doing. When other thoughts come to mind, simply dismiss them and gently return to the repetition.

7. Continue for ten to twenty minutes.

8. Practice the technique once or twice daily.

◆ ◆ ◆ ◆

Activating Your Inner Learner

As peak learners, each of us has a hidden ace—an expert learner at our beck and call, whenever we need help. Where? In our minds' eyes. That's what activating your inner learner is about. It is the same kind of imaginative exercise that Olympic athletes use for training, a kind of mental rehearsal of peak performance called visualization.

This approach is being used more widely in sports and in many other fields as well. You no longer have to be training for the Olympics to get a videotape lesson on golf or tennis that tells you to picture yourself making the stroke.

The basis of visualization here goes back to the power of our minds and brains. Human beings have powerful imaginations. Why not use that power in positive, supportive ways rather than simply leaving your imagination focused on worrying about possible disasters?

Visualization works because when you take the time to picture yourself doing something well and bring to mind each detail of the process, you are strengthening the pattern of behavior in much the same way you do by actually practicing it. Visualizing is like knowing how to play a piece of music and being able to go through the motions of playing it in your head without even touching the instrument.

Life must be lived as a play, then a man will be able to propitiate the gods.

PLATO

We can achieve our "personal best" much more often by vividly imagining what we feel like when we do it. We can also imagine what it might be like to be some master learner we revere. Excellence is contagious. The more time we spend in imagination, "playing" Socrates, Galileo, or Einstein as well as ourselves at our best, the more exciting our own real-life learning will become.

Don Lofland is a teacher of Power Learning. He advises his students to actually give their imagined ideal learner a name. Sometimes he has them actually wear name tags with the names of the master learners they would like to emulate and talk with each other as if they were those people.

Once, when I was using this technique in one of my own seminars, I went all the way and dressed up as Socrates, with a bed sheet toga, leather sandals, and a soda can labeled, "Diet Hemlock." I went around giving advice like "know thyself" and answering questions about "my" life and philosophy. It was great fun, but it also served a more serious purpose. What better way can there be to get people really thinking about the importance of an inquiring mind and challenging issues than to remind them of the great philosopher who insisted he was the most ignorant of men and merely sought to learn?

The following Activating Your Inner Learner exercise will provide a nicely balanced closing to the exercise that started this chapter, Those Slow-Learning Blues. Remember that exercise also used the techniques of imaginative recall to bring back the worst of learning experiences. Now, we are about to look at the other side, the best of learning.

◆ ◆ ◆ ◆

Activating Your Inner Learner

Take a moment to recall the state of mind you had during your best learning experience, a time when learning came easily, naturally, and most pleasurably. Don't think the experience has to be from school days. The state of mind is what is important, not the subject matter you learned. You can use anything, as long as you remember the learning experience as being fun. It might be cooking, learning a sport or hobby, or even exploring a new city.

It also might be one of the skills with which you earn your living. The activity can be relatively simple, such as learning to type or drive, or complex, such as learning the periodic table or financial equations.

1. Start by relaxing in a comfortable position in a favorite chair. Do some deep breathing, using a relaxation technique such as the one you learned in the previous exercise.

2. Now, recall the time when your learning went so well. Where are you? Can you bring back physical sensations, such as the light or the sounds or smells of the place? Who are you with? Picture the faces of people involved, and hear their voices. How do you feel?

    Does this moment stand out from the stream of your life? Do you feel a surge of satisfaction at "getting it"? Did mastering something new make you feel good about yourself? How do you think others felt—the other learners, if any, and the teacher, if there was one?

3. Dwell imaginatively on what you were seeing, hearing, and feeling during your experience. Enjoy this for as long as you like.

◆ ◆ ◆ ◆

That should start to give you a feel for what it means to be a peak learner and for the experience of flow learning. Remember that the key point here is *how it felt*. The more time

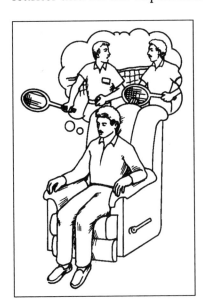

you can spend feeling good about learning, imagining yourself enjoying learning, or imagining yourself as someone you respect who did enjoy learning, the easier it will be for you to enjoy your own learning—and, the bottom line, the easier it will be for you to learn anything!

At this point, you are nearly halfway through reading about those aspects of Peak Learning that deal with emotions. Consider what you have learned so far.

First, you have learned the why and how of the connection between feelings and learning: the many ways in which we can interfere with our enjoyment of learning by allowing out-of-date feelings to trip us up. Practicing the above visualization exercise offers a way to counter those past emotions. Use it whenever you experience any anxiety connected with learning.

Everything begins ... with belief. What we believe is the most powerful option of all.

NORMAN COUSINS

You have seen some of the many deeply held fears that people have about learning and how they often arise because our past educational experience made a number of wrong assumptions about how people learn, assumptions that have been disproved by more recent research. You have also taken a tour through the unfortunate myths spread by the system of schooling we have experienced. Those beliefs were carefully distinguished from the type of learning we want to do as adults, as peak learners choosing to learn as much or as little of what we want in the way that suits us best.

You have taken your first steps toward encouraging yourself to be a better learner, toward retraining your feelings about learning by learning to relax and by activating your "inner learner." The next chapter will continue the retraining process by presenting two more powerful strategies for self-encouragement.

IV.
Building Your Learning
Confidence ◆◆◆◆

This chapter continues the discussion of how to boost the power of the learning process. Once you recognize the negative, subconscious, and hidden beliefs that diminish your ability to learn, you need to take conscious steps to eliminate them.

We are what we think. All that we are arises with our thoughts.
With our thoughts we make the world.

BUDDHA

The ability to learn was once natural for all of us. Watch a toddler poking around a new room, for example. She'll ask a hundred questions a day, want to experience everything, use all her senses, not care if she makes a fool of herself, and concoct her own zany ideas.

At that age, you learned more powerfully than at any period since. First, you had to make sense of that "booming, buzzing confusion," as the great psychologist William James called the world of the newborn. Later, you mastered your native language from scratch.

Two Peak Learning strategies, called affirmations and invocations, make it possible to bring back that power and delight. They cultivate a kind of positive, adventurous, energetic attitude that encourages intellectual abilities and senses. This mental posture endows you with a state of mind that is open to learning and helps you overcome learning fears.

Affirming Your Power to Learn

The first technique, affirmations, is based on the power of autosuggestion. This idea originated with a French doctor, Emile Coué, around the turn of the century. Coué was the person who invented the famous

56

phrase, "Every day, in every way, I'm getting better and better." He believed that by repeating these words to oneself regularly, a person could cure all his or her ills. While his claims for the powers of autosuggestion to cure illness were probably exaggerated, more recent research on placebos and psychoneuroimmunology (PNI) suggest there is a basis in fact for improvements in mental attitude based on this technique, and that such improvements can also have benefits for physical health.

Autosuggestion allows you to internalize new attitudes about learning. It works because our subconscious mind is highly receptive to simple, positive statements that evoke our inner learner. When it hears that you are the kind of learner described below, it increasingly accepts that positive self-image, and that state of mind becomes more accessible to you. Think of autosuggestion as a kind of self-programming, a way to practice the habit of increased self-confidence about your learning abilities. You can also think of affirmations as a kind of ritual in the sense described by Mike Csikszentmihalyi in the last chapter—something you do regularly to encourage the focus and concentration of flow learning.

One of the leading teachers of the autosuggestion technique is Shakti Gawain, author of *Creative Visualization*. "The practice of doing affirmations allows us to begin replacing some of our stale, worn-out, or negative mental chatter with more positive ideas and concepts," she says. "It is a powerful technique, one which can, in a short time, completely transform our attitudes and expectations ... and thereby totally change what we create for ourselves."

Something we were withholding made us weak
Until we found it was ourselves.
ROBERT FROST

Nowhere is this truer than in the realm of learning because we are dealing with the state of our own minds, not external conditions. I'm not sure about how effective affirmations may be in changing the external conditions of our lives—by bringing us riches or friends, for example—although a positive attitude in these areas can certainly be helpful. But I do know, both from my own practice and from the experience of my students, that affirmations can work wonderfully in opening the mind and making you feel more confident and positive about any learning experience.

The affirmations I'm going to suggest are simple and direct. In fact, they may seem simplistic at first. But be patient; they have to be elementary to have an impact on our subconscious minds. As you fill them with your own feelings, these affirmations will have surprising power.

◆ ◆ ◆ ◆

Peak Learning Affirmations

1. Choose a time when you will have complete privacy and no interruptions for at least half an hour.

2. Recall your best personal experience of Peak Learning, the one you used in the exercise on Activating Your Inner Learner in the last chapter. Let yourself reexperience the state of mind and its associated emotions deeply.

3. Now, read each of the following statements slowly to yourself, thinking about how each of them was a part of your recollected experience. After reflecting on each statement for as long as you like, speak it out loud in a gentle voice.

    My learning is exciting to me.

    The more I learn, the more exciting it gets.

    I find each step in my learning enjoyable.

    I understand easily and deeply.

    I enjoy adding to my knowledge and understanding.

    Learning is a pleasure.

    Knowing and remembering are easy for me.

    I love learning and knowledge more and more.

    Learning keeps me mentally alert.

    I am thrilled by the rich variety of my knowledge.

    Every day presents me with opportunities for growth.

    I am enthusiastic about learning.

4. Now repeat the whole list aloud several times. You may want to make your own audio-cassette recording of the statements. Read them slowly, allowing ten to twenty seconds between them. Make any minor word changes you like and skip any statements you don't care for or feel uneasy about. You can also add statements of your own, using the same simple, present-tense format.

5. When you've read the list through, put the recorder on pause, shuffle the affirmations, and read them again in a different order. This will help your mind to stay alert while listening.

6. Repeat until you have filled a thirty-minute tape this way.

Once you have created the tape, you can play it anywhere. You can use your driving time to encourage yourself to learn better all day, or you can play the tape softly, perhaps with a pillow speaker or headphones, just before you fall asleep. Set your own schedule. As with the relaxation exercise, however, it's best to use the tape on a regular basis until you notice enough improvement to feel it is no longer necessary.

◆ ◆ ◆ ◆

Peak Learning Invocations

Invocations are calls for assistance. There is, in fact, a classical basis behind this collection of techniques, namely the myth of the Muses from Greek culture. This myth dramatized the fact that when you want your mind to work at its optimum, in any field from history to sports, you must deliberately put yourself in a receptive but energized state in which the *muse*—the spirit of excellence in that area—can add to your own efforts. The goddess summoned from outside, we now realize, was merely a symbol of a spirit that lies within each of us. But the *process* of summoning that spirit is essential. The following techniques are ways to do that.

These strategies prepare your mind for learning in many ways. You will find yourself relaxed, but braced for an invigorating mental workout. You'll feel your mental powers prepared for action. You will be keenly alert, but not tense. You will be confident of your capacity to rise to the occasion. Collectively, these techniques work to improve motivation, energy, concentration, understanding, retention, and even inspiration.

The invocations are:

> *Fall in love.*
>
> *Stir your soul.*
>
> *Use your experience.*
>
> *Energize your brain.*
>
> *Catch others' enthusiasm.*

You may wish to experiment with each of these over the next few weeks. Then, whenever you need to evoke Peak Learning, you can use the one or two that fit your mood and the task at hand. Doing one or two of these warm-ups can take as little as two minutes. But, properly used, they will increase your productivity, efficiency, and performance.

Because each of us is unique as a learner, you will find some of these invocations more congenial than others. I have intentionally offered you more than you need, so that you can choose the ones you like. Each has its own purpose, as you will see. Some will be useful before, during, or after your learning sessions. For example, "Use your experience" will be useful in enlivening your learning or in thinking about it afterward. "Energize your brain" is helpful when you're actually sitting down to study or are about to start a class or workshop. "Stir your soul" can be done any time to regularly remind yourself of how powerful your mind is.

Invocation 1: Fall in love. The single most powerful thing you can do to foster learning is to fall in love with what you're learning. Socrates insisted that learning begins with Eros—the same appreciation that draws us toward attractive people. In essence, the phrase *love of learning* is not merely a metaphor, nor does it mean simply a lust to understand. Rather, it is a truly profound emotion of respect, appreciation, or even adoration that is necessary to invigorate the process.

In our own times, the great philosopher Alfred North Whitehead described the first stage in any learning project as romance. The subject matter has the fresh impact of novelty, and the new learner catches tantalizing glimpses of something important gleaming through the mass of material. "In this stage, learning is not dominated by systematic procedures," Whitehead believed. Instead, you simply explore, randomly, whatever catches your eye, constantly delighted by unexpected treasures.

The road to new interests is the natural route of fascination and delight.

HILTON GREGORY

This feeling is familiar to most people. We often have such an experience when plunging into a new problem or challenge, discovering a new author or artist who illuminates our life, or visiting a foreign country. Perhaps this is the stage of learning that marks the beginning of flow, when we are captivated by something new.

It is worth noting that Whitehead's second stage, called *precision*, *does* involve a more systematic approach to organizing the new facts we are learning. But his final stage, *generalization*, requires "a return to romanticism with the added advantage of classified ideas and relevant technique." At that point, creative use of the learned material can happen—what we've called building on the relevant information in order to go further.

This invocation suggests the importance of becoming infatuated with our subject, something that traditional education seldom allows. When you tackle any new topic, think of the first get-acquainted phase as one of discovery and delight. You need to explore those aspects of a topic that particularly appeal to you and use them as a springboard. Feel free to skip, scan, and read randomly. Cover only as much as you enjoy. Don't try to store or remember; just get a feel for the subject.

This phase may turn out to be more productive than you would expect. In fact, you may learn some of the most important points about your subject while roaming around it randomly. You often learn the most important points about any new subject at the start, before you know enough to develop preconceptions about it or fears about your ignorance. In many cases, your initial learning makes up more than 50 percent of what you want and need to know. And you learn these points much faster and more easily than the less important 50 percent that follows.

But your primary goal here is enjoyment. See how many and which angles you can find about your subject that delight, intrigue, amuse, and gratify you.

For those who have experienced it, the hour of the awakening of the passion for knowledge is the most memorable one of a lifetime.

COLIN WILSON

You may find it easier to fall in love with a person than with an abstract subject. So keep in mind that every subject, no matter how cut-and-dried it may seem now, was once the passionate preoccupation of some fierce genius who created it out of his or her lifeblood. Discover one of those people, learn about his or her life, and you will find that your subject comes alive.

Tackle mathematics, for instance, by browsing in Eric Bell's *Men of Mathematics* to learn about one of the wonderful characters who created the science of numbers. Or, if you're interested in city planning, read a biography of Robert Moses or the creator of Central Park, Frederick Law Olmsted—men who championed the cause of livable cities against harrowing odds.

The overall aim and effect of this invocation is twofold: to create an attitude toward what you choose to learn that is eager, passionate, enthusiastic, and warmly appreciative; and, at the same time, to give yourself permission to *have fun* as you begin to strike up an acquaintance with your subject matter.

Invocation 2: Stir your soul. I assume that you already value and relish using your mind. But everyone can use a booster once in a while; we need to be reminded in a fresh, vivid way of what we already know. We also need to take time regularly to figure out how our learning can be fine-tuned to the changing circumstances of our lives—to what has happened in the past week and to what we will confront next week.

So, whatever else you are learning, you should also be regularly refreshing your awareness of the enormous potential of your mind. In doing so, you are opening a window through which the great thoughts of others can kindle a fire of inspiration.

The best way to do this is to dip daily into the classics. You will find that reading a page or two of them every morning or evening will give you an exhilarating sense of what humans can accomplish. It will also usually suggest some ways you can make your other current learning easier or more productive.

That which is unique and worthwhile in us makes itself felt only in flashes. If we do not know how to catch and savor these flashes, we are without growth and without exhilaration.

ERIC HOFFER

My basic list of such works includes the *Notebooks* of Leonardo da Vinci (perhaps the greatest learning log ever created), Plato's *Dialogues,* and Aristotle's *Metaphysics.* Look them over the next time you're in the library, see which appeals to you most, and give it a try. You'll want to add the books that work to your permanent library. Other useful works might be found in the *Great Books* series created by Mortimer Adler, but don't feel you have to limit yourself to ancient classics. My own list also includes contemporary books about learning, creativity, and psychology. Even intelligent, well-written fiction can be mentally stimulating.

Another important way to stir your soul is to partake of the vast repertoire of magazines published today. Most of us are familiar with only a few national publications, but there are literally hundreds of provocative and thought-inspiring magazines that can introduce you to new ideas, social trends, and worldviews. Even when you disagree with the writers' opinions, they will challenge you to think and to develop a greater understanding of many issues than you may have had before.

To start with, I recommend that you read at least one periodical devoted to the subject of learning, growth, mental-stimulation techniques, or creativity. Here are some of the best. Sending them a self-addressed stamped envelope will bring you additional materials and possibly a sample issue, so that you can judge for yourself which ones suit your style.

- *Your Personal Best* is a newsletter full of practical methods of enhancing your mental and physical well-being and performance. Rodale Press, 33 E. Minor Street, Emmaus, Pennsylvania 18098

- *On the Beam* is the best newsletter on new teaching and learning techniques using the full range of senses, capacities, and potentialities. 4649 Sunnyside North, Seattle, Washington 98103

- *Adult and Continuing Education Today* is a newsletter for professionals in the field, but useful to anyone involved in the lifelong learning movement as learner, teacher, or program developer. P.O. Box 1425, Manhattan, Kansas 66502

- *The Learning Bulletin* is an excellent source on findings and practices in innovative learning. National Learning Laboratory, 8417 Bradley Boulevard, Bethesda, Maryland 20817

- *The Brain-Based Education Networker* has superb coverage on ways to use your *whole brain* for learning. 449 Desnoyer, St. Paul, Minnesota 55104

Additionally, one of the most interesting and efficient magazines is

---

Experience isn't what happens to you. It's
what you make out of what happens to you.
ALDOUS HUXLEY

---

the *Utne Reader.* This bimonthly magazine is a sort of *Reader's Digest* of the alternative press, in which each issue brings together articles and commentary on a major political or social issue of the times from a diverse group of nontraditional and smaller publications. Its publisher, Eric Utne, also recommends the following magazines and newspapers for those who wish to challenge themselves to alternative thinking:

East West	*New Options*
Extra!	*The Sun*
Granta	*Village Voice*
In These Times	*Whole Earth Review*
Multinational Monitor	*World Watch*
The National	*Zeta*

A good newsstand or your local library is bound to carry most of these, or you can write to the *Utne Reader* (1624 Harmon Place, Suite 330, Minneapolis, Minnesota 55403), who, for a small fee, will send you information on how to order the above publications.

Invocation 3: Use your experience You already have an immense database for learning things to help you cope with your current problems. By reaching back for the most relevant prior experiences in your life, you can locate lessons learned then that apply in the present.

You do this already, of course. One of our most familiar experiences is to be reminded of something that happened in the past when we are going through something similar in the present.

For example, suppose you're applying for a new job. You've made all the necessary preparations, got your resume together, and dressed appropriately, and now it's time for the interview. As it proceeds, you begin to feel a slight sense of uneasiness, not just the usual nervousness about whether your skills and experience will be acceptable to your potential employer. Your mind flashes to past interviews, to stories friends have told you about their own job interviews, or even to similar situations in TV shows or movies. You recall a friend who found herself handling executive-level responsibilities when she'd been hired as a secretary. Suddenly your hunch comes into focus: the way the interviewer is talking seems to suggest the position is a more demanding one than you had supposed, one for which you might have to travel or be available on weekends, if necessary. At the right moment, you can ask a question or two to confirm this and adjust the salary you were going to ask for.

That swift, silent scan of previous experience has helped you to decide how to act in the present moment. You went from a vague hunch, to consulting your memories, to forming a theory based on past experience, to asking a question and changing your plans based on the answer. That's the same kind of learning process a scientist would use in the laboratory.

This process will be discussed in greater depth in Chapter VII, when you will see how to make the most effective use of your recollections to enrich your present learning. For now, the key point is simply that you should allow those flashes from your past to be a part of your present learning. In fact, you should go looking for them.

One of the surest signs of active learning is the ability to take some new bit of information and *connect it* to the rest of your life experience. If you can see how the new data fits in *anywhere*, then you have anchored it in your mind's own cross-referencing system—which is more complicated than any library catalogue or computer—so it can be jogged back into awareness.

Invocation 4: Energize your brain. Whenever you're about to call upon your brain, it's worthwhile to check out the condition of your body. The principle that learning depends on the state of your body has been explored by several leaders in the field of learning how to learn. Don Lofland, for example, insists in his workshops on Power Learning that any study session or other learning occasion "begins with your physiology." He urges his students to do a quick check of their bodily state and make whatever adjustments are necessary in terms of relaxation, the temperature of the room, thirst, or hunger.

One practitioner who has probed this principle is Washington-based Michael Gelb. He bases his High Performance Learning seminars on learning to juggle. "It's a way of making participants aware of how they tense up their bodies when confronted with the challenge of learning something new," Gelb explains. "You wouldn't think people would be intimidated by something as unserious as juggling. I deal with seasoned, thick-skinned executives. Yet you confront them with this playful challenge, and you can see the change in their bodies—and *they* can *feel* those changes! Juggling is just a metaphor, of course. But it gets right to the role of the body in learning. The principle is that the bodily state of the learner is the key to all learning. I want to free the body in order to free the mind."

Gelb urges his seminar participants to notice when they tense up their bodies in learning and to become aware of what messages that sends to the brain. Basically, that message is usually "I can't do this. I'm afraid. I'll feel silly or stupid. But I probably need to feel this way in order to learn." When you get this tense, your brain pretty well shuts down, and new learning is even harder in that state.

As Gelb's work shows, this common, habitual bodily reaction that interferes with learning can be caught, stopped, and changed by consciously relaxing your body to a state more conducive to learning. The how-to details of such a procedure should be learned in an experiential, hands-on workshop with someone who can use nonverbal means of teaching (like juggling) and by watching your body for reactions you may not even be aware of. But you can benefit even before taking such training just by keeping your body in mind, as it were. The basic principles are as follows.

1. Be aware of your bodily state while learning. If you sense tensions, rigidities, or discomforts, take steps to alleviate them. You may need to go back and do the Relaxation Exercise described in Chapter III. A change in temperature or ventilation, a brisk walk, a light snack, or a refreshing drink also can alter your state.

2. Use the active-learning techniques from Chapters VI to give your brain some enjoyable and varied tasks to perform on the material you're learning

3. Be alert to signs of fatigue, tension, or irritation. Rather than suppressing them, attend to them, then throw yourself back into the learning process relaxed and refreshed.

Learning is movement from moment to moment.
J. KRISHNAMURTI

The single most important part of your body for your learning is, of course, your brain, so taking care of it is paramount. The three essentials to this care are exercise, rest, and nutrition.

Exercise provides oxygen, which your brain needs and uses at a disproportionate rate given its size in comparison to other major organs. Weighing in at only 2 percent of your body's total, your brain consumes 25 percent of your intake of oxygen. When a person's oxygen supply is cut off, even if for only a few minutes, brain cells start to die. For these reasons, regular brisk exercise in the midst of your learning sessions (which include everything from reading to attending a workshop) is highly advisable. Regular exercise is also important in maintaining healthy circulation in the arteries leading to the brain, which deliver the needed oxygen.

Adequate rest is also important. Setting a consistent bedtime and wake-up time results in optimum functioning for most people. Disrupting your customary pattern is likely to result in reduced mental energy and acuity, as is experienced during jet lag.

It is now known that individuals differ in the amount of sleep they need to function at their best, and there's a good deal of evidence that most of us could reduce the amount we sleep by one or two hours a night with no negative effects. On the contrary, those who do so and make good use of the extra time in the morning or evening tend to feel better and have improved morale.

Finally, diet is important for the functioning of your brain. Just as the brain uses an amount of oxygen out of proportion to its size, so it is exceptionally sensitive to the effects of different nutritional strategies. It isn't too good an idea to try to learn something complicated after a big meal, for example; it is just too easy to nod off and nap. So much of the body's blood supply is involved in digestion that there's much less available to carry oxygen to the brain for alert learning.

The usual injunctions of nutritionists apply, of course, to learning situations as they do to a normal, healthy lifestyle: Eat a well-balanced diet of generally unprocessed foods, stress fresh fruits and vegetables, and avoid too many artificial ingredients along with sugar, starch, caffeine, alcohol, and unnecessary drugs.

If you want to explore more deeply how what you eat affects your brain, the best book I know is *Eat Right, Be Bright* by neurosurgeon Arthur Winter and science writer Ruth Winter. "A wise choice of food may actually improve your mental ability," the authors contend. While much of the book concerns matters not directly affecting your learning, the authors review all the available research on such matters as eating disorders, problems with dieting, the effects of food additives and of supplementary vitamins and minerals. They suggest, for example, that vitamin B-12, which can be obtained only from meat, dairy products, and eggs (foods that many cholesterol-conscious consumers tend to avoid) is vital to the growth and maintenance of a healthy brain and nervous system.

What kinds of foods can improve mental sharpness immediately? It's important to know this for selecting snacks and meals during periods of intense learning. Dr. Judith Wurtman of M.I.T., author of *Managing Your Mind and Mood Through Food*, asserts that "ups and downs, your mental energy or lack of it, are the result of changes in your brain chemistry." After seven years of research she has concluded that carbohydrates make you sleepy, protein increases your alertness, and fat dulls your ability to perform mentally. In her book she offers A, B, and C lists of foods—the A's being ideal for situations in which you want to sustain peak mental performance.

The general principles Wurtman promotes are to eat lightly—just enough to satisfy your hunger; avoid or minimize carbohydrates to avoid drowsiness; use coffee (in moderation) to keep you wakeful and positive-minded (two separate effects); and take a modest amount of protein to sustain alertness.

To keep the body in good health is a duty ... otherwise we shall not be able to keep the mind strong and clear.

BUDDHA

◆ ◆ ◆ ◆

Exercising

The single best way to adjust your physiological state for learning is to do some brisk exercise. Therefore, follow this simple regimen when you want to get your system geared up for learning.

1. Take a vigorous walk for fifteen to twenty minutes.
2. While walking, focus your eyes regularly on the farthest horizon or on the tops of buildings or clouds in the skies.
3. Also look *around,* taking in as much of the terrain as possible, giving your neck a nice workout.
4. Swing your arms and take big healthy strides.
5. Breathe deeply.

If it's not feasible for you to leave your desk or room, do some stretching.

1. Stretch your arms above your head as far as you can reach.
2. Stretch to the sides, revolving your arms.
3. Bend over sandpaper the floor.
4. Twist your arms to touch hard-to-reach parts of your body.
5. If you're with someone else, have that person give you a little massage of the shoulders and neck and return the favor.
6. Rotate your head.
7. Walk or run in place.
8. Breathe deeply.

Finally, when you get back down to work, check your posture. When I say that Peak Learning is a type of posture toward life, I mean it literally as well as figuratively. Your physical posture reflects and influences how well you learn. Win Wenger, author of *Beyond O.K.,* dramatizes this with the following exercise.

◆ ◆ ◆ ◆

The Learning Stance

1. Stand before a full-length mirror with your legs comfortably spread and your hands hanging at your sides.
2. Turn you feet toes-in, facing each other.
3. Turn your hands with the palms facing front.
4. Open your mouth and let your tongue rest against the inside of your lower lip.
5. Furrow your brow the way you do when you hear something you can't quite understand.
6. Now, say in a firm, loud voice: "I am a sharp, swift, penetrating learner."

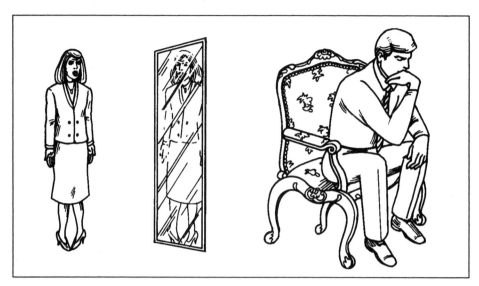

By contrast, adopt this posture.

1. Sit comfortably in a chair with one leg extended out a little farther than the other.

2. Rest your right elbow on your right knee.

3. Rest your chin against your forefinger; hold it with your thumb.

4. Rest your left hand against your left thigh to balance yourself.

5. Look into the middle distance the way you would when absorbed with a problem and getting ideas on solving it.

6. Now, say to yourself: "I'm just not very clever at this sort of thing."

◆ ◆ ◆ ◆

It didn't come out quite right, did it? Your posture worked against it, because you were in the posture of Rodin's *Thinker,* the archetypal symbol of thoughtfulness. The impact of adopting this posture is described by Edward de Bono, a pioneer in teaching people how to think.

> I want you to imagine that … chin-on-hand pose which is supposed to come to any thinker who is being more than just frivolous. As a matter of fact, I believe that thinking should be active and brisk rather than gloomy and solemn. But the traditional image is a useful one for the moment.
>
> Throw yourself into that pose—physically, not mentally—and you will become a thinker. Why? Because if you play-act being a thinker, you will become one.
>
> Adopt the pose of a thinker. Go through the motions. Have the intention and make it manifest to yourself and to those around. Quite soon your brain will follow the role you are playing.

As de Bono points out, posture is one of many subconscious cues our minds read when we decide to learn. And I hope you also caught the similarity to the exercise in Chapter III called Activating the Inner Learner. (That's another example of making use of the invocation *Use your experience).* When we assume a role, we don't have to be on stage or before a camera for the features of that role to appear within us. Even if we have only the foggiest idea of *deep thought,* we can develop the capacity by assuming the physical stance.

Invocation 5: Catch others' enthusiasm. Remember that the purpose of any invocation is to heighten your enthusiasm, your zest for learning. You want to rekindle the adventurous and energetic attitude you had as a child. One way to do that is to catch enthusiasm from other people who are already swept up in your subject. Many of us learn most easily and powerfully from other people. And enthusiasm, like excellence, is highly contagious!

Getting involved with someone who's pursuing the same subject makes for companionable learning. Seek agreeable co-learners when you attend a class. Check for people looking for books in the same section at the library you use and look for other possible intellectual liaisons.

In every community in this country you can find people who are excited about their favorite subject. They often meet, whether the occasion is called a luncheon, reception, or lecture. Just recall the following familiar offerings that you've doubtless seen advertised in your own community. Each of these brings together, as a one-time special event or on a regular basis, people who are eager to share the excitement of their field or skill.

> Business networking breakfasts
>
> Foreign-language societies such as Goethe House,
>   Alliance Française, and Asian Society
>
> Astronomers' sky-viewing nights
>
> Marketing luncheons
>
> Museum and gallery openings
>
> Computer users clubs
>
> Archaeological society lectures
>
> Civil War roundtables
>
> Medievalists or science-fiction fans

There are two kinds of knowledge: knowing something, and knowing who know it.
                                                    SAMUEL JOHNSON

You can also find enthusiasts eager to share their excitement at specialty stores in virtually every field, from photography, dance, the occult, and music to cooking, computers, nutrition, writing, and stage magic.

Just for practice, take two subjects in which you'd enjoy meeting some fellow students or expert practitioners, hearing some good shop-talk, and seeing what local events are upcoming; then, look up the specialty stores in these two areas in the Yellow Pages.

A second way to tap the enthusiasm of a field is to read the liveliest newsletter in that field. (The specialty store you just looked up will probably have sample copies.) What you're after here is the in-group chatter, the sense of camaraderie in which you will soon be able to participate.

Once you've found your source of enthusiasts, you may want to strike up a friendship and spend more time with one. Such people are usually delighted by a newcomer with a genuine excitement about their field; it refreshes their own energy to tell a bright novice what they're letting themselves in for. So it's often possible to strike a mutually agreeable deal in which you serve a mini-apprenticeship by just tagging along and helping with some chores in return for the delights of a guided tour and some first-class instruction along the way.

In this chapter you have seen examples of solid techniques to help you release the full power of Peak Learning in your own life. Because learning is so individual, I wouldn't expect anyone to find that all the suggested techniques work equally well. But, without a doubt, you will find that one or more of these will make a substantial difference in the ease and enjoyment with which you learn. Do not neglect these techniques.

- ◆ Use affirmations to encourage your subconscious mind to find learning exciting, easy, and fun.

- ◆ Fall in love with a field you want to learn by *playing* in it, unsystematically, in order to get a feel for the parts that will be most pleasurable to you.

- ◆ Regularly seek stimulation, support, and inspiration from great examples of learning in the past.

- ◆ Use all of your past experience when you need it to help you in a present learning situation.

- ◆ Recognize that if you want your brain to function at its best in learning, you have to take care of your body as well. The right combinations of food and exercise can help make you a better learner.

- ◆ Remember that opportunities exist everywhere to find others who share your interests and will be happy to help you increase your enthusiasm for learning.

All of these techniques will help you become a peak learner. In exactly the same way that the negative emotions about learning hindered your progress, the positive emotions you develop using these methods will continue to make your learning easier and more enjoyable.

V.
Discovering Your Personal Learning Profile ♦♦♦♦

Many people are surprised to hear that they have a distinctive, personal way of using their minds. There are two reasons for their surprise.

First, we've all been taught to think that our schooling shaped our minds into the one *right* way to learn and think. That's what all those lessons on logical thinking, study skills, and test-taking strategies were all about. The teachers were supposed to be training us to use our minds correctly, at least as far as traditional education goes. However, the way of learning and thinking that we were taught in school is only one way. And it is not the one that is most congenial for the majority of adults.

The second reason why some people are surprised to find that they think in a distinctive way is that other people's thought processes are not visible to us. The brain is the ultimate black box, which we can't open. So we are unaware of how differently each of us thinks and learns.

But four decades of psychological research lead us to conclude that each person has a distinct, individual way of dealing with information and concepts. In fact, if our faces differed as much as the way our minds work, some of us would have eyes like magnifying glasses, others would

---

Exploration of the full range of his own potentialities is not something that the self-renewing man leaves to the chances of life. It is something he pursues systematically, or at least avidly, to the end of his days. He looks forward to an endless and unpredictable dialogue between his potentialities and the claims of life—not only the claims of life—not only the claims he encounters but the claims he invents.

JOHN GARDNER

---

have noses like an elephant's trunk, and still others might have ears like radar dishes!

Professor Robert Smith of Northern Illinois University provides an excellent analysis of learning styles based on his years of monitoring the literature in the field.

> People differ in how they go about certain activities associated with learning. They differ as to how they think. They differ as to how they approach problem solving. They differ as to how they go about "information processing," or putting information through their minds. Some people like to "get the big picture of a subject first and then build toward a full understanding of that picture by details and examples. Other people like to begin with examples and details and work through to some kind of meaningful construct or way of looking at an area of knowledge out of these details. Some like theory before going into practice. Others don't.
>
> With regard to method, one might hear a person say, "I don't like discussion," or, "I went to a workshop and we did role playing—it made me uneasy." With field trips, we might hear, "I fall behind and can't hear what the guide is saying." People differ with regard to the amount of structure and autonomy that they want. Some seem to prefer being told what to do at every stage of learning, while some [only need] some structure and some freedom of choice. People differ, too, in their reactions to competition. When they find themselves in a seminar where the instructor sets them against each other, some experience great anxiety and even drop out, while others appear to thrive. Environmental considerations also come into play—for example, preferred locations and physical conditions for learning. Some like it hot, some like it cold. The amount of light, background noise, and mobility permitted while learning are relevant factors to consider.

Here are three typical examples of differing learning styles.

◆ Andrew Soltise, a new sales representative in pharmaceuticals headquartered in Minneapolis, found himself sinking fast in the plethora of technical information provided by his company and had difficulty keeping up with data on competitors' products.

Variety's the very spice of life,
That gives it all its flavor.
WILLIAM COWPER

◆ Barbara Paar, an attorney in St. Louis, was struggling to master a new word-processing program using legal lingo. "I felt mired in details in the manual," she explained. "I couldn't really get hold of the big picture, so all those details kept slipping away."

◆ Nicholas Naritz, a New York editor for an apparel industry trade magazine, wanted to bone up on everything French—language, popular culture, trends in business—for an upcoming trip to

Europe. But he felt uneasy at the "scraps of knowledge" he was accumulating, as he put it, from an assortment of books he had bought.

Andrew's problem was caused by a different aspect of his learning style from Barbara's. He had fallen into the habit of doing his technical reading in the evening, after his day of calling on doctors and pharmacies. But Andrew quickly discovered from the first exercise you'll be doing that he is a lark, not an *owl*—he learns best first thing in the morning, not late at night. When he swiveled his schedule around to get up an hour earlier in the morning, do his reading before breakfast, and just relax in the evening, he had no trouble in keeping current.

Another simple exercise you will do below revealed that Barbara prefers to learn "from the top down" rather than "from the bottom up." Her problems were readily solved when she called the manufacturer's 800 number, explained the situation, and was referred to a commercially available alternate manual, which explained the whole system in the top-down way Barbara prefers.

Nicholas's problem, too, derived from his preferred way of learning. He discovered from the brain-dominance exercise you will do that the way he likes to learn is to absorb the spirit of a field by talking with people in it. That's how he'd become so knowledgeable about the apparel business, on which there was little to read and study. So he found a more satisfying way to learn all about France. He put away his books and magazines and started going to evening events at the Alliance Française. "I picked up what I needed to know, just by osmosis," he reported.

What does this mean for your learning? It reflects the simple truth that you can make your learning more productive by capitalizing on your personal learning style. Like these three typical learners, you can make your learning easier and more fun by discovering how you like to learn—and then adjusting things so that you learn that way.

We all have times when we think more effectively, and times when we should not be thinking at all.

DANIEL COHEN

In this chapter, you'll explore four important aspects of your personal learning style. The purpose of the exercises is to become more aware of how you like to learn. (As you go along, you might find it useful to make notes on each exercise in your learning log for use later in the chapter, when you put them all together to discover your personal learning profile.) Then, at the end of this chapter, you'll see how you can readily arrange to learn in the style best suited for you.

Test 1: Your Peak and Valley Learning Times

Everyone has a favorite time of day. For some of us it's the early evening, when we are unwinding from work and are eager for the night's activities; we feel more alive and capable, ready to dance until midnight. For others, it's that quiet period at dawn, when few people are up and the day seems fresh and new. A whole new field within psychology, *chronopsychology*, is devoted to researching the patterns of time and energy for each person.

It is now firmly established that each of us is mentally alert and motivated at certain times during the day. Larks seem to wake up singing, mentally speaking, while owls take hours to warm up and may not reach their peak until late afternoon or evening.

Remember that one of Andrew's problems, as we mentioned above, was that his peak learning time came during the early hours of the day just when he hit the office. But although this was the best time for him to be using his brain, he was beset by distractions. By realizing what was happening and planning around it, he dramatically improved his efficiency.

You obtain three benefits to knowing your own peak and valley times for learning and adjusting your learning efforts accordingly.

1. You will enjoy your learning more when you feel in the mood for it.

2. You will learn faster and more naturally because you will not be fighting resistance, fatigue, and discomfort.

3. You will make better use of your "low" times by doing things other than trying to learn.

This exercise will enable you to determine your time preference in learning.

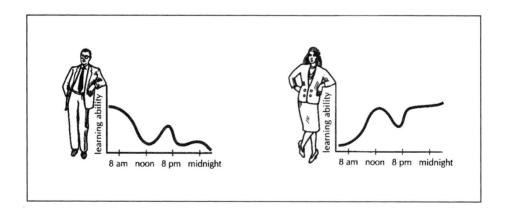

◆ ◆ ◆ ◆

Your Best and Worst of Times

The following questions will help you to sharpen your sense of what time of day you learn best. You may already be generally aware of your preferences, but these simple questions will help spur you to act on them. The questions were developed by Professor Rita Dunn of St. John's University, Jamaica, New York. Answer *true* or *false* to each question.

I dislike getting up in the morning. _True_

I dislike going to sleep at night. _False_

I wish I could sleep all morning. _False_

I stay awake for a long time after I get into bed. _False_

I feel wide awake only after 10:00 in the morning. _False_

If I stay up late at night, I get too sleepy to remember anything. _True_

I usually feel a *low* after lunch. _False_

When I have a task requiring concentration, I like to get up early in the morning to do it. _False_

I'd rather do those tasks requiring concentration in the afternoon. _True_

I usually start the tasks that require the most concentration after dinner. _False_

I could stay up all night. _False_

I wish I didn't have to go to work before noon. _False_

I wish I could stay home during the day and go to work at night. _False_

I like going to work in the morning. _True_

I can remember things best when I concentrate on them

    in the morning. _True_

    at lunch time. _True_

    in the afternoon. _True_

    before dinner. _True_

    after dinner. _False_

    late at night. _False_

◆ ◆ ◆ ◆

Your answers should provide a map of how you prefer to spend your mental energy over the course of the day. To interpret your answers, check whether you answered *true* or *false* for most of the questions that point to a single time of day: morning, noon, afternoon, evening, or night. That will be the period during which you feel that you either work your best or at your worst.

How can you use these results? There are two simple guidelines for Peak Learning that will give your mind an opportunity to work at its optimum.

First, seize your highs. Know when your mind is most likely to click into high gear and prearrange your schedule whenever possible so that you are free to use it undisturbed during that period. Change appointments and hold phone calls to take advantage of the times when your brain does its best thinking.

Second, shut down before you run out of gas. Know when your mind is *least* likely to be ready for action, and plan ahead to do other useful or enjoyable activities at those times, such as socializing, routine work, or relaxing.

More specifically, if you have discovered that you are a morning person, you can enhance your learning by getting up an hour or so earlier than usual. Starting the day with some fast, pleasant learning will give you a good feeling of having met some of your own needs before you move into your daily work. It will also give you grist for thinking during *down times* about what you learned that morning.

On the other hand, if you found that you are an owl, you can make the most of the late hours each day. Think of your learning as the personal reward you've earned by putting in your daily round of work. Take a close look at your late afternoon and evening hours. How would you feel about targeting a specific piece of reading, thinking, problem solving, mental rehearsal, creating, or planning (all learning activities) for your commute home from work? If you know before hand what you want to accomplish, you can have just what you need right at hand on the bus or train (or perhaps a cassette ready in the car). Instead of just nodding off or filling the time with the evening tabloid, you can get your second wind with something you really care about. And by the time you get home, some of the less rewarding TV viewing may not look as attractive as another half-hour or hour devoted to your favorite subject, whether it's reading further or making notes in your learning log. The result will be some fresh food for thought, to be integrated by your mind while you sleep. I guarantee you'll wake up in the morning with a feeling of accomplishment. Often, you're likely to wake up with some fresh ideas of your own about what you were learning.

Test 2: Do You Learn Bottom Up or Top Down?

Here's how Carolyn likes to learn something: Once she has determined what her final result should be—developing a personal accounting system, for example—she plans out what she needs to do to reach it. She lists the information she needs to keep track of and considers the ways she might sort receipts, create ledger books, or whatever. She might decide to investigate computer programs that will do the job for her, or she might consider taking a basic accounting course from a local business college. But her first step is planning her campaign.

Joe learns differently. When he wants to master a new style of cooking, for example, he steers clear of courses and plans. Instead he goes to restaurants, talks to the waiters or cooks, and tastes a variety of dishes.

Then he picks up a cookbook and, after a few experiments, gains a sense of what tastes go together and how much preparation is needed. That's when he starts improvising his own recipes.

The scientist atomizes, someone must synthesize; the scientist withdraws, someone must draw together. The scientist particularizes, someone must universalize.

JOHN FOWLES

The following exercise, developed by David Lewis and James Greene of the Mind Potential Study Group in London, will reveal a basic aspect of your personal learning style. You will find out whether you prefer to tackle new topics from the bottom up, laying a solid foundation first, or from the top down, gaining an overall perspective before filling in the details. Then you will learn how to use this knowledge to design your approach to any learning task.

◆ ◆ ◆ ◆

Are You a Grouper or a Stringer?

Check the phrase in each pair that corresponds more closely to your preferred approach to learning. There are no right or wrong ways to complete these statements; they're designed simply to distinguish your preferences.

When studying an unfamiliar subject, you

____ (a) prefer to gather information from diverse topic areas.

__X__ (b) prefer to focus on one topic.

You would rather

____ (a) know a little about a great many subjects.

__X__ (b) become an expert on just one subject.

When studying from a textbook, you

__X__ (a) skip ahead and read chapters of special interest out of sequence.

____ (b) work systematically from one chapter to the next, not moving on until you have understood earlier material.

When asking people for information about some subject of interest, you

__X__ (a) tend to ask broad questions that call for rather general answers.

____ (b) tend to ask narrow questions that demand specific answers.

When browsing in a library or bookstore, you

__X__ (a) roam around looking at books on many different subjects.

____ (b) stay more or less in one place, looking at books on just a couple of subjects.

You are best at remembering

__X__ (a) general principles.

____ (b) specific facts.

When performing some tasks, you

___ (a) like to have background information not strictly related to the work.

___ (b) prefer to concentrate only on strictly relevant information.

You think that educators should

___ (a) give students exposure to a wide range of subjects in college.

___ (b) ensure that students mainly acquire in-depth knowledge related to their specialties.

When on vacation, you would rather

___ (a) spend a short amount of time in several places.

___ (b) stay in one place the whole time and get to know it well.

When learning something, you would rather

___ (a) follow general guidelines.

___ (b) work with a detailed plan of action.

Do you agree that, in addition to specialized knowledge, a person should know some math, art, physics, literature, psychology, politics, languages, biology, history, and medicine? (If you think people should study four or more of these subjects, score an "a" on this question.)

Now total all the a and b answers.

If you scored six or more a's on the test, you are a *grouper;* if you scored six or more b's, you are a *stringer.* If your a's and b's were close to equal, you find both approaches congenial and can choose the one that better fits the subject at hand.

The higher your total of either a's or b's, the more specialized your learning style is. The descriptions below should illustrate your learning methods closely and clarify how you might follow a grouper or a stringer strategy.

◆ ◆ ◆ ◆

GROUPER

KNOWLEDGE

Groupers. You prefer to take a broad view of any subject under study. You like to search out general principles rather than meticulous details and to relate one topic to as many other areas of knowledge as possible. You are quick to find relationships and to draw parallels among different areas of study.

Because of this learning style, groupers learn most easily and effectively in unstructured situations and do less well if knowledge is presented according to some rigid plan. Because you are able to bring together a wide range of information, you are likely to prove more successful than stringers when an eclectic approach is used.

Very little current teaching is presented in this way. Lesson plans, textbooks, and training schemes, whether in the factory, university, or classroom, are usually designed in a systematic, step-by-step manner that favors stringers. This approach works to the disadvantage of groupers, who prefer to come to grips with overall principles before getting down to the finer details of a topic.

Jump right into the subject you want to study. Go to the library and skim through several books and magazines that look interesting. Feel free to explore several aspects or topics simultaneously. Don't worry about not being systematic, of not mastering the fundamentals first in order to have a solid foundation. You're not building a house; you're creating a rich configuration of facts and concepts that your mind will delight in connecting.

As a grouper, you should keep an eye open for *big ideas, basic concepts,* and *organizing principles.* But as you do this, keep a separate list of the detailed parts of the subject that you will want to master later. This is a necessary aspect of learning, although you can keep it on the back burner when you're starting out. As long as you have your list, you're not likely to get anxious about having too many principles but not enough practical techniques.

Stringers. A systematic, methodical approach best suits you, because you learn most successfully by mastering specific details before moving to more general concepts.

Your best approach is to establish a series of clearly defined goals that allow knowledge to be accumulated gradually. Only facts directly related to the topic under study should be considered, while less relevant information, no matter how interesting, can temporarily be ignored. Stringers tend to achieve good grades in college because the highly structured nature of most academic work favors their particular style of learning.

Devote the initial portion of your time to developing a firmly structured plan with which you feel comfortable. Don't worry about taking all the time you need with this: you will more than make up for it once you get started because you will have the confidence of a detailed road map for your study.

Consult the tables of contents of several good books in your field of study, so that you can define the scope and priorities in that field. Having acquired a rough map of the entire terrain, select those topics you want to master and arrange them in a sensible order.

As a stringer, you should learn about each sub-topic fully before proceeding to the next. You will thrive on a feeling of mastery of each segment and on the cumulative sense of building solidly on the subject as a whole.

What should you do if a learning situation prevents you from using your preferred style? You may be a grouper who prefers to start with the big picture but are in a language course in which you're required to master vocabulary, word by word by word. Or suppose you're a stringer looking for a clear and methodical introduction to art, but your course takes lots of field trips to museums to view and discuss various paintings from many time periods. There are four things you can do.

First, check out whether an alternative arrangement can be made for learning what you want to learn. From our experience in school and college we are all conditioned to accept too readily that the class, course, or program we're in is not something we can control. But as an adult who's in the market for learning, you are much freer to pick and choose. Moreover, there is almost always a range of providers—people and institutions eager to serve learners whose needs diverge from the conventional. If the result will be a more rewarding experience, it may well be worth a few hours devoted to a search for a more congenial learning situation.

A Gestalt is a figure or pattern which can be distinguished against the background or field of perception.... But the term ... carries stronger connotations of significance and meaning [and] applies whenever a significant pattern or construct (the "figure") emerges against the background scene or noise (the "ground").

OXFORD COMPANION TO THE MIND

If an alternative is simply not available, you can bring your preferred style into play by *wrapping* it around the less congenial tasks. In the case of art, you can indulge your strong need for a logical learning style by reading an entrancing book on the kind of artwork you are studying. Dealing with the same subject in an organized, verbal, and analytical way will enliven and inform your experience with the visual aspects. Or you can seek alternative ways to learn. In the case of foreign language vocabulary, you can turn loose your skills at association and imagination to make up all sorts of connections between the words, such as sound associations (*frère* and *fair* or *there*). The holistic methods popularized in Sheila Ostrander and Lynn Schroeder's book, *Superlearning* offer a way of mastering languages that is much more appealing to the grouper than word-by-word study.

Finally, if you find yourself dealing with learning tasks that call for a style with which you are not comfortable, recognize that fact and realize that you'll need to use some of the other Peak Learning techniques to overcome your resistance. Find additional ways to get excited about the subject, practice with friends, review what you want to derive from the learning situation, and so forth.

Test 3: Where Are You Located in the Four Learning Quadrants?

Now that you've explored your preference for the basic grouper and stringer styles, you're ready to dig a little deeper. You also have preferences for dealing with facts or feelings, using logic or imagination, and thinking things through yourself or working with other people. This next exercise will make you more aware of these preferences.

The exercise is based on the pioneering work of Ned Herrmann, whose Herrmann Brain Dominance Instrument (HBDI) is one of the chief tools used by those interested in adapting learning to people's styles of thinking. Herrmann is a living example of the benefits of becoming aware of your brain's preferences and potential. At Cornell, he double-majored in physics and music. Later, while directing Management Education at General Electric, he became a successful sculptor and painter. Today Herrmann is chairman of the Whole Brain Corporation, which offers workshops on the brain and creativity to top corporations.

Herrmann has expressed his personal credo in a colorful book, *The Creative Brain,* in which he tells the story of how the idea of stylistic quadrants first came to him. It's a vivid example of how one's preferred ways of knowing can lead to fresh ideas. Herrmann had been intrigued by both Roger Sperry's work with two different brain-hemisphere styles and Paul MacLean's theory of the three-level brain, both of which were reviewed in Chapter II.

Herrmann administered a homemade test to fellow workers to see

---

Again and again, step by step, intuition opens the doors that lead to man's designing.

R. BUCKMINSTER FULLER

---

whether he could correlate their preference in learning with the idea of brain-hemisphere dominance. The responses seemed to group themselves into four categories, not two as he'd anticipated. Then, while driving home from work one day, he combined his visual images of the two theories and had this experience.

> Eureka! There, suddenly, was the connecting link I had been searching for!... The limbic system was also divided into two separated halves, and also endowed with a cortex capable of thinking, and also connected by a commissure—just like the cerebral hemispheres. Instead of there being two parts of the specialized brain, there were *four*—the number of clusters the data had been showing! ...

So, what I had been calling left brain, would now become the *left cerebral hemisphere*. What was the right brain, now became the *right cerebral hemisphere*. What had been left center, would now be *left limbic*, and right center was now *right limbic*.

The whole idea unfolded with such speed and intensity that it blotted out conscious awareness of everything else. I discovered after the image of this new model had taken form in my mind that my exit had gone by some time ago. The last ten miles had been a total blank!

Note how Herrmann's preference for visual ways of thinking led him to a spatial image, which sparked the new idea. Of course, he followed up on his insight by using his analytical and verbal skills to delineate how the quadrants might work. The moral, notes Herrmann, is that if we want to learn more creatively, "we need to learn to trust our nonverbal right brain, to follow our hunches, and to follow them up with careful, highly focused left-brain verification."

Before I explain the four learning styles Herrmann discovered, try the following exercise.

◆ ◆ ◆ ◆

Four Quadrants for Learning

Start by picking three learning areas. One might be your favorite school subject, the one you had the most fun with. Try to find another that was different—perhaps the subject you hated most. The third should be a subject you are currently starting to learn or one that you've had an intention to begin for some time.

Now, read the following descriptions of four learners' styles and decide *which one was (or would have been, for the subject you hated) closest to your most comfortable way of learning the subject.* Give that description the number 1. Give the one you like *least* a 3. Of the two styles remaining, decide which one might be slightly more enjoyable for you and number it 2. Do this for all three learning areas on your list.

Remember, there are no wrong answers here—all four styles are equally valid. Likewise, don't feel you have to be consistent; if one style seems better for one area but not as comfortable for another, do not give it the same number in both cases.

Learning Area			
Style	1	2	3
A			
B			
C			
D			

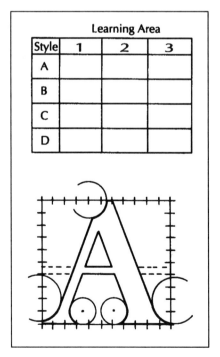

STYLE A: The essence of any subject is a hard core of solid data. Learning is built up logically on a foundation of specific knowledge. Whether you're learning history, architecture, or accounting, you need a logical, rational approach to get your facts straight. If you focus on verifiable facts on which everyone can agree, you can come up with more precise and efficient theories to clarify the situation.

STYLE B: I thrive on order. I feel most comfortable when someone who really *knows* has laid out what's to be learned, in sequence. Then I can tackle the details, knowing that I'm going to cover the whole subject in the right order. Why flop around reinventing the wheel, when an expert has been through it all before? Whether it's a textbook, a computer program, or a workshop—what I want is a well-planned, precise curriculum to work my way through.

STYLE C: What *is* learning, anyway, except *communication* among *people?!* Even reading a book alone is interesting primarily because you're in touch with another person, the author. My own ideal way to learn is simply to talk with others interested in the same subject, learning how they feel, and coming to understand better what the subject means to them. When I was in school my favorite kind of class was a free-wheeling discussion or going out for coffee afterward to discuss the lesson.

STYLE D: The underlying spirit of any subject is what's important to me. Once you grasp that, and really feel it with your whole being, learning becomes meaningful. That's obvious for fields like philosophy and art. But even in a field like business management, isn't the important thing the vision in people's minds? Are they simply pursuing profit or do they see profits as a way to make a contribution to society? Maybe they have a totally unexpected motive for what they do. When I study something, I want to stay open to turning the information upside down and looking at it in a brand-new way, rather than being spoon-fed specific techniques.

◆ ◆ ◆ ◆

Even if you had trouble deciding between two or more styles, the tentative order you put down is important.

Herrmann associates Style A with a "master of logic and reason." The A style is devoted to getting the facts, figuring problems out logically, stating things clearly and precisely, reducing complex issues to simple decisions, and generating new ways of doing things more efficiently. Someone who is strong in this style to the exclusion of all others, Herrmann thinks, is likely to distrust ambiguity, intuition, and emotion.

The only freedom that is of enduring importance is freedom of intelligence, that is to say, freedom of observation and of judgment exercised on behalf of purposes that are intrinsically worthwhile.

JOHN DEWEY

Style B types are similar to A but place more reliance on what has already worked, on getting all the details right, and on procedure, order, and stability. They are more involved in answers and actions—doing things on time and on schedule—than on the questions and theories an A wants to analyze. Both are more verbal than emotional or intuitive.

Style C is primarily sensitive to moods, atmospheres, and attitudes. There is a greater awareness of things as a body process, rather than as visual or verbal information. There is a strong interest in people and communication; logic and theory take second place to feeling and experience.

Style D is where Herrmann finds the most emphasis on originality, ambiguity, and surprise, on the use of metaphor and the ability to picture things in preference to verbalizing them clearly. Style D types thrive on confusion and chaos, enjoying the challenge of many possibilities, and resist coming to final conclusions.

As Herrmann points out, these four styles are exaggerated. It is hard to find someone who uses only one of the four all the time. Even if all of your 1s, 2s, and 3s are on the same styles for all three subjects, your most favored learning style for all kinds of occasions is likely to be a blend of the styles you marked 1 and 2. On the other hand, if the numbers you assigned vary among different styles, you probably have a more flexible approach to learning. Most frequently we find ourselves strong in more than one of these styles and naturally pick the one that's appropriate to a given learning situation.

Your awareness of which of these styles feels most comfortable will enable you to adjust the conditions of your learning to make it more congenial. In much the same way as the grouper-stringer approaches, recognizing that you have a preferred approach allows you to seek learning situations in which that approach works best. Alternatively, you can choose a less comfortable style in order to stretch your learning muscles. And, when you can't find a useful match between what you want to learn and the style in which you'd be most comfortable learning it, you can use your preferred style at the same time. You might experiment with forming an intuitive picture of some subject while building and discarding several logical systems, or you might discuss the views of various authorities in conversation with other students.

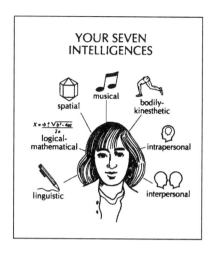

YOUR SEVEN
INTELLIGENCES

spatial
musical
bodily-kinesthetic
logical-mathematical
intrapersonal
linguistic
interpersonal

Recall Nicholas Naritz, one of the learners mentioned near the start of this chapter. He was boning up on everything French but finding the experience frustrating because he was trying to learn in Style A. Once he switched from trying to pick up facts from printed sources to plunging himself into a situation with other people (Style C), in which he could absorb the spirit of the subject (Style D), his learning was greatly enhanced.

Test 4: What Are Your Personal Intelligences?

Most people still believe that their capacity to learn is determined by intelligence. We all recall having our IQ taken at some point in our childhood, and most of us know the results. The IQ test was supposed to measure your capacity to learn and, therefore, to predict your success in school. However, contemporary psychologists have debunked this whole idea of a single capacity called intelligence. You have not one, but at least *seven* intelligences—and you can use most of them to enhance your learning.

Each intelligence in this sense is a particular kind of learning talent that seems to come easily. One person may excel at the eye-hand coordination of sports, playing a musical instrument, or solving math problems; another might find it easy to empathize with others' needs, build a birdhouse, or learn a language. The precise combination of skills can arise from a combination of talent and environmental factors.

The best guide to your multiple intelligences is *Frames of Mind* by Harvard psychologist Howard Gardner. Gardner's seven intelligences are:

1. Linguistic intelligence
2. Logical-mathematical intelligence
3. Spatial intelligence
4. Musical intelligence
5. Bodily-kinesthetic intelligence
6. Intrapersonal intelligence (knowing yourself)
7. Interpersonal intelligence (knowing other people)

Most of us have a pretty good idea of which of these intelligences we've cultivated the most and in which we feel strong. As a reminder, however, here's a simple exercise that will pinpoint some of your strengths.

◆ ◆ ◆ ◆

Which Are Your Strong Intelligences?

Circle the numbers of those descriptions that you feel apply to you.

1. You easily remember nice turns of phrase or memorable quotes and use them deftly in conversation.
2. You sense quickly when someone you are with is troubled about something.
3. You are fascinated by scientific and philosophical questions like "When did time begin?"
4. You can find your way around a new area or neighborhood very quickly.
5. You are regarded as quite graceful and rarely feel awkward in your movements.
6. You can sing on key.
7. You regularly read the science pages of your newspaper and look at magazines on science or technology.
8. You note other people's errors in using words or grammar, even if you don't correct them.
9. You often can figure out how something works or how to fix something that's broken without asking for help.
10. You can readily imagine how other people play the roles they do in their work or families and imaginatively see yourself in their roles.
11. You can remember in detail the layout and landmarks of places you've visited on vacations.
12. You enjoy music and have favorite performers.
13. You like to draw.
14. You dance well.
15. You organize things in your kitchen, bathroom, and at your desk according to categories and in patterns.
16. You feel confident in interpreting what other people do in terms of what they are feeling.

This above all: to thine own self be true.
WILLIAM SHAKESPEARE

---

17. You like to tell stories and are considered a good storyteller.

18. You sometimes enjoy different sounds in your environment.

19. When you meet new people, you often make connections between their characteristics and those of other acquaintances.

20. You feel you have a keen sense of what you can and can't do.

If *all three* of any of the following trios applies to you, you probably are strong in that intelligence, even if you haven't cultivated it.

Questions 1, 8, and 17: linguistic intelligence

Questions 6, 12, and 18: musical intelligence

Questions 3, 7, and 15: logical-mathematical intelligence

Questions 4, 11, and 13: spatial intelligence

Questions 5, 9, and 14: bodily-kinesthetic intelligence

Questions 10, 16, and 20: intrapersonal intelligence (knowing yourself)

Questions 2, 10, and 19: interpersonal intelligence (knowing others)

◆ ◆ ◆ ◆

Whatever your strongest intelligences might be, by selecting among various methods you can assemble a repertoire of ways to learn that capitalize on them. By focusing your learning through your best areas you can make it easier, more rewarding, and more fun. You can build up skills without expecting too much from yourself by challenging yourself to learn something in an unfamiliar way; and by combining skills from as many intelligences as possible, you can learn in a way that is more complete and involving.

Whatever your thinking style, keep in mind that different does not mean defective. Adapt tasks to your way of thinking and take on jobs that can best be addressed by your style.

ROBERT AND SUSAN BRAMSON

Suppose you have a strong spatial intelligence and you're setting out on a study of philosophy. How might you link your learning with your predilection for visual forms, shapes, and patterns?

First, you might seek out the *facts* of the philosophers by obtaining photos of them and their habitats. Find films and videos such as Edward de Bonds series, *Great Thinkers,* which features mock interviews with historical philosophers, or contemporary videotapes of interviews with noted scholars.

You might also try to make diagrams about what you're learning, using various colors for the aspects of each master's thoughts. The metaphor of vision as a symbol for insight and understanding will be of particular interest as you read, and you will come across some books that present philosophical ideas visually, such as *Maps of the Mind* by

Charles Hampden-Turner. You will certainly want to create some fresh visual images of your own that portray the philosophers, problems, principles, or systems you are studying. A diagram comparing Plato to Aristotle, for instance, would be wonderfully illuminating.

Drawing Your Profile

Now that we've explored several concepts of personal learning style, you are ready to bring your findings together in your first sketch of yourself as a learner. You will have fun filling out this personal learning style profile based on the insights you have gained into the ways your mind works best.

Don't worry if your answers don't entirely satisfy you at this point; this exercise is an initial draft. You'll recall seeing in crime films how a police artist composes a portrait of a suspect from descriptions by victims. The first sketch is just a rough approximation, but only after seeing it can the victim say, "No, the nose is wrong. It was much shorter" and "You've got the eyes just right, but the eyebrows were bushier." That's the purpose of this first draft of your personal learning profile. Only by getting *something* down in words can you begin to say, "Yes, I do like to get the overall picture first. But I also like to know that there is a step-by-step way to go through the materials if I want to."

◆ ◆ ◆ ◆

Personal Learning Style Profile

In your learning log, complete each of the sentences below, referring back to your findings from the previous exercises in this chapter. For example, your completed version of the second item might read: "I'm a stringer. I like to learn from the bottom up. I like to focus on solid facts about a new field or topic. When learning about managing for results last year, for example, I recall being bored by the theoretical articles and looking for case studies and concrete instances to begin with."

Continue in this way to complete each of the items. You should return to this profile periodically as you work your way through the book. You will continue to refine this first sketch, and, as you do so, it will become increasingly useful in planning your learning and diagnosing any problems you find.

1. *Drawing on your responses to "Your Best and Worst of Times" exercise:*

   My best time for learning is in the afternoon, so I feel best when I can schedule my learning times from 10-4.

2. *Drawing on your response to the "Bottom-up" or "Top-down" exercise:*

   I'm a (grouper/stringer/combination). I like to learn (bottom-up/top-down), so my preference is to approach a new subject top down.

3. *Drawing on your responses to the "Four Quadrants" exercise:*
   I like generally to learn through (facts/structure/people/feelings), so my preference is to approach a new subject _____
   _____.

4. *Drawing on your responses to "Which Are Your Strong Intelligences" exercise:*
   My two strongest intelligences are *intra and inter personal*,
   so I enjoy learning most when it involves *people*.

◆ ◆ ◆ ◆

Matching Your Style and Learning Resources

Whatever you want to learn, you will be using certain resources. A resource in this sense is anything that feeds or provides the opportunity for your learning. The major resources from which we learn most things are:

- Printed matter, such as books, articles, and papers
- Experiences, particularly ones especially designed for learning, such as simulations, study or action groups, and conferences
- Media: TV, films, audio and videotapes, slides, and graphics
- Nature: Your own investigation of some aspect of your environment
- Other people, especially in situations designed to foster learning, such as lectures, classes, seminars, and workshops

Your preference among these, for any given kind of learning, is a crucial dimension of your learning style. If you can arrange for your learning to involve the resource—the mode or situation—that you prefer, you obviously will find the experience more pleasant and more productive.

Perhaps the most important dimension here is whether you prefer to learn on your own or with other people. Fortunately, it's also one of the easiest to ascertain because you probably have a strong intuitive sense of your preference. Did you seek out others to study with in school? Do you like to go to classes in part because of other people there? Do you feel greatly deprived if you're reading a fascinating book and have no one to talk with about it? Obviously, if your answers were affirmative, you thrive on companionship in learning.

On the other hand, perhaps you relish exploring a new subject by yourself. Do you feel that the presence of other students in a class is likely to slow down your progress or distract from the things you'd like to learn most? Feelings like this suggest that, for you, learning can very satisfactorily be a solo flight with you at the controls.

There are ways to indulge your preference in either case. If companionship is what you want, there are ways to link up with other learners that are more flexible than having to sign up for a class. If you prefer to go it alone, there are new media and resources that can enrich your adventure in learning.

The following exercise has two purposes: first, to illustrate the broad range of resources you can apply to almost any learning goal; and second, to enhance your awareness of your own preferred learning resources.

◆ ◆ ◆ ◆

Matching Learning Resources and Personal Style

Suppose you want to learn more about endangered species. Below is a list of things you can do, each of them resulting in significant learning about this subject. Which three would you feel most comfortable with?

1. Reading a book or two on the subject
2. Participating in a simulation that models the administrative process of getting a species declared protected
3. Attending a series of lectures
4. Interviewing knowledgeable people in the field
5. Viewing video tapes or films
6. Visiting a game preserve, taking pictures, and acquiring relevant materials
7. Writing letters soliciting information and viewpoints on the subject from a range of interested people
8. Writing a paper, article, or speech on the subject, based on any one of the above experiences
9. Role-playing to dramatize the contrasting attitudes different people have about the problem
10. Joining a six-person task force to help plan a local campaign on behalf of an endangered creature
11. Working on your own to design a public information campaign that would spread the word about the general problem and solicit support for a nationally active organization in this field
12. Interning for a week with a zoologist at a nearby university
13. Determining what questions to ask on a survey of community attitudes toward the subject

◆ ◆ ◆ ◆

The person who seeks an education must involve himself in discovering the meaning of his own life and the relation between who he is and what he might become. Without that vision of a personal future and a hard look at the reality of one's own situation, the ultimate purpose of education itself—that is, to grow, to change, to liberate oneself—is almost impossible to achieve.

HAROLD TAYLOR

Learning More About Your Learning Style

If you would like to go even further in exploring your mind's way of working at its best, there are several approaches you can take.

The easiest and most useful is to make notes regularly on your learning style, along with your other ideas, in your learning log. You can distinguish these notes about your learning *process* by writing them in a distinctive color or enclosing them in a box or balloon. Once you get into this habit, you'll find that you quickly become quite sensitive to your distinctive kinds of learning behavior. Here are some typical notes my students put in their learning logs about their own learning processes.

But challenge yourself by occasionally trying something that doesn't come naturally. Everyone can stretch his mind, and it's worth a little effort to learn new thinking strategies.

ROBERT AND SUSAN BRAMSON

The third hour after waking up in the morning is the best one for me. My two cups of coffee have taken effect, my head is cleared up and working in top form. But that's also the time I arrive at the office, and people start distracting me. Maybe for one or two days a week I could warn people away, tell them I have a deadline or something. I know I'd be able to review piles of materials then, much more efficiently than any other time.

Looking up into the sky is a great relaxer after I've been poring over a book. My eyes feel refreshed just from a couple of minutes of tracing clouds.

Discovered I'm the only one in our tennis class that's reading an instructional book outside of class. Guess I just like to get it put in words, too.

The division I've moved into is a whole different ball game, and no one's taking the time to explain the rules. This reminds me of what happened when I first came to the company three years ago. But this time, I realize, I know what's wrong. At this point, I'm at a low point on the learning curve, so I've got to be wary while I wait for the upswing as people get accustomed to seeing me around and let their hair down. I'll catch on just by hanging around.

The second way you can learn more about your learning style is by taking workshops. These usually use one of the major learning style tests in a group setting, with individual counseling about your own style. Among the learning experts who regularly offer such workshops in many cities around the country are Don Lofland, Rita and Kenneth Dunn, Bernice McCarthy, Elizabeth Ruedy, and proponents of such systems as the Myers-Briggs Type Indicator.

There is no book specifically on adults' learning styles. The best treatment of the subject you can read is *In Their Own Way,* by Thomas Armstrong, which focuses on discovering and encouraging children's personal learning styles, but is well worth reading for its application to adults.

You now have a sense of how to capitalize on your preferred style to make your learning more enjoyable and efficient. You can organize materials and structure situations to fit your best way of learning; fine-tune your timing to capture your hours of maximum receptivity and choose learning experiences that match your tastes.

Equally important, however, you can also flex your style by bringing into play those modes of learning that you now use least or find least congenial. If your primary intelligences are linguistic and spatial, you might adventurously tackle an appealing learning project that has a mathematical or musical flavor. If you're a grouper, you can experiment with a stringer approach to a project. If you're a morning person, you might stay late at the office one night and see whether there are tasks you can actually do more effectively during those hours. If you customarily take a class when you want to learn something, try organizing your own learning project instead.

There are three advantages to experimenting with flexing your style. First, some subjects and situations strongly demand one or another style. When that happens, you are at a disadvantage if you can't switch into that mode and operate, if not at your maximum, at least effectively. One example is academic courses, which generally require you to take a stringer approach. Second, you may discover that an alternative approach actually works surprisingly well. Perhaps you have never really given it a try only because some early experiences convinced you that you weren't successful with that approach. All of us have neglected capacities of this kind. Finding yours can be a revelation and add a strong note to your intellectual repertoire. Thousands of people who "knew" they couldn't possibly draw or write—two powerful and gratifying ways of learning—have discovered that they can from two earlier books in this series, *Drawing on the Right Side of the Brain* by Betty Edwards, and *Writing the Natural Way* by Gabriele Rico. And third, practice with different learning styles will greatly improve your capacity to communicate with other people who operate in those styles.

Beyond applying it to your own learning needs, you may find your new awareness of learning styles especially useful with children, if you are a parent or a teacher, and in your career. In both of these areas, chronic problems can be solved through this approach.

In the world of work there is widening recognition of the need to capitalize on different learning styles within organizations. According to Dudley Lynch in *Your High Performance Business Brain* "we can use this powerful new way of understanding people to design better organizations, ... do a more effective and productive job of hiring and placing people, and to frame our management messages so that they can penetrate the natural filters of the mind." That means you should be able to measure how well your learning style fits the tasks that compose your present job. You should also be able to recognize the styles of others, which will make for better communications.

In my workshop we illustrate this by forming a *hemispheric circle*. All the participants seat themselves in a semicircle so that each person's position reflects his or her degree of preference for either the stringer or the grouper style of learning. Those on the left side of the semicircle prefer to learn in a step-by-step, analytical, systematic way; those on the right prefer a holistic, top-down, big-picture approach. Then, we talk about how these two kinds of people can best explain things to each other or convey new information.

Today's successful managers can't spend valuable time in unproductive seminars that are 60 percent old stuff or sit around waiting for someone to offer just the right course. Only those who can design their own learning can cope with constant change.

PAUL GUGLIEMINO

"Hold on, now," one of the left-side folks will say. "I'd really prefer it if you could start out by giving me some basic examples of what you're talking about. You seem to be all over the map instead of starting with first things first." But the next minute someone from the right side will complain, "Hey, I can't see the forest for all those trees you're throwing at me. Could we wrench ourselves up out of the details and get an overview of the subject? What's the point? Where are we headed?"

Often partnerships are profitably forged out of two individuals who complement each other's styles. In my workshops we often see two people who work closely together take seats on opposite ends of the hemispheric circle. In one recent case, a couple in the fashion business found themselves in those places; it turned out that one of them was the idea person and the other the financial wizard. Together they made a dynamic duo indeed.

Creating teams to work together or to solve problems is an important area in which an awareness of styles can assure greater success. Some highly technical problems call for team members who all share the same way of processing information, seeking new facts, interpreting evidence, and coming to conclusions. A narrow fact-finding or problem-solving assignment, such as determining how to expedite the passage of orders through the billing department, might be such a situation. In other situations, however, your success may depend on having the right mix of styles. You may need one or two people who take the top-down, broad view together with others who like to work systematically and logically. Creating a plan for the next year's activities would be a task that could benefit from this mix of approaches.

Another area in which styles of learning and thinking can crucially affect the success of individuals or organizations is boss-employee relations. This typical situation occurs every day in business and industry: a supervisor will complain that a new worker can't seem to learn a routine task. When the suggestion is made that the newcomer might learn it if shown it move by move, the supervisor—clearly a grouper rather than a stringer expresses dismay, exclaiming, "I never give instructions that way. It would be insulting and patronizing—*anyone* can pick it up if they really want to."

Such conflict based on differences in style can extend right up to the executive suite. In their book, *Type Talk*, management consultants Otto Kroeger and Janet Thuesen tell how they helped straighten out troubled organizations by analyzing the disparities among the styles of the managers and executives involved. They even suggest developing a version of the organization chart in which each of the key individuals is identified not by his or her title, but by his or her learning style!

In this chapter you have learned how you like to learn. You've discovered how your brain prefers to process new material, which modes and media of instruction suit you best, which times are best for you, and how to flex your style. You have acquired an awareness of yourself as a learner, which is the first prerequisite of Peak Learning. Now you can make the best use of the powerful techniques and strategies that will make Peak Learning happen for you.

VI.
Improving Your Learning, Reading, and Memory Skills ◆◆◆◆

How can you enhance your learning as you are doing it, day-to-day, minute-by-minute? What can you do before, during, and after learning to increase your enjoyment of the learning process and assure the maximum benefits from the time you spend learning?

The techniques you will learn now are more specific than the general strategies you learned in the last chapter, such as adapting your learning tasks to your personal style and choosing resources. Those strategies set the broad course of your learning, determining where you want to wind up and your general approach to getting there. The new techniques, on the other hand, are your specific *tools*—the compass, sexton, and depth gauge—with which you pilot your learning, steering your path just as an expert navigator conns a ship.

You may have been stopped by that word *pilot* at the end of the previous paragraph. It's not the image we usually apply to the activity of learning; the words that more readily come to mind are *absorb* and *acquire*. Yet I chose the word *pilot* carefully.

What is a good learner? It seems useful to think of him as someone with a certain set of skills. He knows how to formulate problems. He can identify the relevant resources ... that are available in his environment. He is able to choose or create procedures and to evaluate his results. Beyond this, there is a set of higher skills, which we may call "meta-skills." Stated very loosely, they include the ability to know what he wants (or needs) to learn; the ability to see clearly the process of his learning; and the ability to interact with others to help learn these meta-skills. Out of all this, he is able to create useful knowledge.

MICHAEL ROSSMAN

As you use these techniques, you will indeed be in charge of your learning, steering your course as you go.

There are three categories with two techniques each. After you've had a little practice with them, you may choose the technique in each category that most appeals to you. You may also adopt the one that might be most apt for the kind of learning you are doing.

Learning Techniques

I. Before Learning

Pro-Active Reading, a technique to get exactly what you want from books and articles.

The *Vee-Heuristic* technique, to preview in your mind the key questions you want to answer in any learning situation.

II. While Learning

Mind-Mapping, a technique that encourages the use of your natural mental associations to organize incoming information.

Probes, the kinds of questions you can formulate to become actively involved with your information by creatively anticipating where it is leading.

III. After Learning

Memory Improvement, techniques to store factual data in your memory more easily.

Instant Replay, a technique for deep recall and review of any experience to increase what you learn from it.

Before Learning

A principle stressed throughout this book is that the decisions you make *before* you start to learn are crucial for your success.

Your choice of what you want to learn, which resources you want to use, when and where you learn best are all decisive for your effectiveness and enjoyment.

There are also some *specific* techniques you can use when you are just about to start learning something. The two I have found to be most generally useful are pro-active reading, when you are going to learn from a book, and the Vee-heuristic technique, when you want to enhance your learning from some other kinds of experience.

Pro-Active Reading

From our experiences in school, most of us have retained a passive posture toward books. We feel faintly guilty if we don't start on page one and read through to the end. If we decide to quit before finishing, we feel we haven't really read the book. Most important of all, we let the author's priorities and choices of what to emphasize take command of our attention—we hand over control of the learning experience to the author.

The computer is teaching us a better way to read books, quite different from the way most of us were taught in school. That way is *active, self-directed,* and *creative.* When we sit down at a computer, we are in charge. We access the information and procedures we want, choosing from a variety of menus or commands to accomplish our task. We go directly to what we want. We can look over a whole program or database before getting involved, to get a feel for its contents and procedures. We skip around from one part to another. We call up various areas of interest to see what they're like.

When we adapt this style to using books, they take on a different character. Instead of being conduits of data going one way—from author to reader—they become interactive resources for self-directed learning.

Of course, I don't mean to apply this to *War and Peace.* Reading a novel for pleasure is an entertaining experience presented by the author for our enjoyment—even if we often learn quite a bit from it anyway! But for the majority of books most of us use to gain information and understanding, this method of pro-active reading is more appropriate than reading straight through from page one to the end. Instead of tamely following the author's interests in presenting his or her information, we can browse for the exact tidbits of information *we* need to learn for our goals.

The following exercise, developed by Professor Robert Smith of Northern Illinois University for his pioneering course in learning how to learn, will teach you to do this.

◆ ◆ ◆ ◆

Pro-Active Reading

You will need writing material and a nonfiction book that you are not familiar with. The book should have a dust jacket, a table of contents, some front matter (foreword, preface, introduction), and an index.

1. Turn to the inside front of the dust jacket and read what the publisher has to say about the book.

2. Turn to the back of the dust jacket and read what the publisher has to say about the author and his or her qualifications to write such a book.

3. Turn to the front matter (foreword, preface, introduction) and read the author's or editor's orientation to the book.

4. Turn to the table of contents and see how the author has organized the information into parts, chapters, or other subsections.

5. Leaf through the book, rapidly scanning or reading the occasional paragraph or heading that interests you. Try to get the feel of the book.

6. Put the book down and write three questions concerning matters you have become curious about as a result of this preliminary examination.

7. Next, review your first question and find in it a key word or phrase that you think might be in the index. Go to the index and look for the key word; if you draw a blank, try to come up with a synonym. If the synonym isn't there, see if the table of contents leads you to where the question can be answered.

8. Now turn to that part of the book that deals with your question and look for the answer. If the author refers to material in other parts of the book, follow the leads until you have enough information relevant to your question.

9. Use the same procedure with your second and third questions.

Questions

1. How differently did you feel about using a book as a resource for learning from the way you usually feel about a book?

2. Is there any difference in the quality of the information you have gained?

◆ ◆ ◆ ◆

The key point of this exercise is discovering when you formulated your three questions. It wasn't after you had read the entire book, cover to cover. Instead, you did a preliminary scan of the contents. At that point, you could readily decide whether or not this particular book was going to be useful to you—that is, whether the author had something to say that was important for what *you* wanted to learn. If not, there was no need to go further with that book.

Amazingly enough, however, if you have even a general idea of what you want to learn, such a brief scan can stimulate more specific questions that the book should answer. Of course, there may well be more information in the book than those answers, but you decide how much more of what the author wants to present is relevant to your needs. Perhaps digging out the answers to those three questions leads to your decision to read the entire book. On the other hand, those three answers may be all you need from that book and you can go on to your next learning resource.

How you choose to use the book is up to you. As you've seen, the key difference between a Peak Learning life style and your previous, school-based learning is that, in Peak Learning, *you choose whatever you want to do.*

Now that you've gotten the feel of using a book as your personal learning resource, there are some more advanced things you may want to try. For example, you can check the contents of a book in much the same way someone might search through a computer's database of information using key words. An easy analogy would be searching for the name of a client to find out when he or she was last billed. The name is the key word under which the transactions are filed. Many on line information systems allow one to locate all articles that contain a particular key word.

In a book, of course, these key words are listed in the index. Here's an excerpt from a typical book index. Read it as a *graph:* the length of the listing for each item (i.e., the number of pages on which that term is mentioned) indicates how much attention is paid to that subject in the book.

Educational need, concept of, 111

Effort: as motivation indicator, 5, 279–280; and self-concept, 97

Einstein, A., 20–21

Ellis, A., 68, 73, 87, 296

Elstein, A. S., 236, 296

Emotions. *See* Affect

Empathy: and affect, 186; and attitude, 76; defined, 24; by Instructors, 22–28; and learners' level, 26–27; and learners' perspective, 27–28; and understanding of needs and expectations, 24–26

Enjoyment, and motivation, 8, 279

Enthusiasm: caring and valuing in, 32–33; defined, 29; emotion, animation, and energy in, 33–38; indicators of, 34, 36–37; by instructors, 28–38; loss of, 35, 38; research findings on, 30

Of the items on this list, only *two* are covered in a major way: *empathy* and *enthusiasm*. If you took five minutes to scan the whole index this way, you'd end up with the twenty-five key words for this book. Usually these key words will constitute about 15 percent of the entries; the other 85 percent will have only one, two, or three pages following them. By reading a book's index this way, you can get an immediate answer to the following crucial questions:

1. What are the dozen most important ideas covered in this book?

2. Which of these important ideas might provide good starting points for me to get into the book because of my familiarity with them?

3. What ideas are covered that are entirely new to me, and do they sound intriguing and useful?

4. Given the above, and my learning goals, do I have enough reason to continue with this book or should I seek information elsewhere?

The mere formulation of a problem is often far more essential than its solution, which may be a matter of mathematical or experimental skill. To raise new questions, new possibilities, to regard old problems from a new angle requires creative imagination and marks real advance in science.

ALBERT EINSTEIN

To summarize the value of the pro-active reading technique just described:

◆ A quick scan of the book's description, introduction, table of contents, and index can give you an immediate sense of whether the book will be useful in meeting the learning goals you have set. If the book is not going to help you reach those goals, you can safely discard it.

◆ If you quickly scan, using suggested questions you'd like the answers to, you can read only those parts of the book that provide those answers (and any cross-reference necessary to understand them) and go on to the next learning resource. There's no need to feel any guilt because you haven't read the entire book—no one is testing you on it!

◆ Analyzing the index of a book can help you decide whether to spend any further time on it and where the best place for you to start might be. There is no danger that the "book police" will catch you because you didn't start on page one!

Turning Any Experience Into a Learning Opportunity

It is sometimes said that the experiences we go through in life make us what we are. That's not entirely correct, however—it's what we manage to learn from those experiences. Few people have developed a method for learning from their experiences in a systematic way. The best we do, most of the time, is try to be alert to what's going on during the experience, then think about it later—if we ever find the time to do so. The result is that we fail to gain the full learning value from many of our most significant experiences. There's a simple technique by which we can do better. The "Vee-heuristic" technique enables you to:

1. Identify upcoming experiences from which you want to learn.

2. Marshal your existing knowledge and understanding so that you can draw on it during the experience.

3. Formulate interesting, useful, powerful questions you want to answer by learning from the experience.

4. Plan your own behavior so that the experience yields the answers you are looking for.

The original Vee-heuristic technique was developed for students in school by Joseph Novak and Bob Gorwin, two Cornell University professors who explain it in their book, *Learning How to Learn.* (The term *heuristic* refers to techniques that help us find or discover something.) The diagram that follows is my simplification and modification of theirs, based on the needs of adult learners.

The *Vee* provides a framework that enables you to think creatively about what you might learn from an upcoming experience. You can explore how to pose questions or to behave in ways that will yield the knowledge or understanding you want from the experience. You can use the technique to learn from a meeting you will be attending in two hours or from a stint of jury duty that starts in three weeks.

While information may be infinite, the ways of structuring it are not.... Your choice will be determined by the story you want to tell.

RICHARD SAUL WURMAN

Use the example of jury duty to see how we might enjoy it more and learn more from it by using the Vee. Start by drawing a sample of the Vee diagram in your learning log. On the left side, write down what you already know or feel about jury duty—facts, impressions, opinions, and questions.

One of my workshop student's entries for this exercise included remembering the classic film *Twelve Angry Men,* a textbook she had used

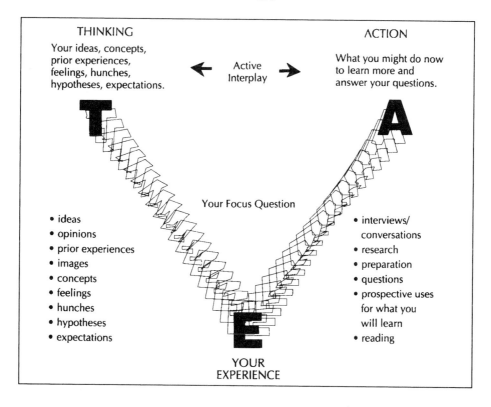

THINKING

Your ideas, concepts, prior experiences, feelings, hunches, hypotheses, expectations.

ACTION

What you might do now to learn more and answer your questions.

← Active Interplay →

Your Focus Question

- ideas
- opinions
- prior experiences
- images
- concepts
- feelings
- hunches
- hypotheses
- expectations

- interviews/ conversations
- research
- preparation
- questions
- prospective uses for what you will learn
- reading

YOUR EXPERIENCE

in college on the American legal system, a magazine article on the jury's role in a recent newsworthy trial, some rules of thumb she had learned about how leadership emerges in small groups, and her feelings about this intrusion on her family and professional life. Each of these pieces of past knowledge or feeling could be the basis for deeper learning from this actual experience of jury service. For example, you might note the differences and similarities between the actual experience and the dramatized portrayal of a jury in *Twelve Angry Men*. Or you might formulate three or four theories about how a leader emerges in a small group like a jury and see which ones are borne out. It might be interesting to discuss, during break times, the jurors' different attitudes about taking time away from their families and jobs.

That's where the focus question comes in. Once you've identified what you already know and feel (left side of the Vee) and decided what you'd like to learn from the experience, you can formulate the question you'd like to explore.

Clustering taps the childlike, wondering, innocent, curious, playful, open-ended, flexible, pattern-seeking design mind, allowing us to play with language, ideas, rhythms, images, sounds, and patterns creatively before committing ourselves to a fixed course. In short, we avail ourselves of choices.

GABRIELE LUSSER RICO

The following questions are but a few that have been formulated by my workshop participants. An anthropology major who is now in market research asked, "How does a jury trial serve the same function as rituals in primitive societies?" A question posed by a secondary-school teacher considering a career shift into industrial training was, "How does a 'natural' leader emerge in a small group, and how does he or she relate to the officially designated leader?" An actor-director in a regional theater asked, "How does a theatrical portrayal of a courtroom differ from the mundane reality?" And this question was posed by a manufacturer with an accounting background: "Are there ways the trial process could be expedited without a loss of integrity, in order to increase its efficiency and speed trials?"

Having identified your own question, go to the right side of the Vee and list some actions you can take to gain the information you seek. For example, you might do some preparatory reading or even see the movie *Twelve Angry Men* again. Or you might decide you want to watch the behavior of your fellow jury members to see whether you can predict which one will most affect how the others decide. Or perhaps you will want to talk with other people in advance about their own jury-duty experiences.

Sometimes the preparation you do will cause you to rethink your focus question. Often you may recall some bit of relevant experience you forgot to list initially, or you may come up with some new sources of information to pursue during or after the experience. The key feature of this technique is that *any experience to which you apply the Vee-heuristic method is one in which you are actively involved in the process of learning as much as you can.*

Most people spend most of their lives simply going from experience to experience. However, as active lifelong learners—as peak learners— we can use any experience we have in the cause of furthering our learning and enhancing our enjoyment of life. With just a little advance planning, your life can become a rich storehouse of potential learning experiences.

During Learning

While you are engaged in learning—whether you are reading, listening, or discussing—your mind should not be passively trying to absorb information. Rather, it should be *active.* You should be posing questions to yourself, organizing the incoming information to fit your own interests, learning goals, and needs.

Two of the best techniques I know for activating your mind while learning are mind-mapping and probes.

If the brain works primarily with key concepts in an interlinked and integrated manner, our notes and our word relations would in many instances be structured in this [mind-mapping] way rather than in traditional "lines." Rather than starting from the top and working down in sentences or lists, one should start from the center or main idea and branch out as dictated by the individual ideas and general form of the central theme.

TONY BUZAN

Mind-Mapping

Mind-mapping will appeal most strongly to those with high visual intelligence, who may feel stifled by the need to outline subjects in a linear order, one topic after another. They, like groupers, will prefer to see a more complex overview, with branches in many directions. However, mind-mapping is a simple enough process to be easily used by the rest of us as well, and therefore it's a good way to flex your own learning style in the visual, top-down direction. Even if your preferred style is highly linguistic or mathematical, you will find mind-mapping an intriguing alternative way to look at information and ideas.

Mind-mapping was first popularized by Tony Buzan, a leading British learning coach, in *Use Both Sides of Your Brain.* Gabriele Rico, in her book, *Writing the Natural Way,* pioneered using the technique to make writing easier and more enjoyable; she calls it *clustering.* The idea has been applied to problem-solving and idea generation in business and industry by Charles Hess and Carol Colman, Anne Robinson, and Dudley Lynch, who call mind maps *brain webs*. In modified form, it has also been recommended by many educators for teaching youngsters in school.

Mind-mapping is also suitable for advanced learning: one of the most dazzling mind maps in my personal collection organizes connections among the main thinkers behind contemporary culture. Created by Maurice Stein and Larry Miller at the University of California at Santa Cruz, this giant map links such figures as Sigmund Freud, Karl Marx, and Charles Darwin with more recent figures such as Herbert Marcuse and Marshall McLuhan. Following is an example from Tony Buzan of a British student's mind map of concepts in economics.

At first glance it may look confusing, a hodgepodge of branches and arrows and labels. But as you study the map, it starts to make more sense. The place to start is in the center, where you will start shortly when you make your own mind map. The central circle, labeled *economics*, is where this map begins.

As we move away from that center we see a series of labeled branches for concepts, in no particular order. These are the first few terms that occurred to the student in connection with the idea of economics. There is no rule that requires this list to be complete or academically accurate; after all, it's the student's own map! Some of these secondary ideas spun further branches, others didn't—again, the amount and distribution of information is up to the person making the map. One can always return and add new branches anywhere. Finally, the arrows around the outside show links between various branches that this student wanted to stress.

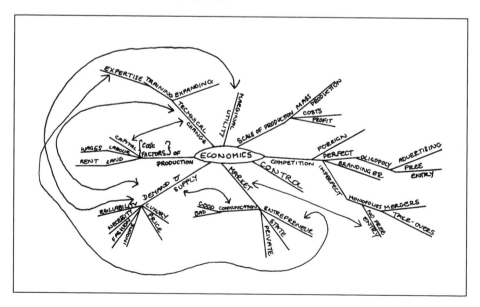

Sometimes people ask why mind-mapping is superior to the standard outlining technique we all were taught in school. There are several reasons why it is more effective and enjoyable for most people.

1. It's *visually* pattern-oriented and, therefore, it activates an additional area of our brain in the service of our learning.

2. It's open to creative additions at any point, thus encouraging us to think about a topic in more directions than simply *before* and *after.*

3. It invites use of color and design in ways that make it easier to remember later.

4. It allows us to see connections among widely disparate elements of the subject (since they're all right there on the same page). Interconnecting arrows can suggest complex relationships among parts of some idea or field we might otherwise have missed.

The following exercise will be your guide to creating a mind map.

◆ ◆ ◆ ◆

Mind-Mapping Something That Matters to You

Develop a mind map for an idea, issue, problem, or situation of current concern to you. Your area of focus might be a business problem or a subject you are studying in school or on your own.

To start your mind map, put the key word you want to work with in an oval in the center of a sheet of paper that is 8 1/2 by 11 inches or larger (the larger the /better). In Peak Learning workshops, participants work on flip-chart-size sheets of paper (27" by 34"). At first they are daunted by the size, but once they get rolling they find they have so many ideas that they can hardly fit them all on the page. Work in pencil so you can easily erase and change items as you find more precise words for your thoughts.

Now, begin to create branches to other ovals that are your main sub-ideas. (Initially, it is easier to read the labels for sub-ideas if each one has its own oval rather than simply assigning the label to the branch itself, as our earlier example did.) It generally helps to arrange the sub-ideas you think are most closely related to your central concept as direct branches from it; less significant ideas can then branch from those sub-ideas. However, don't worry about whether you're sure an idea is important enough or not—you can always erase it, move it to the periphery, and insert a new, more important idea in that oval. And leave room for new ovals that will occur to you later.

Each time you create an oval that interests you, add spokes to it to capture related ideas. These may be specific examples, references, or thoughts implied by the sub-idea. Note that in some cases these spokes will themselves develop spokes, as in the lower right-hand corner of our example, where *competition* led to *imperfect* and on to *monopolies,* which subdivided into *mergers* and *take-overs.*

As you can see, the rules of mind-mapping are made to be broken; the whole point is to create and capture your own thoughts in your own way, reflecting your personal image of the idea you are mapping. Use any resources and techniques that appeal to you.

A worthwhile graphic should reveal data by:
- *inducing you to think about the substance rather than the form*
- *encouraging the eye to compare different pieces of data*
- *revealing the data at several levels of detail*
- *avoiding distortion*

EDWARD TUFTE

I like to use three to five colored pencils (or felt-tipped pens) when doing a group mind map or when I want to further distinguish the kinds of branches into types. For example, I might use one color for all the people who have written about my subject, another for sub-ideas that come from my own experience, and a third for connections I need to research.

Feel free to use visual symbols as a conceptual shorthand. You might use a little cartoon image of a brain to refer to all the ways in which brain functions relate to your idea, or a drawing of a book next to a name might suggest a text for reference. You may want to create special symbols for how you feel about various ideas sparked by your key term. Benefits and promising applications, for example, could be flagged with a smiling face, a rising sun, a light bulb, or a dollar sign. Danger points or reservations could be designated by a question mark, a downward-pointing arrow, or a skull and crossbones.

◆ ◆ ◆ ◆

Don't be surprised if one mind map leads to another. The way this usually happens is that one of your ovals begins to emerge as very important to you. It has a lot of spokes, many of them are important ideas that generate their own spokes, and the whole thing looks like it's going to get out of hand! That's the time to start another map with the sub-idea from your original map in the center.

Naturally, you'll have to do a few mind maps just to get the feel of the process before it comes naturally. You have an interesting experience to look forward to. The creative climax of mind-mapping at its most successful can actually give you more information than you started with! You may find, while connections are spilling onto the page and radiating from the center, that something suddenly strikes you that you hadn't seen earlier. As Gabriele Rico describes it in *Writing the Natural Way:*

You are clustering, seemingly randomly, when suddenly you experience a sense of direction. The moment between randomness and sense of direction is the moment of shift....

You suddenly perceive a direction to follow. Something stands out as significant for you here and now ... it is like looking through the eye of a camera at a total blur only to discover, as you turn the focusing mechanism, a sudden broad vista ... or a grouping of clearly defined figures. Not only is the image focused, but it is *framed* to give you a sense that the objects you are focusing on somehow belong together.

Were all maps in this world destroyed and vanished under the direction of some malevolent hand, each man would be blind again, each landmark become a meaningless signpost to nothing.

BERYL MARKHAM

That is the point at which Rico advises her students to start writing a brief summary paragraph describing what insight has just occurred.

Notice what is going on here. We started with a subject—whatever it is we have decided to learn about. We gained some information about it, one way or another. By mind-mapping or clustering we created our own personal pattern, an image of a network showing how our various bits of knowledge might relate to one another. Then, when the moment felt right, we returned to our usual style of verbal thinking and wrote a summary paragraph that captured the new insight.

We have actively used more of our brain's capacities to make connections that help us learn. How?

We can now approach our newly learned information from several directions. We can use the image of the map, and any secondary maps we create, as a literal map that reminds us of the overall territory we've traveled. A list of the concepts used in the map can supply key words to guide our search for further resources (which can be used, for example, to check the index of a book). Even the pattern of connections shown by the map—the branches and arrows—can tell us what we need to check further or assist us in reformulating a focus question to gain new information.

The pattern can also help us to organize data in a way more suitable to a standard outline or report, where our summary paragraph can find a proper home. If you wish to write up what you've learned in an essay or article, the summary paragraph will probably (but not always) be easier for others to grasp than your personal map would be.

You will find mind-mapping useful when you are:

- planning a speech or an article, as an alternative to standard outlines;

- taking notes from reading, lectures, workshops, seminars, TV documentaries, or meetings;

- bringing your prior knowledge, ideas, and feelings about a new subject to the surface;

- summing up or recalling what you've learned about a subject so far;

- ◆ generating new ideas about a problem, situation, or issue that concerns you; and

- ◆ brainstorming applications of new concepts you have learned.

Probes

Probes are ideas and questions you develop while you are learning but *before* you have learned much about any new field. The idea of probes affronts most people because we all learned in school that you needed to learn what had already been established in any field before you could even think about contributing an idea of your own. On the contrary, you can and should come up with ideas of your own right from the start for two reasons. First, they will help you learn the subject by keeping your mind actively involved with what you're studying.

... shall I teach you what knowledge is? When you know a thing, to recognize that you know it, and when you do not know a thing, to recognize that you do not know it. That is knowledge.

CONFUCIUS

That would be a good enough reason in itself, but there's a second, even more intriguing justification: occasionally, one of these early probes in a new field will contain an insight you would have missed if you had waited until you knew more.

This is called the *novice effect,* which Michael Hutchinson identifies in his book, *Megabrain.* One's first exposure to a new field, Hutchinson points out, causes changes in the brain's chemistry. He cites the frequency of "late bloomers" who made original contributions to a field, even in the sciences, where the usual pattern is that the best discoveries are made early in one's career.

Leo Szilard, for example, was a leading physicist who became a biologist as he approached fifty. Szilard suggested that scientists could actually harness this novice effect by changing their fields every five or ten years, plunging into something about which they know nothing. A similar pattern is found in the career of Gregory Bateson, who combined the fields of biology, anthropology, systems theory, and psychology (among others) to produce intriguing new insights in each field.

"Subjected to a novel barrage of experiences and stimulations," Hutchinson writes, "the brain is forced to grow, to make neural connections, to forge new chemical pathways, to retain its youthful plasticity, to see the world with fresh eyes." In that youthful freshness lie the seeds of insights that are not likely to come to those who have been mired in the same field for twenty years.

A more mundane use of your own probes is to learn more effectively by actively engaging your mind with the material. Your mind works faster than you can read—and much faster than any lecturer can talk. It likes to keep busy, so after it takes in what's being conveyed, it looks around for something else to do. The result is that you experience distractions. Eventually, you could get so irritated by the difference between your own speed of comprehension and the rate that information is being presented that you lose track of what you're reading or hearing.

A powerful remedy is to put your mind to work in a productive way. Give it something to chew on to keep you focused, to spark your own creative responses, to leap *ahead*. I call such leaps *probes*. You can think of the word as standing for *propositions before*—that is, before the text or speaker gets to the point, before the facts and arguments are presented, and before you get distracted.

Consider probing whenever you begin to sense that the argument is moving along a little too slowly for you. Start to go beyond simply taking notes on what's being said or read; instead, start to make notes about what's coming next. Just *guess* what the speaker or writer is leading up to. I call these *pre-notes*—notes made *before* you're exposed to the material.

Then, as you proceed through the text, watch for how you need to modify your proposition in light of what you're reading. You will, in effect, become a co-creator with the author, absorbing what he or she has to say as well as exploring your own ideas and expectations. The result is an active dialogue, a conversation, which tends to be far more absorbing, stimulating, and pleasurable than passively absorbing information as it is handed out.

Probes are such a powerful learning tool that they are often used by authors as they write. An author will formulate an initial proposition, present it as a hypothesis, and then examine the evidence to see how well it stands up.

For example, Professor David Perkins of Harvard uses this as the organizing principle of *The Mind's Best Work: A New Psychology of Creative Thinking*. Here's how he explains its usefulness:

> I have found it helpful to organize most chapter sections around "propositions" and "revised propositions." A proposition, which usually occurs near the beginning of a section, is a concise statement of a familiar or plausible view about creating. The revised proposition, arriving near the end of a section, is another statement on the same issue, sometimes a direct contradiction of the original proposition and sometimes a qualification of it. The text of the sections is mostly a journey by way of evidence and argument from the original to the revised proposition. This device has helped me to keep the issues explicit and focal.

Thus, Perkins opens one chapter with this simple proposition: "There must be something special about the mental processes that lead to discovery." He explains why this is a proposition worth investigating:

"Extraordinary outcomes, like moments of discovery, ought to involve extraordinary means."

Later in the chapter, Perkins shows how creative discoveries can often be adequately explained by quite ordinary mental processes such as remembering and noticing. By the end of the chapter he is revising his initial proposition. If there is something special about the mental processes that lead to discovery, he realizes, it's *not* what we usually think: some unusual, hidden work of the unconscious or some special mode of mental functioning. He then gives his revised proposition:

> Revised Proposition: Discovery depends not on special processes but on special purposes. Creating occurs when ordinary mental processes in an able person are marshaled by creative or appropriately "unreasonable" intentions.

This happens to be a good description of what happens when you put Peak Learning principles to work.

As you can see, using probes is a superb way of making sure that you have a clear idea in mind of what is being discussed. It's no accident that this is essentially the basic method of scientific experimentation: formulate a hypothesis and test it.

Probes can also be developed from your prior knowledge and awareness of the subject you are studying. When you bring such prior knowledge to the surface by using mind maps and/or the Vee-heuristic technique, you may then find a variety of ways to formulate and reformulate focus questions that you can use as probes to be tested as you continue to learn. The following exercise will help you in developing your own probes.

◆ ◆ ◆ ◆

Developing Probes

Asking a question is the simplest way of focusing thinking ... asking the right question may be the most important part of thinking.... A fishing question [is] exploratory (like putting bait on a hook but not knowing quite what might turn up).... A shooting question [is] used to check out a point and [has] a direct yes or no answer (like aiming at a bird and hitting or missing).

EDWARD DE BONO

This exercise has two parts. In the first, you'll go over a sample text and explain the steps you might use to formulate probes about where the author is headed. In the second, you'll cover some guidelines you can use on a text you choose for yourself.

PART 1

This sample text is a selection from a chapter called "Role Playing" in Edward De Bono's book, *Six Thinking Hats,* which will be returned to in the next chapter.

Read the following two paragraphs.

> People do not mind "playing the fool" so long as it is quite clear that they are just playing a role. They even take pride in putting on a good performance and playing an extremely foolish fool. That now becomes a measure of achievement and excellence. The role has taken over and the ego is now the stage director.
>
> One of the problems with Zen Buddhism is that the harder the ego tries "not-to-be-there," the more present it becomes in its "trying." One style of actor loses his or her ego identity and takes on the ego of the role (method acting). Another style of actor directs his or her own performance. Both are good actors. Both are having an ego holiday. One is having a holiday abroad and the other is having a holiday at home.

Now turn to a fresh page in your learning log and formulate a probe. Your first one might be, "What is this author talking about?" Is it about being a fool? About problems with Zen Buddhism? About acting styles? The role of ego?

When you have an answer that feels right, make a guess about where this might be leading. How is it going to relate to styles of thinking, which would seem to be the topic of the book? Here are some possibilities, but take a few minutes to think up your own.

◆ He's going to argue that ego gets in the way of thinking.

◆ He wants to show that there are different styles of ego development in playing a role.

◆ He is trying to convince us that playing a role is a process in which we rate our performance in a different way than we would if we felt our *self* was being judged.

Now close this book and think of your own probe and answer. When you are ready, return to the selection and read the next two paragraphs.

> To play at being someone else allows the ego to go beyond its normal restrictive self-image. Actors are often quite shy in ordinary life. But a role gives freedom. We might have difficulty in seeing ourselves being foolish, wrong, or outsmarted. Given a well-defined role we can act out such parts with pleasure in our acting skill rather than damage to our egos. There is prestige in being considered a good actor.
>
> Without the protection of a formal role, the ego is at risk. That is why habitually negative people claim the role of devil's advocate when they want to be negative. This means to imply that they are not normally negative, but that it is useful to have someone play this role and that they intend to play it well. . . .

How well did your probes match up with the next selection? Clearly, De Bono is saying more than "ego interferes with thinking." These paragraphs provide a further explanation of why playing a role is a way to allow the ego to feel safe. Instead of feeling guilty for continually pointing out why something won't work, a nay-sayer can feel pride for scrupulously playing devil's advocate because *someone* has to tie down excessive optimism and enthusiasm in order to prevent thoughtless mistakes.

Now revise your probes. You are still trying to understand how this issue of role-playing might be relevant to how we think. Write any guesses in your log. Here are a few possibilities.

Questions are the creative acts of intelligence.
FRANK KINGDON

◆ Maybe he wants us to believe that actors make the best thinkers.

◆ Perhaps he is going to tell us that looking on the dark side of any idea is a bad thing because the people who habitually do it pretend they're being "devil's advocates" as an excuse.

◆ Perhaps this is a similar kind of role-playing to that in the exercise in Chapter III about "Activating Your Inner Learner." (Using a Vee-heuristic technique might help to recall this and other past experiences that could be relevant here.)

Now that you've revised your probes and leaped ahead, read some final paragraphs from De Bono.

> To role-play being a thinker in the general sense of that word is a valuable step towards becoming a thinker. [Aha!] But we can go further by breaking down that large role into more specific parts. These become character parts like the character parts in a good pantomime, a good TV soap opera, or a traditional Western movie. …
>
> The broad-thinking hat role is broken down into six different *character roles,* represented by six differently colored thinking hats.
>
> You choose which of the hats to put on at any one moment. You put on that hat and then play the role defined by that hat. You watch yourself playing that role. You play the role as well as you can. Your ego is protected by the role. Your ego is involved in playing the role well.…
>
> Thinking now begins to flow from the *acted parts* and not from your ego. …

How did you do? This is not a question of whether your guesses about where the author was going were correct—such a question would turn this into a test. My question is about whether you gained more from the material by actively anticipating what would be presented and noting not just what you read but what these passages *suggested to you as new thoughts to follow up.* My bet is that using the probes enriched your reading immensely.

PART 2

For the second part of this exercise, pick a new text on your own—perhaps an editorial from today's newspaper or a nonfiction book you're about to start reading. Do all the pre-noting and Vee-heuristic work you'd like to before reading a short opening section of the piece. Now stop, turn to your learning log, and begin to create the same sort of probes just used.

◆ What is the point of this first section? What is the author trying to say?

◆ What past knowledge of or experience with this subject do you have that leads you to suspect where the author is going?

◆ Is the author taking a stand on some issue? If so, what kind of supporting evidence or argument do you think will be presented to justify that stand? If no definite position has been presented so far, do you think the author is leading up to some position? How?

◆ What kinds of information do you expect the author to present next as relevant to the topic discussed? (Who, what, where, or when something happened? How or why some situation came to be?) What kind of result can be expected with this issue?

The true art of memory is the art of attention.
SAMUEL JOHNSON

As you can see, each of these general patterns for probes can spawn many more, all specific to whatever you're reading or hearing. Even considering a small fraction of the possible probes you can raise will keep your mind happily occupied while waiting for the next bits of information to arrive.

◆ ◆ ◆ ◆

This section has covered two important Peak Learning tools for becoming actively involved with what you're learning while you're learning it. Mind maps let you build personal pictures of the relationships you can see in the material, while probes allow you to anticipate where your learning is going and correct your understanding "on the fly." Now it's time to turn to the tools you can use to retain what you learn.

After Learning

No matter how clear we are about our learning goals, no matter how well we've matched a learning plan to our personal style, and no matter how carefully we take notes and keep them organized, sooner or later we all have to remember something of what we've learned so that we can put it to effective use. What can you do to strengthen your retention of what you're learning or have just learned?

For factual material, there are numerous techniques to assist memory retention. These mnemonic devices are an intriguing and enjoyable way to improve your memory. When you've had a rich experience from which you feel there's more to be learned, the instant-replay technique will enable you to distill further learning from your recollections.

Memory Improvement

We all tend to be uncomfortable about remembering. From our school days, most of us recall having to memorize material that seemed boring, irrelevant, and uncongenial—whether vocabulary lists or mathematical equations. Naturally, we had trouble doing so. From that experience we overgeneralized the difficulties and unpleasantness of the process.

However, it's entirely different when you are working with information that you know you want and ideas that excite you. When you use the Peak Learning approach and techniques in your self-directed learning process, remembering becomes astonishingly easy. Learning in these active, multisensory, personally congenial ways, your mind absorbs information without strain. The following strategies and techniques can help to make your learning more memorable.

Choose your own goals. This assures that you know *why* you're learning and have immediate uses to which you can put your knowledge. What you're learning isn't an alien mountain of material you are trying to cram into your head. Your keen interest, by itself, will facilitate recall. Understanding your subject in some depth will further strengthen retention, and your immediate use of your new knowledge will make it stick. "Understanding the subject, and relating what you learn to something you already know, makes for powerful memory and storage," declares Toronto psychologist Endel Tulving.

Employ techniques that activate your mind. This enlivens what you are learning and makes it more personal and memorable for you. You are asking questions, responding creatively, and processing new information in other ways. In doing this you are automatically storing the information in a richer, more elaborate form, connecting it with other data. "The more you organize information, the greater the likelihood that you will be able to retrieve or remember it," says Dr. James Staszewski, research psychologist at Carnegie Mellon University.

Three other Peak Learning approaches and techniques previously discussed also further reinforce your retention.

Get into the "flow" of learning. As you saw in Chapter III, flow learning sidesteps any resistances or anxieties, thereby opening your mind to input and understanding, which promotes maximum retention.

Invoke your enthusiasm and commitment. Invocations stir your feelings and emotions in support of your learning, thereby giving the material a more powerful impact.

Use your strongest style. This permits you to approach learning in the way that's personally most comfortable and efficient, thereby facilitating study.

The result of all these factors is less struggle and easier learning. "My favorite word about learning is *ease*," declares Elisabeth Ruedy, who conducts "Learning How to Learn" workshops in New York City. "The right attitude and the right skills result in ease in learning. Easier learning is largely a matter of changing self-limiting attitudes and acquiring more effective skills."

Of course, there are special occasions when you need to rely on your memory *per se.* You might want to remember the names of a number of people you are introduced to at a party or meeting or need to memorize a list of items being rattled off in a situation in which you can't take notes. Or perhaps you want to memorize your long-distance telephone credit card number and others you use often. These aren't parts of learning projects, and you can't use most of the strategies and techniques that have been discussed. For such situations, there are two powerful techniques you should add to your repertoire. These techniques will also be useful when you are involved in a learning project.

Association. The first is association in its many various forms. By association, you aim to associate meaningless names or numbers with something significant that will help to recall them to mind.

Tony Buzan, who was introduced earlier in connection with the technique of mind-mapping, lists several key principles for making memory associations easier. They include:

What memory has in common with art is the knack for selection, the taste for detail. Memory contains precise details, not the whole picture; highlights, if you will, not the entire show.

JOSEPH BRODSKY

◆ Involving as many senses as possible. Create colorful, moving, three-dimensional mental images, complete with sound, rhythm, touch, and even scent to associate with the thing you want to remember. Writing, speaking, drawing, touching, listening—the more you can use all of these in the process of memorizing something, the better your recall will be.

◆ Creating an organized sequence of associated images for a list of things to be remembered. You can simply number the items or use the ancient method of imagining each item in a particular place. This allows you to create a state-specific kind of recall—if you lose your place, you can go back to the start of the sequence and work forward again.

◆ Using exaggeration, absurdity, or even sexuality to give your associated image an impact you won't forget soon.

◆ Keeping it simple. Too witty or convoluted a link between your image and what you want to remember is confusing; make the link direct.

Here are a few examples of these principles for the association method of memorization.

To remember the name of a new person you meet, say it a couple of times during your conversation (which adds the physical act of speaking to the sense of hearing), learn something distinctive about the person, and associate the name or face with something visually fanciful. Harriet Goddard will be much more memorable when you have worked her name into the conversation once or twice, learned that she studies comparative religions as a hobby, and pictured her parachuting out of a plane as a kind of "goddess with long hair" ("Hair" and "God-ard").

To remember a set of unrelated items, such as groceries on a shopping list, try associating each of the items with a part of your house or room. Picture a bunch of carrots sitting on the table in the foyer, a can of coffee right next to the phone, bananas hanging from the standing lamp, and so forth. If you have trouble recalling an item, you can start at a familiar spot and mentally walk through your house until you find it.

To recall an important formula or list, devise a sentence with words based on its first letters; for example, you might remember the planets via "My very excellent mother just sells nuts until Passover" (Mercury, Venus, Earth, Mars, Jupiter, Saturn, Neptune, Uranus, and Pluto) or the familiar "Roy G. Biv" for the colors of the spectrum (red, orange, yellow, green, blue, indigo, violet). This is called the *acronyms* technique.

In the practical use of our intellect, forgetting is as important as remembering.
WILLIAM JAMES

Those who cannot remember the past are condemned to repeat it.
GEORGE SANTAYANA

To remember important numbers, link them to patterns that are meaningful to you. An avid cross-country runner might turn the formula for her bike lock, 3–4–3–9, into 3:46.39, close to the world record for the mile.

Sophisticated test-takers use state-dependent learning by studying in the room in which they will take the test or by calling up the visual look of the book and the page on which they read the material. The brain apparently encodes much of the context together with what you are learning, and any one of the contextual pieces can serve as a key for unlocking the rest of the information.

If you wish to develop a more systematic approach to this kind of memorization, there are a number of fine books available, such as Tony Buzan's *Use Your Perfect Memory*. However, I urge you to examine such books before you get lured into their intriguing systems. Pay particular attention to the examples offered and decide whether you really want to be able to do these stunts. Whole chapters in Buzan's book, for instance, deal with memorizing an entire pack of playing cards, lists of telephone numbers, historical dates (three chapters), birthdays, and anniversaries. Will doing this be useful or enjoyable to you?

Mental review. The second approach to better memory, mental review, also enables you to retain more complex data with remarkable reliability. In fact, you can actually reverse the *curve of forgetting* and increase your recall over time. The usual curve is shown top right.

It sweeps distressingly downward: after only five minutes, a significant amount of new learning is lost; an hour later, about two-thirds; and a day later, you have lost 90 percent.

The good news is that this curve can be turned around. You can train yourself to recall more with the passage of time. Much of what's forgotten in five minutes can actually be recalled in an hour, and the loss on Day One can be rectified on Day Two. The resulting curve is shown below right.

Your remembering can peak after a couple of days, and you can end up retaining, instead of forgetting, 90 percent of what you want to memorize.

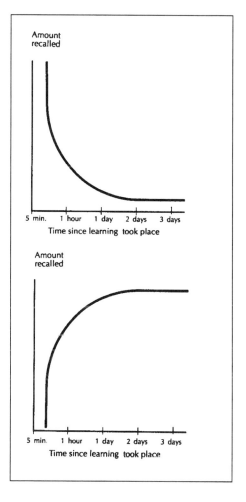

The discoverer of this phenomenon, and of the technique that follows, is Professor Matthew Erdelyi of the City University of New York. Memory review is most effective for "nailing down" well-organized expository presentations, such as speeches, workshop presentations, or classroom lectures. Following is an exercise to help you learn how to use this memory technique.

◆ ◆ ◆ ◆

Mental Review

1. Select a task. As you read, listen, or participate in a meeting or conversation, make a mental note (or written note) of the key points. (Because this technique does not require taking written notes, it is a favorite of many top executives, who often need to keep track of important information in conversations over lunch or at other social occasions where taking written notes would be awkward.) Keep a running total of how many points you want to remember.

2. Five minutes later, take two or three minutes by yourself, undisturbed, and go through those main points. Say each one to yourself, but just once. Relax and enjoy this session. Don't worry about or strain to recall anything you've forgotten, but "guesstimate" what the missing points might have been.

3. About an hour afterward, hold a second session doing exactly what you did before. Again, relax and simply say each item once to yourself. Note that these sessions are only a couple of minutes long and can be done anywhere, including in the car going home after a lecture or during a commercial while watching a documentary on TV.

4. About three hours later, hold a third session.

5. About six hours later, hold a fourth.

6. Hold a final session right before going to sleep.

7. Repeat this procedure three times on the second and third days, spaced evenly throughout the day.

8. From then on, you can keep the material fresh in your mind by having a recall session every three or four days.

Needless to say, the above procedure can be enhanced with any of the mnemonic tricks covered earlier. You can associate your items with visual images, particularly unusual and vivid ones.

◆ ◆ ◆ ◆

Instant Replay

After going through some new experience, you may feel that you missed some of the significance of what happened. You realize that there were facts, insights, or new ideas that you were aware of but didn't quite pull into focus. Perhaps events were moving too fast or you were understandably preoccupied with the task at hand. It's not review that you need—you're concerned with catching important things you simply didn't learn the first time around.

Fortunately, there's a straightforward, enjoyable way to extract such learning from any experience, after the fact. You can replay your experiences, recapturing what you might have missed the first time around. In fact, you can often perceive and understand *more* than you possibly could while they were occurring. While similar to the visualization tech-

---

It was a mental state of happiness about as complete as I have ever known in life. Ideas came in an uninterrupted stream and the only difficulty I had was to hold them fast. The pieces of apparatus I conceived were to me absolutely real and tangible in every detail, even to the minutest marks and signs of wear.... When natural inclination develops into a passionate desire, one advances towards his goal in seven-league boots.

NIKOLA TESLA

nique we used in Chapter III to activate your inner learner, this approach works by recalling subconscious images in all their detail. Because you recall *pictures,* this exercise may seem a little difficult at first. Most of us tend to remember words. But with a little practice, you will find that the technique becomes easier and is well worth it.

The benefits of instant replay are similar to those of instant replays of ball games on TV. You can see the experience from angles that were not observable at the time it occurred. You also can analyze it to understand the structure and process, as the TV commentators do by highlighting the nuances that you couldn't follow while watching the action. The key is summoning up as clear a picture of the experience as possible.

"Instant replay isn't merely recall," notes Win Wenger of Project Renaissance. "You will actually *increase* your perceptions and insights from the experience by three to five times."

The following exercise will guide you in learning the instant-replay technique.

◆ ◆ ◆ ◆

Instant Replay

Select a recent experience, preferably from the past 48 hours, which you feel has additional significance to be plumbed. It might be an encounter with a person, a movie, or a television show, or simply a moment of observing a scene or an image.

Close your eyes and describe this experience aloud to someone else or to a tape recorder, following these guidelines.

1. Begin with sensory details and your feelings—what you saw, heard, felt, touched, or otherwise perceived. Stay in the present tense throughout this exercise. ("I am having lunch in the company cafeteria with the marketing team.")

2. Describe the items in such detail that the person listening will almost see, hear, and feel what you did. ("Bill is wearing a plaid shirt and has loosened his tie. Janet's blouse is yellow. Frank is fiddling with a pen. I see strong sunlight reflecting off the next table.") Make a real effort to plumb the reality of the experience. Devote three to five minutes to this.

3. Having done your best to evoke the scene and the situation, try to move in closer. Ask yourself questions about half-glimpsed details. ("In the corner of my eye, I see Frank's fingers suddenly clench around the pen. Was there something wrong?") Try to connect these new details with your other recollections in several ways.

Often some new insight about the significance of the experience will present itself. ("Bill laughed at Janet's choice of colors for the new packaging. Maybe Frank agreed with Janet, or maybe he was irritated by Bill.")

4. Continue for at least ten minutes, or as long as half an hour, if you like.

5. Review the tape or jot down any notes you have about your new perceptions and insights.

◆ ◆ ◆ ◆

At such points where deep human emotion, identification with other beings, and perception of reality meet lies the crux of creativity—and also the crux of the most mundane thoughts. Spinning out variations is what comes naturally to the human mind, and is it ever fertile!

DOUGLAS R. HOFSTADTER

Once you have mastered instant replay, you can add another angle to it. It's called the SubjuncTV and is the imaginary invention of Douglas Hofstadter. The SubjuncTV is an imaginary TV set on which you can dial alternative *possibilities*—what might have happened. Here's how you might use this technique.

1. Select a recent experience you'd like to have had happen differently. Follow the same pattern as with instant replay: close your eyes, start with sensory details, stay in the present tense, make the situation vivid and real for the listener. "I approached that interesting person at the party, noticing particularly his tweedy professorial jacket and smelling the pipe tobacco."

2. Now, imagine reaching out and switching the channel to an alternative version of the same incident. "Instead of pausing awkwardly, reconsidering whether to say something or walk past him to refill my plate, I caught his eye and went directly up to him, and said...")

3. Now, be just as concrete about what happened, as you were with the version that actually occurred.

4. Finally, enjoy the feeling of how the incident went this time.

This chapter discussed several key Peak Learning tools you can use to make your self-directed learning more powerful and effective. It covered techniques you can use before you start in on a learning project, such as pro-active reading and the Vee-heuristic technique, to ensure that you get the most out of the time you spend. It also covered things you can do while you are in the midst of learning, such as mind-mapping and probes, which keep you actively involved in your learning process and help to make the process itself a creative and enjoyable activity. Finally, I've mentioned several techniques you can use after having learned something to retain the information you want to keep. With these tools at your command, you're well on the way to your Peak Learning pilot's license!

VII.
Developing Your Critical
and Creative Thinking ••••

Most of us unconsciously *narrow* the range of mental powers we use when we learn. One reason for this is that we were taught in school to concentrate on what we had to learn and that process often stifles the broader range of mental powers we have available: imagination, intuition, making associations and connections to relevant (and irrelevant!) experiences, questioning, and synthesizing new insights. Ignoring all these natural responses tends to drain our energy and undermine our learning.

In this chapter, you'll learn how to bring the full spectrum of your mental skills to bear on what you choose to learn. Tapping these additional learning tools is as easy as knowing the *right way* to use such thoughts as:

"I have a gut feeling about this topic . . ."
"I could imagine it working this way if . . ."
"This reminds me of the time I . . ."
"I still have this nagging question about . . ."
"When I put it all together, I think the bottom line here is . . ."

Intellectual independence at the earliest possible age should be the object of education. . . .
The initiative should be transferred to the student himself at the earliest practicable stage. . . .
The educational ladder should hoist the climber up from the child's passive role to the adult's active one.

ARNOLD TOYNBEE

The following techniques will show you how to do that. You are going to explore ways to think about your learning experiences that will let you focus the power of your whole mind to make your learning even more your own. Using these strategies, you will be able to:

◆ *Do more with what you learn,* by evaluating your learning in terms of outcome.

◆ *Generate penetrating and insightful questions* derived from all of your past experience.

◆ *Spark your creative flow of ideas* through conceptual strategies such as morphological forced connections.

◆ *Orchestrate your mind's full range of powers,* including your imagination, intuition, and feelings, in a coordinated way.

Climbing the Ladder of Learning Outcomes

As was seen earlier, *learning* means different things to different people—even among teachers and experts in education. These differences provoke heated debates about what schools and colleges should be doing. Some people feel the focus should be on basic facts; others want the emphasis to be on general training and life skills; still others stress understanding or analytical abilities. The debates rage from local schoolboard meetings to national presidential campaigns.

Fortunately, when it comes to our personal learning as adults, we don't have to choose. And we shouldn't! *All* kinds of learning are vitally important to us at different times and in different situations. Moreover, becoming aware of the different ways to think will enable you to expand your abilities in any learning situation.

Happenings become experiences when they are digested, when they are reflected on, related to general patterns, and synthesized.

SAUL ALINSKY

There are six major outcomes of learning, according to Professor Benjamin Bloom of the University of Chicago and his associates. Their taxonomy is widely accepted as the most useful way to think about the results of learning.

1. *Recall.* Remembering bits of information, terminology, techniques, usage, etc.

2. *Comprehension.* Understanding what you read or hear, so that you can summarize or explain it.

3. *Application.* Using what you've learned in concrete situations.

4. *Analysis.* Breaking a subject down into its component parts, so that you can see how they fit together and spot any logical gaps where you might need more information to understand the subject better.

5. *Synthesis.* Putting all the pieces back together in a new, personal way that combines information from many different sources and creates new insights and ideas about the subject.

6. *Evaluation.* Judging the value of material for a given purpose.

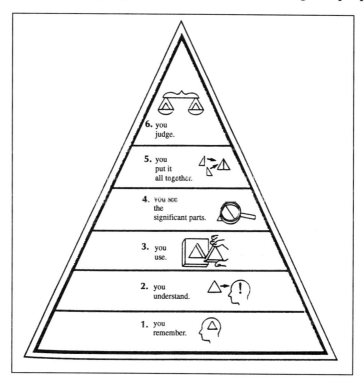

I prefer to turn this list upside down and see it as a ladder of increasingly complex outcomes of your learning.

These steps are listed in rough order of complexity, of course. You have to absorb some facts before you can begin to understand a subject, and understanding usually precedes application. However, this hierarchy is remarkably comprehensive; almost any cognitive outcome of your learning can be fitted under one of the six categories. It is therefore useful in thinking about what you really want to get out of any learning situation.

For example, we're all familiar with the kind of person who "learns more and more about less and less" but never gets to the point where the learning becomes *useful* in his or her life. Such people are stuck at the lowest level of this hierarchy of learning outcomes: simply remembering facts.

Recognizing the need to move up the list to more complex learning outcomes gives rise to some of the most accepted truths about learning. Everyone agrees, for instance, that at a certain point in one's study of anything, the best learning experience is to *teach* what you've learned to someone else. This principle applies to every kind of learning, from learning to be a gourmet cook to mastering differential calculus. In shifting from learning to teaching, you also have to climb the ladder. You are moving from remembering and understanding to *using*. Moreover, to teach you have to go even higher: you must *analyze*, or break the subject down into its parts, and *synthesize*, or put it together again. Finally, if you're doing a conscientious job of teaching, you will need to *evaluate*—to judge not only which parts of the material will be most useful to the person you are teaching but also *how* well you are conveying information.

One learns from books . . . only that certain things can be done. Actual learning requires that you do those things.

FRANK HERBERT

Consider the application of this hierarchy to your reading. Suppose you've read a popular treatment of some scientific subject and a friend asks you about it. What would you say?

You might start with stating whether or not you liked the book and why—in other words, giving your *evaluation* of the book, focusing on how useful it was in explaining the subject. You then might offer a short summary of the author's message—that is, provide your own *synthesis* of the book. (This is probably the best test of whether you really understood the book.)

Responding with several significant parts of the authors argument would let you explain how the conclusions you or the author reached depended on certain facts or assumptions. This would be your *analysis* of the book. If the book is, for example, the instruction manual for building a ham radio, showing that you understand it would involve actually building it, or *using* the information.

Finally, you may *remember* only bits and pieces, specific facts or interesting points raised. Depending on your goals, that may be all you need to absorb from the book.

Other ways to practice and use these learning processes will occur to you once you start looking for them. You will benefit from knowing how to *adjust* the kind of learning you are doing, so that you can advance from merely learning more and more facts to beginning to cultivate insights, applications, and new ideas from what you are learning.

Playing with Categories

At the upper end of the learning ladder, when you turn to analysis, synthesis, and evaluation, there is an important skill you can master that will help you to think more clearly about your subject: categorization. It seems to be a natural human function, and one which has paid off in a big way for civilization! We all make categories about simple things in our lives, such as what foods to buy or what clothes to wear, but when it comes to learning we may take that skill for granted. Whether we are explicitly learning or simply experiencing events, becoming aware of the categories we use—and revising them whenever we choose—is the key to being able to analyze a subject, synthesize new insights about it, and evaluate how suitable something is for our purpose.

We must remember that our categories are not rigid pigeonholes, but useful tools. They provide a way to make a tentative organization of a mass of data, much like the mind maps discussed in Chapter VI. It is usually a mistake to apply an old category to a new experience without considering what is different about the new situation. Likewise, we must be careful not to assume that our tentative categories cover all aspects of a subject and never have to be revised.

Most [scientists] have never considered how it is that human perception and categorization underlie all that we take for granted in terms of common sense, and in more primordial ways that are so deeply embedded that we even find them hard to talk about. Such things as: how we break the world into parts, how we form mental categories, how we refine them certain times while blurring them other times, how experiences and categories are clustered associatively, how analogies guide our intuitions, how imagery works . . . and so on.

DOUGLAS R. HOFSTADTER

Here are two examples of ways my wife and I taught our children to use categorization.

One fall when they were about seven or eight, we wanted Peter and Elizabeth to notice the wonderful differences among leaves—shape, color, and so forth. But instead of trying to *teach* them that, or even urge them to look closer, we went on a leaf hunt, looking for as many different kinds of leaves as possible. You scored points by finding a leaf that was different from any that others had already found.

Then, instead of just urging them to look carefully at the leaves to detect differences, we set them to devising a *classification* system for them. It could have any criteria they wanted, as long as they could both agree on where each leaf belonged and provided that every leaf fitted under some category. The categories had to do with such factors as size, color, shape, and number of points.

Suddenly, by operating on the *analytic* level of breaking the leaves down into categories, the children were keenly observing and comparing. This was, of course, an introduction to the basic scientific process of *taxonomy*, which resulted in organizing the elements into the periodic table and classifying animals and plants into different species.

Later on, when we wanted the children to learn about the propaganda techniques they were seeing in TV ads, we turned again to this climbing-the-ladder approach. Instead of trying to teach them the techniques abstractly, we just asked them to identify any one technique used in each ad as it came on, giving it whatever name they liked. When they had generated ten or so categories, we scrawled them on a piece of cardboard and taped it to the side of the TV set. Some of the categories they came up with were "Famous Person," "Fear of Smelling Bad," "Having a Better Car Than Your Friends," and "Everybody's Doing It."

Then the game changed. When each ad came on, the challenge was to figure out what category it went under or to devise a new one. Within a week, the kids themselves—using the learning skills of analysis, synthesis, and evaluation—had refined their own set of propaganda categories. You can imagine how much more interested they were, then, to see what the books said on the subject. They were intrigued to find out where the experts' categories duplicated theirs and where they had come up with different ones, or just different names. Needless to say, they hadn't come up with textbook terms like *argumentum ad vercundiam* (meaning "an appeal to an authority"—their "famous person"), *argumentum ad populum* ("everybody's doing it"), or *argumentum ad misericordiam* (an argument from fear or weakness). But you can imagine how delighted they were to discover that these were the Latin tags for the same categories they had created.

Educators and employers tend to ignore the immense amount of learning that almost everyone does outside of school and college. This is often a personal tragedy and it prevents our society from benefitting from the "hidden credentials" which Americans could be contributing to business and social life. We are blighting lives and hobbling our progress by failing to find ways to discern, harness, and reward these "hidden credentials."

PETER SMITH

This game of categories can be played in all kinds of situations, from the frivolous to the serious. The important feature *is not* whether your categories are "right," nor is it whether the experts agree. Categorization is *your* analytic tool to serve *your* learning purposes." Actively categorizing your experience is a way to pay attention to what's happening so that you can learn from it.

Learning From Your Experiences

You have an immense database from which you can learn things to help you cope with current problems. By reaching back for the most relevant prior experiences in your life, you can locate lessons learned then that apply in the present.

You do this already, of course. One of our most familiar experiences is to be reminded of something that happened in the past when we are experiencing something similar in the present. Many of us inevitably remember a particularly unpleasant elementary-school teacher every time we happen to see the wicked witch in the classic movie, *The Wizard of Oz*. We can also be reminded of a friend's experience with a certain store when we are about to decide whether or not to make a purchase there.

This process of being reminded of a relevant past experience was identified as basic to all learning by the great psychologist William James. A contemporary psychologist, Professor Roger Schank of Yale University, was as intrigued as James with this simple "reminded-of" phenomenon. He collected examples from coworkers, asking them for recent instances in which they had found themselves using past experiences to learn lessons that applied in the present.

One of Schank's coworkers reported seeing a TV commercial for a new video game in which an announcer offered the viewers a free game for buying two games at the normal price. The first thing it reminded him of is that the flip side of a hit record is often an awful song that nobody wants to hear. Then he thought of the free tickets offered to subscribers to our regional theater, which are usually to a play they can't sell out. He also remembered how the excerpts from new movies used in TV ads are sometimes the only part worth seeing. Putting all those together, he remembered an aunt of his who used to take him shopping and warn, "The strawberries on the top of the basket are the best ones you're going to get in that basket."

Schank points out that this person has created a whole category of events he can mentally access. This category might have a label like "getting stung when promised something for free," "examples of the principle that you get what you pay for," or "sellers who mislead you by featuring the only good part of their product." Having created such a file in his mind, and fitting experiences into it, the viewer made his past experience as a consumer useful in the present.

While such "reminded-of " experiences occur constantly to all of us, we usually do not consciously learn from the information. We are reminded of past situations on a random basis, and often the accessing mechanism is subconscious. Sometimes the past experience is clearly relevant, as in the case just cited; but more often, the past experience that comes to mind appears irrelevant: observing the color scheme of a room, smelling a man's cologne or a woman's perfume, hearing a tone of voice or noting a quick turn in the weather, for example.

What we really need, Schank explains, are techniques to *control* which past experiences are called up. By making our recollections more conscious we can benefit far more from the lessons learned. He continues:

> If we can find ways to be reminded *when we want to*, we can have a very powerful set of data available to us at any time we wish, not just at the whim of our unconscious. Our own experience, when called upon at the right time, can allow us to learn a great deal. . . . We can come across events in our past that allow us to compare current events to ones in our past. What we want is to be able to take full advantage of history, both personal history and cultural history. [my italics]

The following exercise is based on several ways in which Schank suggests you can access your own past experience, more powerfully and consciously, using the analysis of a past event to help you understand more deeply a current event or solve a problem.

Time present and time past
Are both perhaps present in time future,
And time future contained in time past.

                                                                    T. S. ELIOT

◆ ◆ ◆ ◆

Using Your Past Experiences for Present Learning

Identify a current situation, opportunity, or problem in your life that you feel might be understood better on the basis of your past experiences. It might be dealing with a troublesome person, deciding on a change in your work life, or understanding why you feel so positive or negative in a certain kind of situation.

Write or speak into a tape recorder in free-association style for two to five minutes about the situation you have identified. Your purpose is to bring it vividly to mind in all its aspects, bringing thoughts, feelings, assumptions, and projections to the surface. You might start by completing one of the following sentences or an appropriate version of your own:

> What makes this problem hard to solve is . . .
> What bothers me about this situation is . . .
> It would help if I could think of ways to . . .
> I'm wondering why I'm reacting by . . .
> What's going on here might be explained by . . .

Now choose one or two of the following kinds of reminding that are most appropriate to your situation, and use the questions below to stir up recollections of comparable experiences you have lived through. Write a sentence or paragraph on each of them.

Era-Based Reminding
Focus on a past era in your life. Recall past experiences that are relevant from when you were in college or high school; in your first job; in one of your early relationships; a young child; in one of the places you've lived for an extended period of time; on a vacation or trip; beginning childraising; living through a historical period that meant much to you; or listening to certain popular songs or performers of a past era.

Question authority.

TIMOTHY LEARY

Feature-Based Reminding
Focus on what features are important about the present situation. Recall past experiences that involve the same kinds of people or problems and ask yourself the relevant questions:

◆ When did you deal with a person or people who share this dominant characteristic?

◆ When were you involved in the kind of organization that had the features of this one?

◆ When do you remember feeling the same kinds of emotions as you feel now?

◆ When did you face the same kind of pressure as you see in this situation?

◆ When did you hear the same words or terms that you are hearing in this situation?

◆ When did you feel in the same position vis-à-vis the problem as you do now?

Goal-Based Reminding
Ask yourself if the goal you are after now has been pursued by yourself in other situations or by others you know of.

◆ When and how have I pursued this goal before?

◆ Who else do I know who has pursued a similar goal?

◆ Whom have I read about or seen portrayed in plays, on TV, or in literature or the press who shared this kind of goal?

◆ How would people I admire for their skills and abilities go about reaching this goal?

Explanation-Based Reminding

Ask yourself what similar situations you have experienced in which you sought to explain things in a similar way. How might your strategy in those situations be helpful here?

◆ How have I explained this situation before?

◆ What explanations of this kind of situation have I read or heard about?

◆ What explanations of related situations might be applicable here?

◆ How could this situation be explained using various theoretical perspectives, such as psychological or philosophical systems, political beliefs, or business principles?

Once you have exhausted all the questions you can come up with that remind you of related past experiences, apply them to the present situation. Which reminders have the strongest similarities to your current subject? Can they help to resolve the problem? Can you find parallels between how you behaved in a previous situation and what you might do now? How would you have to change your past approach to meet the differences in the present problem?

For example, if you are uncertain about whether to suggest some idea to your boss, you may be reminded of her reaction to a previous suggestion made by a colleague. You might remember how that suggestion seemed tentative or half-hearted and how it opposed a policy your boss had endorsed strongly. Thus, you might decide to approach her firmly, but only after first finding out whether she is open to the kind of modification you want to suggest.

◆ ◆ ◆ ◆

You will derive benefits from using this technique that go beyond insights into your current problems. Getting into the habit of accessing past experiences will affect the way you store your current experiences. You will actually begin to classify experiences and situations more and store them in more detail, thus developing your skills of contrast and comparison.

Ask Penetrating Questions

A questioning attitude is the prime factor in the incredible learning we do in our early years, notes Professor James Adams of Stanford University in his classic *Conceptual Blockbusting*.

> Everyone has a questioning attitude as a small child because of the need to assimilate an incredible amount of information in a few years. The knowledge that you acquire between birth and the age of six, for instance, enormously exceeds what has been consciously taught. A great amount of knowledge is gained through observation and questioning. Unfortunately, as we grow older, many of us lose our questioning attitude.

But that attitude is basic to Peak Learning. If I had to define the primary characteristic of a peak learner, it might well be the capacity to ask lots of questions, good questions, and know how to get answers. The model for this is, of course, Socrates, who launched our Western intellectual tradition not by propounding a new set of answers, but by insisting on asking penetrating questions.

'Tis a lesson you should heed
Try, try again.
If at first you don't succeed,
Try, try again.

Can we regain that questioning attitude and thereby turn our learning curve back, toward the way we learned as a child? Adams is convinced that we can:

> You merely need to start questioning. An emotional block is often involved here, since you are apparently laying your ignorance out in the open. However, it is a block that will rapidly disappear once you discover the low degree of omniscience present in the human race. No one has all the answers and the questioner, instead of appearing stupid, will often show his insight.

One of the best guides to developing this questioning attitude is Roger Schank, who was introduced in the reminding section. His book, *The Creative Attitude: Learning to Ask and Answer the Right Questions* is full of useful advice and explanations.

One of Schank's most interesting points involves the degree to which creative thinking is based on failure. He suggests that the *cycle of understanding* begins when an expectation we have fails—something doesn't occur the way we thought it would. As a result, we ask why. Then we create an explanation, which often reminds us of another event. These lead to another question: How are these two events similar? This in turn suggests a new, more general explanation for *both* events. Since that generalization leads to a new expectation, we've gone back to the beginning of the cycle.

In summary, *failed expectation* leads to *question* ("Why?"), which leads to *explanation* ("Because . . ."), which leads to *reminding* ("Seems like when . . ."), which leads to *new question* ("How are these the same?"), which leads to *generalization*—and that sets a new expectation.

This might seem like an exercise in futility. Why come up with explanations if our expectations fail? But that isn't how it works in practice. Some expectations *don't* fail—and then we can add the explanation for their success to our personal knowledge. The key issue is this: by actively creating many explanations throughout the learning process, you have a better chance of finding one that works. Every failed

s out some possibility, and every successful one is
n in similar circumstances.

uggests, your ongoing Peak Learning process involves
ng things to yourself, applying those explanations that
ation to new experiences, and evolving still more accu-
is that can, in turn, be tried out again in the future.

In "Twin Peaks," David Lynch and Mark Frost have understood
that America, as we live it every day, is ... an environment of
anomaly.

MICHAEL VENTURA

This idea will be applied in the next exercise, "Questioning an Expert." It's an opportunity to sharpen the Peak Learning skill of creating
and discarding explanations to enhance your learning.

Questioning an Expert

Through this exercise, created by Adams, you will experience the power of
working with a *questioning attitude* instead of merely listening to an expert tell
you about his or her field. Questioning is especially important in problem-finding
and problem definition.

To do the exercise you need a cooperative person who is in a profession
with which you are not very familiar. This exercise may take a certain amount of
time, but if the person is a friend of yours or is interested in activities such as
this, he or she probably will not object.

Begin by asking questions until you have isolated and defined a specific
problem in the person's profession. Don't be satisfied with a vague overly general, big-picture problem (for example, "medical care for the aged" would be too
broad). Try for a specific problem statement that is obviously solvable with a
small amount of effort, such as "Why does the sight of a hypodermic needle
scare people?"

As you ask your questions, be aware of where your difficulties lie. Are certain types of questions more difficult to ask than others? What is your subject's
response to different types of questions? Were you able to go from a very general problem statement to a specific one? Did you work with several problem
statements on the way to your final one?

Now, having had this practice in using the questioning attitude, you
may want to learn more about how to formulate, hone, and answer
questions. Schank points out that understanding can arise only from
not understanding. For him, the key to creative thinking is something we
don't understand, an *anomaly*. (As I wrote this, I found the word
anomaly itself anomalous, so I looked it up in a dictionary. The word

derives from Latin and Greek roots meaning "irregular, uneven, or incongruous.")

We've all seen those children's puzzles that ask for the number of things that are wrong with a picture. With great glee, a child will start counting upside-down cows, fish flying through the clouds, and so forth. That's a fairly simple example of training someone to spot anomalies. A somewhat more sophisticated example of the same principle is found in various psychological tests that ask you to decide which object is out of place in a group. Schank emphasizes anomalies because:

> To be creative in an area, you must learn to find anomalies in that area and make explanations of those anomalies. New ideas will start flowing. What does it mean to try to find anomalies? It means taking the experiences of a normal day and turning them around, treating them as if they were new. It means discovering why the normal day wasn't normal at all. . . .
>
> We can *decide* to see nearly anything as anomalous. When we do this, we effectively take *active* control of the understanding cycle, employing it in situations where previously it operated only unconsciously and passively.

Schank has a good point, one that is basic to the questioning attitude that peak learners develop. If you are able to find anomalies in everything instead of seeing daily events as just the same old stuff—the status quo—your experience of life is immensely richer and you develop a broader attitude toward learning. I also hope you noticed a recurring theme in both the Adams exercise and Schank's explanation of the importance of anomalies: *active control.* The more we are able to consciously direct our questioning and reminding skills, the easier it is to refine both our questions and our explanations. It is also quite a bit more *fun* to be learning in this way than to be a passive sponge only soaking up whatever an expert thinks we ought to know!

Thinking, willing and judging are the three basic fundamental activities. They cannot be derived from each other and although they have certain common characteristics, they cannot be reduced to a common denominator.

HANNAH ARENDT

The following exercise will offer some ways to help develop your skills at picking up on subtle anomalies.

◆ ◆ ◆ ◆

Hunting for Anomalies

Schank presents four tools to assist in spotting anomalies. Select any three things that happened to you over the course of your day. They can be perfectly normal and ordinary things, events you might never think to question. Using the tools below, describe each of these events as if they were anomalies.

1. Assume everything is anomalous until proven otherwise.
   Ask questions such as:
   "What makes spicy Mexican food different from spicy Thai food?"
   "Why would someone open a new restaurant on that corner?"
   "How is that TV commercial trying to get me to buy their product?"

2. Propose alternatives to everything:
   "What if I used Oriental hot peppers in a Mexican salsa?"
   "Where would I open a new restaurant in this area?"'
   "What information in a TV commercial *would* get me to buy their product?"

3. Reject standard explanations. Remember that the goal here is not simply to criticize everything, but rather to come up with new alternatives. Something "everybody knows" is a great target for your own original thinking.

4. Pretend you're a foreigner or a person from another planet. This is one of my favorites. How would you explain to ET, for example, such common earthly events as traffic jams or soap operas? What would you have to make clear?

◆ ◆ ◆ ◆

Schank's Maxims

This section closes with a final list from Professor Schank, one that sums up the best strategies for creative question-asking, as well as for Peak Learning as a whole. Some of them may appear obvious, something you already do from time to time. But that's the point here: while none of the following points is very hard to follow intellectually, Schank believes that *social* pressures keep us from being as creative as we can be. Either we're afraid of showing ignorance and looking dumb or we feel under pressure to accept what we were told without questioning—the don't-make-waves feeling that often seems so pervasive. As Schank puts it, "The difficult part is changing one's attitude toward one's own ability to think."

Most people think about things in only one way. Yet there are different types of thinking for different situations. Learning to distinguish and choose the right style of thinking is an art that can enhance your success, help you achieve your goals, influence others, and avoid making errors.

ALLEN HARRISON AND
ROBERT M. BRAMSON

If you like, you can invent your own exercise to go along with Schank's Maxims, following the same pattern we used in the last exercise. In the following list, any comments I've added are in square brackets.

Schank's Maxims

1. *Look for anomalies.* Anomalies are where the action is, creatively speaking.

2. *Listen.* You can't find anomalies if you weren't paying attention to what was going on in the first place.

3. *Find data.* Before you make a theory [or an explanation] look to the world around you, ask yourself what is happening. [Starting with a theory can prevent us from seeing important data.] The more you know, the more you can create.

4. *Classify and invent new classifications.* Their real value is the generalizations they capture. [We can know why a category makes sense if we created the explanation behind it.]

5. *Make rash generalizations.* The idea behind making a rash generalization is not to be right, but to be thinking.

Nothing is so useless as a general maxim.

LORD MACAULAY

---

6. *Explain.* When we learn something, it's because we have invented an explanation for it. We have explained it to ourselves.

7. *Refuse to learn the rules.* You must pick your spots for rebellion, be sure that you have reason on your side, and be prepared to take the consequences. [Being creative depends on discovering things for yourself.]

8. *Reject old explanations. Ask why.* [Authorities tell us to believe simple answers to complex issues.] . . . it is important to learn to distrust these explanations, not because someone is trying to fool you, but because the standard wisdom might be wrong.

9. *Let your mind wander.* . . . the process of letting your mind go where it wants can be useful if where it wants turns out to be an interesting place to go. . . . If you don't give your mind a little freedom every now and then, it may stop wandering.

10. *Fail early and often.* Failure is a good thing. We learn from failure. Take a chance. Have an idea and allow the possibility that it

might be a bad idea. [Wisely Schank also adds the following to his list:] The Eleventh Maxim: *Reject all the above maxims.* Who says I know what I'm talking about? Can we really enhance our creativity? That's a good question.

Orchestrate Your Mind's Full Range of Powers

Most of the techniques that have been covered in this chapter and the last are *cognitive*; that is, they refer to ways of improving the knowledge we get from our thinking process. What about the other ways your mind functions? Some of them were explored earlier in this book, but here you will learn how to *coordinate* them—to orchestrate them to get the best from each.

Take, for example, your emotions—how do you *feel* about what you're learning? What's your "gut reaction" to new knowledge, new ideas? You always have *some* strong feelings about whatever information you are dealing with. Becoming aware of these feelings—and using them as cues to your instinctive reactions—can often be crucial for good learning.

To understand is to invent.

JEAN PIAGET

Similarly, what about your imagination? Your mind is never constrained by the facts at hand. It's human nature to make multiple connections to other things. How can you enlist fantasy, metaphor, humor, and other uses of the imagination to enrich your learning?

Then there is *intuition*, which is derived from a Latin word that means "to see within, to consider or contemplate." Intuition generally refers to a process of knowing that seems more like a feeling than an intellectual response—it is immediate, it "feels right," and we don't know (consciously) how we arrived at our knowledge.

The next few sections will explore several techniques to weave emotion, imagination, and intuition in with our more rational, cognitive learning tools.

Sparking Ideas with Imagination

Creativity might be defined as getting lots of *different* ideas about something. Yes, I know we are all taught to believe that one *good* idea is worth a thousand bad ones, but how can you tell which is the good one if you don't have a considerable number to choose from? In short, real creativity means allowing your mind to generate as many ideas as possible without prejudging their worth.

Another aspect of creativity is the ability to generate as many ideas as possible across a *broad* spectrum, not just one or two narrowly relevant lines of thinking. In an exercise in which you are asked to think of as many uses as possible for a brick, you could, for instance, generate *lots* of ideas by listing such activities as "build a home," "build a shopping center," and "build a garage" and continuing along this line, but you'd be lacking in diversity. You'd be outscored by someone who came up with "make an artwork," "break a window," or "reach higher."

How can you get ideas about what you're learning that are numerous and different—and also relevant and perhaps important?

One of the best methods is Morphological Forced Connections, a forbidding name for a delightful procedure. Here are the rules and an example of the procedure, as laid down by the inventors, Koberg and Bagnall, in their offbeat, life-planning manual, *The Universal Traveler*.

1. State the problem.

2. List the attributes of the situation.

3. Below each attribute, place as many alternates as you can think of.

4. When your list is completed, make many random runs through the alternates, picking up a different one from each column and assembling the combinations into entirely new forms of your original subject. (After all, most inventions are merely new ways of combining old bits and pieces.)

EXAMPLE:

Subject: Improve a ball-point pen.

ATTRIBUTES:

| Cylindrical | Plastic | Separate Cap | Steel Cartridge, etc. |

ALTERNATES:

Faceted	Metal	Attached Cap	No Cartridge
Square	Glass	No Cap	Permanent
Beaded	Wood	Retracts	Paper Cartridge
Sculptured	Paper	Cleaning Cap	Cartridge Made of Ink

INVENTION: A Cube Pen; one corner writes, leaving six faces for ads, calendars, photos, etc.

When I am, as it were, completely myself, entirely alone, and of good cheer . . . it is on such occasions that ideas flow best and most abundantly. Whence and how they come, I know not; nor can I force them.

WOLFGANG AMADEUS MOZART

Another useful starting point to stimulate new ideas about your subject is a book called the *Strategy Notebook*, published by Interaction Associates in San Francisco. They present sixty-odd thinking strategies that can apply to any project you have, helping you to generate ideas. Any time you find yourself at a dead end, at a loss for where to go next, you can pick one of these notions at random and see what your imagination does with it. Here's their list and a sample of how you would use one of the strategies to generate ideas in a common business situation.

Build up	Display	Simulate
Eliminate	Organize	Test
Work forward	List	Play
Work backward	Check	Manipulate
Associate	Diagram	Copy
Classify	Chart	Interpret
Generalize	Verbalize	Transform
Exemplify	Visualize	Translate
Compare	Memorize	Expand
Relate	Recall	Reduce
Commit	Record	Exaggerate
Defer	Retrieve	Understate
Leap in	Search	Adapt
Hold back	Select	Substitute
Focus	Plan	Combine
Release	Predict	Separate
Force	Assume	Change
Relax	Question	Vary
Dream	Hypothesize	Cycle
Imagine	Guess	Repeat
Purge	Define	Systemize
Incubate	Symbolize	Randomize

Strategy for *Eliminate*

ADVANTAGES: The advantage of the technique of elimination lies in the possibility that you may be more sure of what you don't want than of what you do want. This strategy requires beginning with more than what you need or want in the solution and eliminating elements according to some determined criteria. There is an element of safety in this strategy because you have not overly extended yourself by deciding what you don't want in the solution.

LIMITATIONS: This strategy assumes that within the realm of possibilities you are considering, there is a good solution. However, after you've finished eliminating, it's possible to end up with nothing. Another difficulty is that it is easy to infer that you want the opposite of what you have eliminated (i.e., you don't want rain, therefore you must want sunshine, leaving out the possibilities of snow, fog, hail, etc.). Thus elimination must be tempered by caution and good judgment.

The following exercise presents a structure for the stimulation of new ideas.

◆ ◆ ◆ ◆

Who Needs Our Product?

Have each member of your group make a list of all the possible customers for the product you want to make. Don't leave out any ideas or associations anyone suggests, no matter how remote or incongruous. Write down all the ideas.

When everyone agrees that they cannot think of any more possibilities, each member of the group should go through the total list of ideas you've recorded. They should eliminate any potential customers they don't consider reasonable and write down their own personal lists of whoever is left. When all members have completed their own elimination lists, pin up all the personal lists on a display board so that everyone can share one another's ideas. This exercise has the advantage of allowing participants to get personally involved in the subject by using the strategy of elimination, and it can be modified to encompass a variety of subjects.

◆ ◆ ◆ ◆

By now you should be aware that generating a great many ideas about some subject is a good deal more like a game than like following some rigid formula or set of rules. Imagination involves *play*, letting the mind wander and seeing what it comes up with on its own. Since imagination is crucial to creativity, it should come as no surprise that creativity is just as playful.

The readiness is all.

WILLIAM SHAKESPEARE

Both of our previous examples referred to *conscious* processes—things you do with your mind. We now turn to what may be the greatest storehouse of creativity we all possess: the mysterious unconscious processes of intuition.

Using Intuition

Precisely because our intuition operates outside our conscious awareness, it remains difficult to say much about it that can be scientifically verified. Intuition also lies on the border between the emotive learning techniques discussed in Chapter III and the more cognitive skills covered above.

For the purposes of this book, however, I want to emphasize only that using your intuition can make a significant difference to your learning. It allows you to leap over detailed reasoning steps to reach a conclusion, emphasizing what your whole brain tells you is right without slowing down your thinking by forcing you to check each minute detail for flaws. Intuition can give you that sudden flash of insight that is the key to solving the whole problem. In many cases, this may be all you need for some learning project. As self-directed peak learners, the in-between steps just may not do much for you, but if and when necessary you can always go back and fine-tune the details later.

The keystone to intuition in Peak Learning is the recognition that learning is not just something you do, it is also something you *allow to happen.* Chance and luck can help your learning, if you let them. So you shouldn't be afraid to follow your hunches, even if you can't completely explain how they will work out in advance. How can you encourage this attitude?

First, welcome serendipity. We've all had experiences where we learn something new, such as an unfamiliar word, and suddenly find several opportunities to use it in the following few weeks. If you remain open to the opportunities fate sends your way, chances are at least some of them will be helpful. This is why peak learners make a habit of trying new things, reading books on subjects they never thought to study, talking with chance-met acquaintances like fellow passengers on a plane trip, and generally keeping an eye out for interesting anomalies. All these things help keep us open to serendipity and luck. When we take the time to think over such experiences, to consider what they might mean to us, we can find amazing treasures we would never have thought to look for.

The main difficulty of thinking is confusion. We try to do too much at once. Emotions, information, logic, hope, and creativity all crowd in on us. It is like juggling with too many balls. What I am putting forward . . . is a very simple concept which allows a thinker to do one thing at a time.

EDWARD DE BONO

Second, use your learning log to record any faint stirrings of thought that you might ordinarily dismiss as irrelevant, odd, or unproven. Remember, we've all been conditioned to believe that we have no right to our own judgment in some subject until we've mastered what the so-called experts already know. As you've seen in Chapter VI and in Schank's Maxims, the "Novice Effect" can actually deliver new insights *because* we are looking at some subject with fresh eyes.

Writing down such traces of creative thought may lead to useful new insights because your intuition can function as an early warning system. You will have plenty of chances to test out the ideas as you learn more, and you may learn more from a wrong idea than from one that proves to be correct.

Third, consult your intuition. Explore how you *feel* about a learning project, the goals you set, the resources you consider, and the actions you are preparing to take. If you find yourself uneasy about any of them, look more closely and see if you can figure out why.

For example, you may be trying to solve some business problem and get a sudden flash about how to do it while taking a shower one morning. Your intuition may be telling you to try that solution first, rather than investing several hours in preliminary research. Why not give your sudden flash a try? Or you may be browsing in a bookstore when a particular cover suddenly strikes your eye. It may not be a book you would normally choose, but your intuition may be suggesting this book is worth looking at. In short, your intuition is a direct channel to the combined skills of your entire mind, a subtle whisper telling you something that you didn't realize you knew.

Initially, this may take some effort on your part. All through our school years, we were told to disregard feelings of discomfort; after all, learning was supposed to be hard work, not feel good. We were supposed to adjust our preferences to the teacher's plans. Happily, that is no longer true for us as adults.

Our feelings can serve as informative meters, providing feedback based on clues that escape our conscious gaze. Learning to make the most of this information—by letting it come to the surface of our minds without prejudging what it "should" be—is a valuable habit. The more we can do this in our learning, the more we encourage ourselves to exercise our intuitive skills on our own behalf.

Six Thinking Hats

I'll close this chapter with one of the best ways I know to orchestrate feelings, imagination, intuition, and rational thinking in learning, a process developed by Edward de Bono called Six Thinking Hats. De Bono is generally regarded as a world pioneer in directly teaching thinking as a skill. He is best known for his term *lateral thinking* which refers to the process of coming at problems *sideways* instead of following a strict, step-by-step approach in order to stimulate creative solutions.

De Bono has a unique capacity for devising simple, *usable* methods for better thinking. Of the Six Hats system, he says: "I could have chosen clever Greek names to indicate the type of thinking required by each hat. That would have been impressive." (De Bono was a Rhodes Scholar at Oxford and holds a Ph.D. from Cambridge, so he wouldn't have too much trouble doing it.) "But it would have been of little practical value, since the names would be difficult to remember. I want thinkers to *visualize* and to imagine the hats as actual hats."

De Bono asks you to imagine (or actually obtain) six colored hats, each representing one of the major roles your mind plays in its learning process. Each of these hats encourages you to see your subject in a unique way. Used together, they enable you to choose the best ways to think about your subject, to switch from one way to another, and to know that you've covered all the major ways by the time you've finished.

Hats are a familiar metaphor in our learning history. From our school days, most of us can still remember allusions to the dunce cap that early American schoolteachers made slow pupils wear, or to the injunction to "putting on your thinking caps." In this case, we're using the hats to stand for roles. (You may wish to go back to Chapter VI, pages 110–113, to review De Bono's explanation of mental role-playing as part of the exercise on probes.)

Now, start by forming a mental picture of the six hats, each one representing an essential way of thinking about any problem or issue:

◆ *White hat*—used to think about facts, figures, and other objective information. (You may wish to associate the color with a scientist's white lab smock.)

◆ *Red hat*—used to elicit the feelings, emotions, and other nonrational but potentially valuable senses, such as hunches and intuition. (Think of a red heart.)

◆ *Black hat*—used to discover why some idea will *not* work; this hat inspires logical, negative arguments. (Think of a devil's advocate or judge robed in black.)

◆ *Yellow hat*—used to obtain the positive outlook; sees opportunities, possibilities, and benefits. (Think of the warming sun.)

◆ *Green hat*—used to find creative new ideas. (Think of new shoots sprouting from seeds.)

◆ *Blue hat*—used as a master hat to control the thinking process. (Think of the overarching sky, or a "cool" character who's in control.)

The hats are particularly useful when you're attempting to solve a problem or make a decision, such as whether to take a certain job, rent an apartment, vote for a candidate, enter a relationship, or select a vacation spot. In situations like these, keep the hats in mind as you gather information for your decision and again at the point when you actually make it.

Things learned on earth we shall practice in heaven.
ROBERT BROWNING

The following exercise provides a taste of the benefits you can gain with de Bono's playful *hat trick*.

◆ ◆ ◆ ◆

Using the Six Hats

1. Select a problem or issue on which you need to make a decision based on the facts, your feelings, what might happen in the future, and risks—in other words, virtually any significant decision from making an investment to entering a new relationship.

2. Express in one sentence what you'd like to accomplish in this little thinking exercise. Use your learning log or a pad, but be sure you have at least six separate sheets—one for each hat.

3. Decide which of the hats would be good to start with for this problem. Do you need to bring your real feelings to the surface? Figure out what you need to learn next about the situation? Project the future consequences of a decision? Clarify the risks that are bothering you? (These first three steps are, of course, made using the blue hat—you are deciding what to think about and how to approach your problem.)

4. Using one page for your notes on thoughts prompted by each hat, go through all six hats. Take as much time as you like, but put down at least three items under each. Your thoughts should address the following questions.

WHITE: What facts would help me further in making a decision? How can I get them? (From whom? Where?)

RED: How do I really feel? What gut feelings do I have about this situation?

BLACK: What are the possible downside risks and problems? What is the worst-case scenario?

YELLOW: What are all the possible advantages? What would be the best outcome?

GREEN: What completely new, fresh, innovative approaches can I generate? What creative ideas can I dream up to help me see the problem in a new way?

BLUE: Finally, review your thoughts. Sum up what you've learned from this comprehensive display of your thinking about your chosen subject, and decide what your next steps need to be.

When you finish, collect all six sheets and look them over. You will probably discover that "putting on the hat" led you to generate more ideas in each area and to do so with greater freedom.

◆ ◆ ◆ ◆

These last two chapters have presented the meat and potatoes of the Peak Learning system—proven exercises for significantly increasing your ability to learn and to actively manage your learning. From proactive reading and probes to anomalies, categories, questions, and hats, it has been a whirlwind tour. If you've been reading straight through for an overview, I hope you'll take the time to go back and try at least those exercises that intrigue you.

With this chapter, we have covered two of three areas of Peak Learning we set out to explore: the affective, or emotional, aspects of learning (Chapters II, III, and IV), and the cognitive, or thinking, aspects of learning (Chapters V, VI, and VII). What's left?

In the next chapter, we'll deal with *environmental* aspects of learning. We'll see how you can design your best learning space.

VIII.
Designing Your Optimal
Learning Environment ◆◆◆◆

There probably has been a time when you've gone into someone's study or workroom and thought, "This place *works! No* wonder she's so productive. *Anyone* would be up for learning and creativity in this environment." The right learning place can do the same thing for you. It can be anything from an elaborate office in your house to a room in your apartment or a corner of your bedroom. However modest at the start, a comfortable learning place is an important step in taking command of your own growth. When asked, "What does a woman need in order to be able to write?" Virginia Woolf responded with a phrase that became the title of one of her books: "A room of one's own."

Perhaps that's why the word *study* means both the *process* of learning and the *place* where it occurs. Many of history's greatest learners created for themselves an ideal place to learn. Even today's most effective executives are known for the care and the flair—with which they have designed their offices to facilitate learning, thinking, and decision-making. When you're serious about something that requires study, you want to be in a place where you can be at your best, where you can retire to your own thoughts and ideas.

I spent a lot of time creating the environment where I work. I believe people should design a world where they will be as happy as possible.

B. F. SKINNER

The dual meaning of the word *study* expresses an important truth: when you go to your study, you go not only to a specific place but also to a mood and attitude that is productive of a state of mind—Peak Learning. The way you design and arrange the space can help greatly to evoke both the feelings and state of mind conducive to high performance, making learning easier and more enjoyable. Environmental psychologist Franklin Becker puts the principle well in his lively book, *The Successful Office.*

> Plumbers have wrenches; surgeons, scalpels; carpenters, hammers and chisels: the tools of their trades. Good tools make for good work. For knowledge workers—lawyers, writers, executives, accountants, professors, managers, therapists, stockbrokers, journalists, people who work with ideas and information rather than with wood, pipe, concrete, or steel—the tools of the trade are the office and all its equipment and furnishings. In fact, your office can be as important to your job as a scalpel is to a surgeon. When you realize this fact, you will take your office more seriously. You will become aware of the whole psychology of workspaces and workstyles that extend far beyond the conventions of decoration or design.

Whether you are designing an executive corner office or one corner of the dining-room table after the dishes are cleared, the act of dedicating a certain space to learning and arranging it to your specifications is crucial. It can mean better concentration and discipline, more ease of learning and enjoyment, and less interruption from others.

The best office space will be a space where you want to work. We all have our idiosyncrasies and preferences, and the right place for one person can be a disaster for another.

PAUL AND SARAH EDWARDS

Over the years, I've had the privilege of visiting with some of the most notable learners of our times, among them futurist Alvin Toffler and philosopher Sidney Hook. What always strikes me is the way their learning/working environment expresses so much about their style.

Toffler's study is an immaculate high-tech room with state of-the-art word-processing and computer equipment from which he can monitor and tap into information sources throughout the world. On the other hand, philosopher Sidney Hook's study is an old-fashioned, cluttered professor's hideaway, with books, magazines, and manuscripts strewn about in a system known only to the proprietor. Both of these environments work for their creators. Both are ideal learning places. Both say: "This place works."

Learning in the right environment has made a major difference for participants in my Peak Learning workshops. In one participant's words: "I never realized how much support a learning environment would give to my reading and thinking. Now that it's set up, I feel it calling to me first thing in the morning for some brain aerobics, then again in the evening to do some journal writing. And on the weekends for some of my larger projects . . ."

Another participant noted, "Before I created my learning environment, everyone seemed to feel they could interrupt me for any reason if I was *only* reading or writing or listening to tapes. Now, I get much more respect for the fact that I'm engaged and shouldn't be interrupted."

And a third participant had the following comment: "I simply get twice as much work done in the same amount of time from having everything I need—including the proper attitude—right at hand."

Designating a place as your study and making it your own is a way of taking yourself seriously. In effect you're saying to yourself and others, "The growth of my mind is as important a part of my life as eating, sleeping, socializing, and working—and I need a special place to do it." It strengthens your sense of yourself as a self-directed learner and signals that commitment to others.

Creative space . . . is the sum total of what nurtures, supports, inspires, and reinforces our creativity.

NED HERRMANN

There's an additional reason why your learning place is crucial to your most effective performance. Psychologists now know that learning is *state specific* in some important respects. This simply means that our learning is connected to the specific state and situation we are in when we do it. For example, students who learn a subject and also take the final exam *in the same room* generally do and feel better than if they learn it in one place and are tested in a new, alien environment. Apparently the visual, auditory, and other cues in the environment are associated with the learning, which becomes easier to recall when those cues are present.

An even more commonplace experience is going into your kitchen to do two or three things and finding that you forgot one of them on the way. If you're concerned enough to try to remember the forgotten item, you probably instinctively go back to the room where you thought of the three things and find that being there enables you to recall it.

Be thine own palace, or the world's thy jail.

JOHN DONNNE

This principle is applied in several ways in what follows. I'll discuss how color, sound, and graphics can all contribute to your productivity and learning effectiveness. You will learn how to harness these factors for your learning by *creating* the state-specific cues that work for you.

Your Personal Vision

Start by simply identifying some of the elements that make up your ideal learning environment. First, recall one specific instance of feeling impressed by someone's workspace or office. What gave the room you're thinking of its distinctive qualities of both comfort and energy? When I ask my students this question, these are the qualities they usually recall in such rooms. How many apply in the case you've thought of?

◆ *Decor*—including light, color, and sound as well as evocative and intriguing pictures, photos, charts, sayings, objects, or plants.

◆ *Furniture*—the right chair, desk, shelves, work tables, and lamps.

◆ *Tools*—exactly what's needed, right at hand, nicely designed (computers, typewriters, pens, and so on).

◆ *Resources*—depending on what kind of office or workroom you want, the resources may range from a comprehensive and current dictionary (for wordsmiths) to the equipment of, say, a photographer's studio and darkroom.

We can begin to experience fulfillment as soon as we choose to create environments permitting us to do so.

BOB SAMPLES

Continue by doing a visualization of your ideal learning place in the following exercise. This visualization will be your baseline image. At the end of this chapter, after exploring some of the resources you might not be aware of, you will have a chance to revise that initial image, enriching it with new details that can make it work for you.

◆ ◆ ◆ ◆

Visualizing Your Learning Place

Make notes in your learning log or on a separate sheet of paper in response to the following questions:

1. Where would you like your learning place to be located? (In your home? If so, where? As part of the place you work?)

2. How large would you like it to be?

3. What kind of acoustics would you like? (Quiet or with some sound, and if the latter, what kind? Acoustically private or open to sound from the surroundings?)

4. What kind of lighting and color scheme would you like? (Strong or subdued? Lamps or diffuse lights? Natural or artificial?)

5. What kind of decor would you want? What kind of color scheme, floor covering, decorations, or art?

6. What kind of equipment would you want? (Typewriter or computer, drawing table or photography tools, etc.?)

7. What kind of furniture would you want? (What style of chair, desk or work table, bookcase or tool cabinet, etc.?)

Now, on another piece of paper, do a rough sketch of how all this would look. Don't worry about any lack you feel in drawing or designing ability—this is merely for your own reference later at the end of this chapter

◆ ◆ ◆ ◆

Tuning Your Learning Environment

It is time to explore some options and resources you may not have thought of. As you read, keep handy your notes on your ideal study, but jot down any thoughts you have for changes as you learn more about what questions you might ask and what possibilities are available.

You can start with decor, under which I include, as my students usually do, the use of light, sound, and decoration.

Sound

For decades, teachers have been telling students that they can't learn well with the radio or TV on, yet many successful students have gone right ahead and done so. Now, psychologists are catching up with the kids' awareness of what works for them.

According to Professor Rita Dunn, one of the leading authorities on learners' preferences, "teachers and counselors frequently project their own preferences for sound or quiet onto students during learning, assuming that if *they* require the absence of sound to concentrate, the same condition must hold for everyone." She cites studies suggest-

Comfortable learning area off living room.

ing that "inherited differences in nervous system functioning require that extroverted individuals learn in a stimulating environment, while introverted persons prefer a quiet, calm environment with few distractions." Another study found that when sixth-grade students were matched with their "preferred acoustic environments" (with the presence or absence of sound), these students scored significantly higher in reading achievements and evidenced more positive attitudes toward school than did students who were mismatched.

So you should feel free to suit your own stylistic preference in your learning place. Fortunately, you can do this even if you do not have acoustical privacy. If you prefer sound but want to avoid bothering others in your acoustical space, there are headphones such as those used with Walkmans. If, on the other hand, you prefer quiet but your learning place does not provide acoustical privacy, simple earplugs can very effectively muffle external noise to a degree to which you can easily disregard the residue.

Full room study with filing area and wall shelves.

Still another aspect of sound in your learning place relates to state-specific learning. You can actually *use* specific sounds, such as music, to cue your learning and creativity. Here is how Liza Cowan of the New York Training Institute for Neuro-Linguistic Programming does it.

> When I'm writing an article or working on a design I always listen to music. I will listen to several tapes before I find one that has just the right sound to accompany me for the specific work I'm doing. Once I've found it, I like to stick with it. I find as I go along that if I switch tapes I lose the mood and momentum; so I listen to the same tape over and over again. If I have to leave the work-in-progress for any length of time, which I frequently do, I find that when I put that tape back in the machine, I re-access the state of creativity for that particular piece I'm working on. I have had people ask me how I can stand to listen to the same music over and over again. It seems boring to them. But I'm not really listening consciously. I'm feeding my unconscious mind, my creative part, keeping it on track.

There is even more evidence that sound can improve your learning. A Bulgarian doctor and educator, Giorgio Lozanov, was a pioneer developer of techniques for accelerated learning. In one study, Lozanov worked with students who were learning a foreign language. He discovered that if he played Baroque music in the background while they studied, the students were able to learn more vocabulary words than they could in a silent room. The background music seemed to significantly enhance their learning skills.

And life is color and warmth and light
And a striving evermore for these.

JULIAN GRENFELL

Whether or not you have been raised to believe that learning requires silence, feel free to experiment with sound as part of your Peak Learning environment. Try several different kinds of sounds for different learning projects and see if any of them allow you to feel more relaxed and focused on the subject you are learning. Remember, the basis of Peak Learning is discovering how *you* learn best.

Light

One of the simplest exercises I use in my workshops is simply to sit a student down in front of a book and ask him or her to read a page. Then, before asking the student to repeat the performance with the next page, I replace the 60-watt bulb near the chair with a 90-watt bulb. "That's wonderful," the student invariably exclaims. Particularly as we get older and our vision becomes a little less sharp, simply increasing the wattage in our reading lamps can be a blessing.

But there's a broader aspect to the question of light and learning. Psychologists have discovered that many people suffer seasonal depressions when the natural light of the sun wanes in the winter. This depression can be successfully treated merely by increasing bright, white light in your environment. Think back to any seasonal differences in your learning behavior. Do you generally find, for example, that you rack up a rash of reading over the summer, even during the times you're *not* on vacation and just as busy as during the winter? Or that your ambitious September learning plans, inspired by school openings, freeze up by early January? You may be unconsciously disinclined to read or engage in other learning activities in the lower lighting levels of winter.

If any of the examples rings a bell, you can use a number of different approaches to improve your learning environment. Try to take advantage of natural light by moving your desk or reading chair beside a window or by replacing your usual light bulbs with stronger ones. You might also consider full-spectrum lighting that reproduces all the wavelengths found in natural sunlight.

Color

The influence of color in our lives has recently been discussed in books, courses, and workshops around the country. The uses of color are being explored by psychologists in areas ranging from healing to personal success. For example, if you've visited a hospital recently you'll likely have noticed that bright colors are now widely used to improve morale and promote recuperation. You can even hire a color consultant to tell you which colors are best for you. They usually suggest different colors for different seasons of the year and, if you're female, which colors to use in your makeup. This know-how can be applied to learning as well, although some of the ways will surprise you.

First, you can choose a color scheme for your learning that pleases you. More important, though, you can select colors that actually trigger the state of feeling in which you like to learn.

For example, here are some powerful feeling states that many of my students like for their learning. Each is associated with the kinds of colors that seem to reinforce that feeling, according to the Nippon Color and Design Research Institute.

◆ *Energetic*—orange–white, yellow–green, green–purple, gray–red, blue–orange:
"There is a lot of energy in colors such as these, and they transmit that energy to whatever they are applied to."

Color helps determine whether people feel their surroundings are cramped or spacious, and how hot or cool the room feels. For a sense of excitement, cheer, and relief from boredom, use warm colors. Reds, oranges, yellows, and browns increase heart rate and respiration. . . . If you want to create a calmer, more serene, and restful environment use cool colors. Blues, greens, and grays slow down body responses.

PAUL AND SARAH EDWARDS

◆ *Dynamic*—red–orange, orange–blue, black–yellow, red–black, black–orange:
"Brilliant, energetic colors such as these suggest vitality, health, aggressiveness, humor, and youth."

◆ *Fresh*—yellow–green, blue–gray, blue–white, green–light green, green–white:
"Use these color combinations to brighten and give a cool and refreshing look."

Needless to say, you can express your color preferences in many parts of your learning place: the walls, rug, furniture, and accoutrements. Just imagine for a moment the difference between a study space in which the palette is red, black, and white (perhaps with a white formica desk top, black filing cabinets, and a red chair and desk accessories) and the same set-up in lavender and brown: a wooden desk, lavender chair, and light brown rug. Obviously color schemes like these suggest different styles of learning and thinking, since each of these two palettes would put you in different frames of mind for learning.

---

*A man should keep for himself a little back shop, all his own,
quite unadulterated, in which he establishes his true freedom
and chief place of seclusion and solitude.*

MICHEL DE MONTAIGNE

Colors can also be used to make the very *materials* of learning better organized and more stimulating. You can color-code your four or five major interests by using one color for each. Thus your red folders, notebook, and even pens can identify one major area of interest, whereas blue or yellow or green supplies can signal another. Such a system speeds up locating materials on each project—particularly when you're grabbing for the right folders as you run out to a meeting.

But far more significant is the psychological impact, yet another manifestation of state-specific learning. The unique *color* of each project energizes you for working on it. The color triggers feeling states and recollections about what you've been learning in that area. Recall the discussion of Edward de Bono's six thinking hats in Chapter VII. Color serves to activate a different part of the brain for each hat in order to help you think differently.

Some notable thinkers of the past and present have used colors this way: students of philosophy are familiar with the philosopher Wittgenstein's notebooks known by their colors; students of literature will recall Doris Lessing's *Golden Notebook*; and psychologists are familiar with Carl Jung's *Red Book*, in which he transcribed his inner learnings after his break with Sigmund Freud.

Graphics and Display

Your learning place should welcome you and stimulate you with vivid reminders of your interests and passions. You can inspire yourself by displaying photos, drawings, and other visuals

Informal sun room converted to a learning area.

about the people, places, and events in your field, or by posting mind maps of what you're learning and key words that have emerged from your study, or even mounting affirmations about your learning or key quotes from people you admire.

The great French essayist Montaigne created one of the first "ivory towers" as his personal learning space (he actually constructed a tower on his property, which he reserved for reading thinking, and writing). He decorated its beams and columns with maxims and adages from the writers who had meant the most to him. There were fifty-seven quotes in all, such as this one from the Latin writer Lucian: "Preserve measure, observe the limit, and follow nature."

Professor Robert McClintock comments:

> Fifty-seven sayings upon the wall, upon the *study* wall. [Montaigne] sustained himself in a life of continuous self-education. The sobering sentences that surrounded Montaigne as he worked helped direct and sustain his formation of self; they reinforced a regimen of self-culture, speaking to him sagely as he cut his quill, shelved a book, stoked his stove, or gazed in silent introspection. Such sayings . . . set forth the ends and means of study, of meditation, inquiry, and self-formation.

Furniture

Most of us have a limited imagination when it comes to the kinds of furnishings now available from contemporary designers. If you haven't looked at fine furniture design recently, seek out the nearest outlet for it at office-supply and home-furnishing stores. You will find that your imagination will be stimulated by the many novel ways in which designers are using new materials, colors, and shapes to combine comfort and efficiency. And sometimes you'll be pleasantly startled by how some great old designs can be revived to good effect.

Roll-top desk in living room.

For example, several decades ago designers rebelled against the old-fashioned roll-top desk and introduced the contemporary ideal of the clean-as-a-whistle slab of wood, formica, or glass. Recently, the most avant-garde designers realized that the old roll-top was actually an aid to learning. By leaving your materials as they are when stopping work and simply closing the top, when opening it when you return, you gain a wealth of cues about where you were and what to do next. Cleaning up by sweeping everything into a file folder or an in-basket, on the other hand, breaks up the patterns in which you've organized what you were doing and may necessitate a lot of time spent finding where you left off.

Coping with Environmental Problems

All of us run into obstacles when we're learning. For some they may be interruptions, in person or by the omnipresent telephone; for others they may be noise, visual distractions, or even irritations within one's own body due to posture.

All I want is a room somewhere,
far away from the cold night air,
with one enormous chair.
Oh, wouldn't it be loverly!

LERNER AND LOEWE

The best way to deal with such problems is to treat them as one-time mistakes that provide the impetus to take corrective action. To treat them this way, simply identify whatever it is that is interfering with your learning on a given occasion and consider how you can alleviate the problem. There's almost always a practical way. Eighty percent of the problems raised by participants in my seminars involve one of these five, for which I suggest the following solutions.

◆ *Background noise.* Earplugs may do the trick.

◆ *Visual distractions.* A simple screen may work.

◆ *Discomfort.* Consider your posture, your chair, and the height of your chair and desk or work table.

◆ *Interruptions by phone.* Try having an answering machine take messages or screen calls.

◆ *Interruptions by people in your environment.* Let them know simple signals will indicate that you're at work and that you would prefer not to be disturbed.

Revising Your Vision

After covering the information about environmental effects and resources that improve learning, many of my workshop students rethink their plans for a personal learning space. To stimulate your own imagination further, I'd like to share four examples of what they came up with, ranging from the simplest to the most ambitious.

The first plan was drawn up by Marge Raymond, a purchasing agent and poet living in Lincoln, Nebraska.

I don't have the luxury of extra space to claim for myself, so I knew my place wasn't going to be ideal, right away. But you said we should start, so I did, and it paid off. Just making the following small improvements made a big difference in my learning and my self-image.

I was working with severe limits on the two things you need most to do this right: space and cash.

I looked at desk surfaces that you can push up flush with the wall and latch closed when not in use, the old door stretched-over-two-filing-cabinets trick, and making the dining-room table double as a desk. I did the manual work myself, including scraping, plastering, and painting the walls.

It's quite a feeling to have worked successfully within the constraints to create the best possible solution for myself. To me, this personal place symbolizes that I'm now doing my personal learning. After all those years of using my mind for others in their space, I'm doing my work, for myself, in mine.

A place for everything, and everything in its place.

SAMUEL SMILES

Here is a plan created by Jane Coos, a computer programmer and amateur stand-up comic who is studying for a B.S. in business administration at Pace University in New York City.

Some of my happiest hours were spent in the library carrels at the Smith College library when I was a student. So after going through the two visualizations, I realized that replicating that would suit me just fine. It would evoke the warm, supportive, secure yet intellectually venturesome feelings I usually had when studying or doing research as a student. So I bought a carrel in lovely blond wood (nicer than the ones at Smith, I noticed when I returned recently). Since the walls of my apartment are a little thin, I also use earplugs when necessary. The sides of the carrel are covered with corkboard and serve as a bulletin board with a changing selection of sayings, pictures, and other visual stimulations. I have a wonderful cactus which sits on top and reminds me of how much you can do with each little bit.

Albert Bosker teaches and works with environmental activists in Racine, Wisconsin. He describes how he planned his new work space.

The look I was after was the one I'd seen several times at Wingspread, the Frank Lloyd Wright house hereabouts, built for the Johnson Wax family and now a conference center. From the first time I visited that building I had that feeling that "this place *works*—I could learn, create, and solve problems here." Maybe that's why they turned it into a conference center in the first place, actually. Anyway, what I did was choose that Wright-type wood decor. In fact, I bought some beautiful photos of Wingspread, and an architectural drawing, and used them as my decorations. I also have several wonderful quotes by Wright up on the wall because he's an idol of mine such as "Early in life I had to choose between honest arrogance and hypocritical humility. I chose honest arrogance and have seen no occasion to change."

My key inspirational books on the environment are right at hand, but the reference materials are tucked away in files to keep that clean-desk look that makes me feel everything's under control, and I can focus on the topic I want to put under the mental microscope. I don't think it would suit others, but for me the space and what I've made of it is perfect. Whenever I sit down at my desk there, I feel a little bit of Wright's spirit inform what I'm reading, studying, writing, or planning.

On the threshold [of my study] I slip off my day's clothes with their mud and dirt, put on my robes, and enter, decently accoutered, the ancient courts of men of old, where I am welcomed kindly and fed on fare which is mine alone . . . and for two hours I forget all my cares.

NICCOLO MACHIAVELLI

Andrew Payton, a retail store manager and amateur astronomer from Modesta, California, describes his work environment.

My learning place is built around my computer because most of my learning is through communications, nationwide and occasionally international, via modem and telecommunications. For that reason the space has to be insulated from the outdoors, and rather antiseptic. Naturally, I've got storage bins for print-out paper, and bookcases built the right size to hold my manuals. The color scheme suggests the computer age—it's beige and gray. But I like it that way. *Colorless* might be the word other people would use, but for me it's both restful and exhilarating to enter my little cocoon. I've found fellow-enthusiasts for the topics of major interest to me right now—lunar transient phenomena (that just means shifting light on the moon's surface, which can be very revealing about the lunar landscape), and an amateur astronomer named Kinnebrook (who was fired from the Greenwich Observatory in 1796 in a disagreement with his boss).

What makes this style of learning perfect for me is that I'm a night owl. Now, instead of searching around for the late-night movie on TV, I can spend an hour or two inputting my contribution to ongoing dialogues with others via modem. Then, the next day, at their convenience, my co-learners access my work on their computers and respond. The next night, there'll be two or three comments, references, thoughts, criticisms, or whatever, in my computer's in-basket. I find that the half-dozen people in each of these little networks can come up with the relevant data I need on virtually any topic within these fields. For me, that's a much more agreeable way to learn than poring through books at the library, or even searching on-line data bases, to find what I'm looking for.

Every idea is a source of life and light which animates and illuminates the words, facts, examples, and emotions that are dead—or deadly—and dark without them. Not to engage in this pursuit of ideas is to live like ants instead of like men.

MORTIMER J. ADLER

Now, with the example of these four students fresh in your mind, it's your turn again. You had a chance earlier in this chapter to do a baseline visualization and plan for your learning place. Now that you've learned about other ideas and possibilities, you might want to reconsider your plan. This time, you will bring to the following exercise an enlarged sense of the possibilities.

◆ ◆ ◆ ◆

Your Ideal Learning Place—Not-So-Instant Replay

Visualize once more your optimum learning environment. Given some of the suggestions you have just read about, and engaging all of your senses, what additions or subtractions would you now make to the "room of your own"? How would you alter its decor, furniture, location, equipment, supplies, lighting, and color? How would you further enhance your study?

Think back to what you learned about your personal learning style and read the profile of yourself as a learner that you wrote at the end of Chapter V. Does it suggest anything about how you might design your best place and conditions for learning?

The revised list of questions that follows is designed to draw on what you've just learned about your ideal learning environment. Note your response to each question on a separate sheet of paper.

1. Describe the location and size of your ideal learning space.

2. What type of acoustical environment do you prefer for learning? What kind of sounds, if any, do you feel might stimulate your best learning?

3. From the previous discussion, what color combinations do you think will enhance your comfort and ability to learn?

4. Describe the type of lighting and furniture that would most assist you in achieving your learning goals.

5. What kinds of decorations—pictures, mottos, mementos, objects, or whatever—will inspire your best learning?

6. What kind of equipment will you need—from an easel to a computer—to support and implement your learning projects? How can those tools best be arranged in the space described in your answer to question 1 to make them easily accessible when you need them?

◆ ◆ ◆ ◆

Now, what can you *do* with what you've learned—and dreamed—about your ideal learning place?

First Learning Project: Your Personal Learning Space

As an initial example of a learning project, this chapter can provide the basis for a project on this very subject. It will guide your further inquiries over the next few weeks as you drop into stationery and furniture stores; browse in bookstores and libraries for books on interior design, personal organization, and study systems; and talk with people you admire about *their* learning places (visiting them if you can). The result will be a design for your personal learning space that is congenial, inspiring, and practical.

Here's a sample outline for such a project. It is only one example of how you might organize your learning. Feel free to change this in any way to make it more in tune with your own personal learning style.

Purpose. To design a desirable and practical learning environment for myself.

Rationale. I've decided to take my learning seriously enough to do it as effectively and enjoyably as possible—and that includes the physical aspects.

Prior knowledge and experience. I've had some good and bad experiences with learning environments in the past, which I'll re-examine for leads to what works for me.

Environment. Thats what this is all about!

Style. I'll approach this using what I've learned about my learning style (head for the nearest store with up-to-date furniture, equipment, and supplies; read up on interior design at the library; begin sketching alternative arrangements and showing them to friends who are sensitive to design. . . .)

Resources. In addition to the ones just mentioned under *Style:* stores that sell especially attractive furniture or supplies for my field (stationery store, art-supply store, etc.), art galleries and print shops, and computer outlets; books and magazines on interior and industrial design, available at the library; interior designers among my network of friends, acquaintances, and professional colleagues.

Results

1. A listing of the essential furniture, equipment, resources, and supplies for my learning space.

2. A layout plan for their placement.

3. An evaluation of items 1 and 2 above by someone knowledgeable in the interior-design field.

This chapter has discussed a number of the environmental factors that can help to make your learning easier, more enjoyable, and more productive. You've witnessed how color, light, and sound can combine to stimulate a state in which you can learn and remember better. You have also seen that designing your own personal learning space can be tremendously rewarding, a way to show yourself that you take your own learning seriously.

At this point, perhaps you are beginning to catch a glimpse of a pattern of habits that can encourage lifelong learning and improve the quality of your life. The next chapter will consider exciting new developments in the technologies available to support your personal learning.

◆ ◆ ◆ ◆ ◆ ◆ ◆ ◆

Excerpts from

Overview
of the Internet

Virginia Mayer Chan

◆ ◆ ◆ ◆ ◆ ◆ ◆ ◆

Introduction ◆◆◆◆

You're sitting at your desk in the office. You look at your company's website to see how many people have visited it during the last week. During the afternoon, you take a break to read news headlines and sneak a peek at movie reviews of the latest releases. Then, you read and respond to messages from your spouse who's visiting relatives 3000 miles away and check to see how your stocks are doing. Later that day, while preparing to leave the office, you check to see what the traffic's like for your evening commute by calling up a real-time traffic map of your area. Before leaving the office, you post a note to a "newsgroup" to see if anyone out there knows a good recipe for chestnut dressing. When you get home, you look up information that you need for classes you're taking and print out the articles on your home printer, saving you a trip to the library.

The reason you can accomplish all of these varied tasks without leaving your seat is that you're connected to the Internet, which means you have access to tens of millions of computers and untold numbers of Internet users world-wide.

In addition to drawing upon the wealth of information available to Internet users, University of Phoenix students are urged to take advantage of the Internet resources provided to them by the University. The purpose of this article is to introduce those resources, which are enormously beneficial in pursuing one's educational and professional goals. At the same time, for those students who are not yet Internet-literate, introductory information on basic Internet services, search vehicles and terminology is provided below, along with recommendations on how to locate and choose a suitable service. Therefore, the approach has been to remain as generic as possible in hopes that the principles noted below will remain applicable, even as the details change.

University of Phoenix Internet Resources

First and foremost, you'll want to visit the University-provided research databases. At the time of this writing, University of Phoenix provides access to three major databases which have indexes to over 9000 foreign and domestic journals and periodicals. When you search using key words, not only do you get lists of articles on your subjects, complete with abstracts, but in thousands of cases you get the articles downloaded right to your computer, or faxed copies sent immediately to your fax. If you want to access this feature, start with the University of Phoenix website with the following web address: **http://www.uophx.edu**. The link to the research database is currently labeled "Electronic Library," which takes you to "Online Collections." From there you're prompted to forward your requests. If it's your first time accessing this site, you'll be asked to register and will be prompted through a registration screen which will ask for your name, address, student ID number, and so forth. If you're already registered, you'll be asked for your name and password. There is no fee for registering. Once you are registered and are recognized by the system, the prompts for accessing the various databases are quite "user- friendly" and you should have no trouble searching for articles and receiving them instantly. As busy working professionals, you can imagine the advantage of having thousands of articles at your fingertips, without ever having to dig through library stacks!

Secondly, there's the University of Phoenix website itself. Now that you've visited the research facilities, you may want to look at other available features—information on each campus, an alumni network, University publications, Apollo Group news, and more. Eventually, course information by academic discipline and interaction with faculty will most likely be available, too.

Internet Basics

(Note: If you are already comfortably surfing the 'Net, read no further.)

I. How to Get Started

Let's step back for a moment. If you're not yet at a point where you can access the University of Phoenix resources on the World Wide Web, you might benefit from reading the basic information provided below so that you can get started.

You'll need a modem, a computer, and a phone line. The modem needs to be at least "14.4 bps" and the computer needs to be at least a 386. Those are at the low end of what's available today, and it goes without saying that a faster modem (say, 28.8 bps or above) and a 486 or above computer would be preferable. As for the phone line—if you have a telephone, you have a phone line. But if you're going to be online for long periods of time, you'll be blocking incoming calls and faxes, so you'd probably need a second line, or at least a "call waiting" feature to save incoming messages.

In order to get started, you will need to sign up with a "service provider." Some of the more well-known providers include America Online, Netcom, and Compuserve. They will provide software, usually in the form of a diskette, that will prompt you through an installation. These service providers aren't the same thing as the "Internet," they are your link with it, which means that they make it possible for you to connect with the millions of computers, programs, and computer users that make up the Internet. Just as the Internet is growing at a very fast rate, the number and variety of service providers is growing. A few questions to ask when selecting a provider are as follows:

◆ Are they "user-friendly"? (especially important for beginners)

◆ How wide an audience do they reach?

◆ How much do they cost? (flat fees are generally preferable to hourly rates)

◆ Do they have toll-free phone numbers regardless of where you're calling from?

◆ Are they compatible with all "browsers"? (software by which you "surf the 'Net")

◆ Do they readily provide technical assistance?

◆ Do they provide special services? (i.e., space for a personal website?)

◆ Do they have sufficient phone lines to carry heavy traffic?

◆ Do they allow you to select your "user name" or do they assign a number?

These are a few of the important considerations to ask if you are choosing an Internet service provider. Also, note that the so-called "commercial online services" (as against direct providers) offer many resources in a controlled environment, which tend to be more user-friendly and screen out adult-oriented material, as well as providing access to the Internet. Please bear in mind that the Internet is a hodgepodge of information shared by millions of users, so that you're likely to encounter something "inappropriate" from time to time.

II. Introduction to Internet Services

In the section below, we'll be discussing some of the commonly used Internet services which will benefit you in your educational, professional, and recreational pursuits. These include the following:

- E-mail

- World Wide Web

- Gopher

- Newsgroups (Usenet)

1. *E-mail* ("electronic mail) is reportedly the most commonly used feature of the Internet. You can write and receive messages (and attached documents) to and from anywhere in the world for the same cost as your basic fee. This feature has made it possible to maintain long-distance correspondence on a more intensive level than previously possible, as well as enabling low-cost, instantaneous dissemination of information on a wide scale. The instructions for using the electronic mail feature will vary depending upon the service provider.

2. The *World Wide Web* is a tool for accessing various sites which all share a set of standardizing conventions identifying them as "World Wide Web" sites as against other types of Internet services. These standards frequently include a designation beginning with "http://www...." The Web is currently very visible in the public eye because businesses and individual users are rushing to establish their own "web presence" and advertisements are increasingly urging you to visit their products' websites. However, please take note that it is NOT synonymous with the Internet, it is simply a segment of it. Generally speaking, you access the World Wide Web by selecting that pathway as instructed by your service provider, then typing in the location in the long rectangle provided. In the instructions given above for accessing the UOP web site, the address shown was "http:/www.uophx.edu."

   World Wide Web sites increasingly feature multimedia displays, including sound and animation, so additional software products such as Netscape and Microsoft Internet Explorer are often required to "browse" these sites.

3. *Gopher* is also a tool that will search areas of the Internet that recognize certain standardizing conventions (as distinct from the Web, for example). Unlike the Web, which has a large commercial presence, Gopher targets sites offered by government and academic institutions, and is primarily "text-based," meaning that you're less likely to find the graphics, sound, and animation which are gaining prominence on the Web.

4. *Newsgroups* (through the feature known as "Usenet") are Internet sites in which messages are displayed concerning a specific subject of interest to the users. They typically form around

news-related subjects, entertainment offerings such as movies, TV programs or music groups, various hobbies, and computer-related topics. Participants read entries by others and can "post" responses or initiate new discussion topics. The method of posting a note is similar to that used by a given service provider's e-mail system, but the messages will be displayed for public viewing and responding rather than sent to a private mailbox (unless otherwise specified).

III. Finding What You Want—Basic Searching Advice

The subject of searching for specific subjects is a science unto itself. However, a good first step is to use "search engines" which are available on the Internet, and a highly-recommended starting point is "Yahoo," accessible through the World Wide Web at **http://www.yahoo.com**. A Yahoo search will locate Internet sites whether on the World Wide Web, Gopher, in a Newsgroup, or elsewhere. Other highly effective search tools include AltaVista, WebCrawler, Excite, and many others. Another approach is to check your newspaper—nowadays many devote space to introducing the latest websites or Internet directories, which can be found in bookstores. However, given the rapid obsolescence on the 'Net, online resources such as Yahoo may be your best bet.

Using the above information, you'll see how easy it is to find all of the items mentioned in the first paragraph, such as stock quotes, traffic reports, cooking clubs, and news headlines—and of course, research articles for your UOP course work! Enjoy!

◆◆◆◆◆◆◆◆◆

Excerpts from

Business and Professional Communication

Wallace Schmidt
and
Greg Gardner

◆◆◆◆◆◆◆◆◆

Group Problem Solving and Meeting Dynamics ◆◆◆◆

Learning Objectives

◆ To identify and describe the types and functions of small groups found in organizations

◆ To show the relationship between group and systems functions

◆ To define small-group activity, focus on the nature of small groups; the laws of their development; and their interrelations with individuals, other groups, and larger institutions

◆ To recognize what constitutes a small group and be able to increase effectiveness in groups by understanding what produces group facilitation and group effectiveness

◆ To discuss group identity, structure, norms, roles, networks, methods, and cohesion

◆ To recognize the needs and demands of conference dynamics and apply appropriate techniques when conducting meetings

People in organizations must inevitably spend at least some of their time as members of various groups—social, information-sharing, learning, and problem-solving groups. The coffee break, cocktail party, departmental meeting, training seminar, in-house management program, and task group are all typical discussion situations. Each discussion type represented here is going on in hundreds of organizations right now and these are only a few of the types of situations and groups from which discussions emerge. Of all types of sustained direct oral communication, none is more common or important to our way of life generally and that of an organization specifically than small-group discussion and conferences. This chapter examines the different types and functions of groups in organizations, reveals groups to be effective in solving problems, and presents practical conference techniques useful when conducting meetings.

Meetings account for much of the time spent in organizations. Rollie Tillman, Jr. found that 94 percent of organizations with more than 10,000 employees and 64 percent of those with less than 250 employees had formal committees that met regularly.[1] Other studies indicate that over 90 percent of the *Fortune 500* companies used problem-solving and decision-making groups in their daily operations, and that executives typically spend an average of ten hours per week in formal committee meetings.[2] Then there are the many informal meetings conducted daily, weekly, and monthly. It is likely that in your lifetime, regardless of your occupation, you will spend more than 9,000 hours—roughly one year— in meetings.[3] Norman Maier describes the situation well when he notes that "executives hold conferences at all levels in an organization; scientists work in teams; educators serve on committees; parents serve on action groups; teachers educate by the use of participation methods; psychologists and psychiatrists practice group therapy; and teenagers hold meetings."[4] So, despite the criticism often leveled against small groups in organizations, they do represent one of the most prevalent forms of communication within the organizational structure. Additionally, in the last decade telecommunications has become a fact of organizational life with conference calls and videoconferencing becoming common. This unequaled technological development has led E. K. Clemons and F. W. McFarlan to observe that if organizations "don't capitalize on the promise of telecommunications, laggard companies may find themselves in trouble."[5]

Small Groups Defined

A camel, some say, is a horse that was built by a committee—the implication being that group solutions are far less effective than those made by individuals. Max S. Marshall suggests in *The Hydra of the Campus* that a "committee is a body of men [or women] who can do nothing individually, but who can collectively decide that nothing can be done. A committee is a group of the unwanted chosen from the unwilling by the unfit to do the unnecessary." And many would agree with Lewis Carroll's description of small-group activity, when he wrote in *Alice's Adventures in Wonderland:* "I don't think they play at all fairly ... and they all quarrel so dreadfully one can't hear oneself speak—and they don't seem to have rules in particular; at least, if there are, nobody attends to them—and you've no idea how confusing it is all the things being alive...." Despite the fact that group associations can prove difficult, you can avoid creating "camels" and reap enormous rewards and benefits. Now, more than ever before, it is important that groups perform their functions well if the larger system is to work.

Ernest Bormann defines group discussion as "one or more meetings of a small group of people who thereby communicate, face-to-face, in order to fulfill a common purpose and achieve a group goal."[6] Stewart Tubbs and Sylvia Moss present an even more complete definition when they observe that a small group is a "collection of people who influence one another, derive some satisfaction from maintaining membership in the group, interact for some purpose, assume specialized roles, are dependent on one another and communicate face-to-face ... *small group communication* may be regarded as *the process by which (three or more) members of a group exchange verbal and nonverbal messages in an attempt to influence one another.*"[7] The key terms common to these traditional definitions of small groups as well as the current literature in group dynamics are a "process" involving a "face-to-face interaction" of a "collection of people" for a particular "purpose" and/or "objective."[8] Small groups develop characteristics that differ from the sum of the characteristics and personalities of its members. Referred to as synergy, the recurrent finding that the whole is more than the sum of its parts has revealed that groups often come up with solutions that are superior to the thinking of any one member.[9]

A group is not just any collection or aggregate of people. Consider five people standing on a street corner waiting to cross or seven people working in the same setting—are these small groups? Certainly each situation has few enough people to qualify, but there is no communicative bond or interdependent purpose so these are not small groups. "Groupness" emerges from the relationships among the people involved, thus a small group is a collection of people who relate to one another in ways that make them interdependent to some significant degree. If an automobile accident should occur and the five pedestrians waiting on the street corner in our earlier example should join together to help the injured, then a group has been formed. Or, if our seven employees combine their talents to work on a particular project, again a group has emerged. Groups possess specific and definite sets of characteristics. John Brilhart identifies five characteristics common to small groups:

1. A sufficiently small number of people so that each will be aware of and have some reaction to each other (from 3 to rarely more than 20).

2. A mutually interdependent purpose in which the success of each person is contingent upon the success of the others in achieving this goal.

3. Each person has a sense of belonging or membership, identifying himself/herself with the other members of the group.

4. Oral interaction (not all interaction will be oral, but a significant characteristic of a discussion is reciprocal influence exercised by talking).

5. Behavior-based norms and procedures accepted by all members.[10]

Marvin E. Shaw points to six characteristics and raises six questions that serve to define group activity:

1. *Perception*—do members make an impression on other members?

2. *Motivation*—is membership in the group rewarding?

3. *Goals*—do group members work together for a purpose?

4. *Organization*—does each member have a specialized role—moderator, note taker, and so on?

5. *Interdependency*—is each member somewhat dependent on the others?

6. *Interaction*—is the group small enough to allow face-to-face communication between members?[11]

Groups may, then, be viewed as systems or interdependent subsystems. "They are a set of units bound by a definable context within which the component units interact with each other."[12] Groups are open and dynamic, having a multiplicity of purposes, functions, and objectives. B. Aubrey Fisher developed an Interact System Model to describe the sequence of phases that groups experience. This concept depicts group activity as a continually evolving process moving through four phases of decision emergence—orientation, conflict, emergence, and reinforcement.[13]

The first phase is orientation and is characterized by large amounts of clarification and agreement. It reduces uncertainty and allows disagreements to be aired without disturbing the peace. The clash of opinions, formation of coalitions, and solidification of roles occurs during the second phase, *conflict*. The move to phase three, *emergence*, is more prolonged but eventually the group attains a unanimity of opinion. This is the longest-lasting phase. Finally, phase four, *reinforcement*, serves to build solidarity and real agreement among members. These phases describe groups moving through a developmental process. Bruce Tuckman and Mary Ann Jensen further confirmed Fisher's view when they synthesized previous research and concluded that groups go through a developmental cycle of forming, storming, norming, performing, and adjourning.[14]

Although many theorists accept this classical view of group development which assumes that all groups follow the same sequence of phases, a growing number of researchers are examining a multiple sequence model. A *multiple-sequence model* suggests that groups do not pass through a uniform, graded sequence of stages en route to a decision or problem solution, but rather that different groups can experience different developmental sequences. It assumes that the stages are not distinct and groups do not necessarily progress in the same fixed sequences. From this perspective, ideas may be introduced, anchored, shelved, and readvanced in a group's halting progress toward a final solution. Consequently, various orderings of phases are possible depending on the group.[15] Whatever the process, groups do experience some cycle of evolving and dissolving.

Small groups involve a mutually motivated aggregate of individuals, cognizant of accepted norms and procedures, orally interacting, purposefully, interdependently, and systematically. Communication in groups is complex with all of the dimensions operating simultaneously and basic dimensions continuously changing during the interaction.

Group Norms, Roles, and Networks

The outcomes of small-group problem solving are very much dependent on the group norms that evolve, the group roles performed by members, and the group networks employed. A group is more than a collection of individuals working toward some common purpose; it consists of people who relate to one another in many ways. Each person in a discussion group holds a definite position in relation to the others in the group and together they all work to achieve a group purpose.

Group Norms

Norms are rules or patterns of behavior that develop over time. Edgar Schein defines norms as "a set of assumptions or expectations held by the members of a group or organization concerning what kind of behavior is right or wrong, good or bad, appropriate or inappropriate, allowed or not allowed."[16] Group norms constitute the conventional methods a group uses to deal with both task and interpersonal concerns. According to Muzofer Sherif, every social group, small or large, with some degree of in-group and out-group delineation, has an "organization defining the roles (statuses and functions) of individual members ... and requires certain conformities in action and aspiration from the individuals who belong. All this is determined or regulated by a set of standards or norms of the group."[17] Groups develop norms about a variety of activities and events, such as meeting times, attendance, leadership, and rules of order governing participation. The norms may be formal or informal, explicit or implicit. The former often take the shape of written bylaws to a constitution or a statement of standard operating procedures; the latter are transferred from established group members to newcomers by word of mouth. Thus, the new member will be wise to identify group norms and wait until they become evident before charging into meetings with ideas, suggestions, and particularly with recommendations for change.

Norms do not emerge on their own, but are the products of the group. Consequently, groups maintain and perpetuate norms through indoctrination and enforcement. Indoctrination consists of socializing new members in the ways of the group and against those group members who violate group norms—fail to conform. John Wenburg and William Wilmot have identified five sequential steps taken by groups to handle deviants:

1. Delay action (do nothing and hope that the member will automatically "get back in line");

2. Talk among themselves and use light humor with the deviant;

3. Ridicule the deviant (recognizing his/her behavior as different and shameful);

4. Apply "serious" persuasion (severe criticism or even threats); and

5. Ignore, isolate, and finally reject the deviant.[18]

Whether formal and explicit or informal and subtle, all groups include procedures for indoctrinating new members to group norms and for enforcing adherence to them. The more closely a group conforms to its norms, attitudes, and values, the more cohesive it is. Cohesiveness is a process in which group members are attracted to each other, motivated to remain together, and share a common perspective of the group's activities.

A natural consequence of group norms, then, is conformity of member behavior. Conformity can contribute to the development of group cohesiveness, but it does not exist without certain liabilities. The desire for conformity can lead to group pressure being exerted on members who hold dissenting opinions. Stewart Tubbs and Sylvia Moss, in summarizing studies of conformity research on individuals distinguish between private acceptance of a judgment or opinion and public compliance, i.e., between whether people change their thinking as a result of hearing opinions different from their own or whether they say they agree with the group when in fact they disagree. Public compliance usually results from a desire to avoid social pressures and the unpleasantness of conflict. Individual characteristics of compliance reveal dependence, need for social approval, and a lack of self-confidence. The influence of conformity is increased when members have a high degree of salience toward the group—a perception of the importance of the group and the personal desire of members to belong to a particular group.

Conformity can also affect group behavior in a number of ways. One effect of conformity is a tendency for members to increase their individual willingness to assume risks as a result of group activity. This inclination away from conservatism and toward risk-taking when in groups is referred to as the *risky-shift phenomenon*. Several explanations have been proposed ranging from the suggestion that Western culture values risk-taking over conservative behavior to the possibilities that members arguing in favor of risk-taking are more persuasive or that the diffusion of responsibility among the group members promotes risky actions. Although research findings seem to agree that the risky-shift phenomenon is real, some exceptions have been noted in the group behaviors of managers and executives tackling business-related problems. In these instances, a measure of individual decision making proves to be more risk oriented than the end product(s) of small groups involved in the same task(s). When queried, such managers and executives express a willingness to personally accept the responsibilities of risky decisions and their accompanying praise, rewards, or punishments. However, when acting as a part of a group, there is reticence to impose undue risk on or jeopardize the other group members. Consequently, groups in organizational settings may not necessarily experience the risky-shift phenomenon to the same extent as groups in other settings.

A second effect of conformity on groups is the *Pollyanna-Nietzsche effect*. The Pollyanna-Nietzsche effect refers to the overwhelming belief by group members that their solution is indeed the "best" and will work flawlessly. Certainly, the energy and commitment required of group members, along with agreements made through consensus, contribute to explaining this effect. However, effective group problem solving does not always produce finely tuned solutions, and perhaps there are even better alternatives that have not been advanced or considered. Groups must carefully evaluate the implementation of any solution and constantly be vigilant to other alternatives. Problem solving is often an ongoing activity.

Finally, Irving Janis has been studying for a number of years a phenomenon he calls *groupthink*. Groupthink is "a mode of thinking that people engage in when they are deeply involved in a cohesive in-group, when the members' strivings for unanimity override their motivation to realistically appraise alternative causes of action."[19] It occurs only when cohesiveness is high and represents a "deterioration of mental efficiency, reality testing, and moral judgment that results from group pressure."[20] Janis is convinced that a group's cohesiveness can make their desire for conformity exceed their task interest to reach a high-quality decision. Discussion members may be troubled by conflict, doubts, and worry, and consequently seek complete concurrence without regard for the decision(s) at hand. Examples of groupthink include the failure to prepare for the Japanese attack on Pearl Harbor, the Bay of Pigs invasion, and the disastrous helicopter attempt to rescue the Iranian hostages.

Although Janis sees groups that are highly attractive to group members as especially prone to making bad policy decisions, he doesn't believe that all cohesive groups end up succumbing to groupthink. Groups can take the following positive steps to avoid groupthink:[21]

◆ The leader should be impartial and avoid endorsing any position until after complete, active discussion by all participants who act as "skeptical generalists."

◆ The leader should instruct everyone to critically evaluate ideas and encourage the expression of objections and doubts.

◆ One or two group members may be appointed as devil's advo-cates; playing the role of critical evaluators, they guarantee "hard-hook" assessments of cherished ideas and proposed plans.

◆ The group may, from time to time, be subdivided to work sepa-rately on the same question and to air their differences.

◆ Outside experts may occasionally be invited to attend meetings and provide interpretive insights.

Implementation of these suggestions prevents easy consensus and can help close-knit groups avoid making terrible decisions—becoming vic-tims of groupthink.

Group Roles

Every member of a discussion group will perform a variety of functions; the profile of all these functions and the relative frequency of each in relation to the behaviors of other members describes one's group role. Group roles are most often classified into one of three broad categories: (1) task roles, (2) group-building and group-maintenance roles, and (3) individual self-serving roles. In 1948, Kenneth Benne and Paul Sheats explained these communication roles in their classic article, "Functional Roles of Group Members."[22]

Task behaviors are purpose oriented and refer to goal-related activi-ties serving the accomplishment of the group's objectives:

1. The *initiator-contributor* suggests or proposes to the group new ideas or an alternative way of regarding the group problem or goal.

2. The *information seeker* asks for authoritative information and facts pertinent to the problem being discussed and seeks clarifi-cation of suggestions.

3. The *opinion giver* asks for a clarification of the values pertinent to what the group is undertaking or of the values involved in a suggestion made or in alternative suggestions.

4. The *information giver* offers facts or generations that are authori-tative or relates his or her own pertinent experiences to the group problem.

5. The *opinion seeker* states his or her beliefs or opinions as they relate to a suggestion made or to alternative suggestions.

6. The *elaborator* spells out suggestions in terms of examples, offers a rationale for suggestions previously made, and tries to deduce how an idea or suggestion would work if adopted by the group.

7. The *coordinator* clarifies the relationships among various ideas and suggestions, tries to pull ideas and suggestions together, and

generally works to coordinate the activities of various members or subgroups.

8. The *orienter* defines the position of the group with respect to its goals by summarizing what has occurred, pointing to all departures from agreed-on directions or goals, and raising questions about the direction the group discussion is taking.

9. The *evaluator-critic* examines the group's accomplishments and critically subjects them to some standard or set of standards functioning in the context of the group task.

10. The *energizer* prods the group to action and stimulates or arouses the group to greater or higher-quality problem solving.

11. The *procedural technician* expedites group movement by doing things for the group, such as performing routine tasks.

12. The *recorder* writes down suggestions, maintains a record of group decisions, and generally serves as the "group memory."

Group-building and group-maintenance behaviors maintain cooperative interpersonal relationships, cohesiveness, and a group-centered orientation. They contribute to the social well-being of the group:

1. The *encourager* praises, agrees with, and accepts the contributions of others.

2. The *harmonizer* mediates the differences among other members, attempts to reconcile disagreements, and works to relieve tension in conflict situations.

3. The *compromiser* operates from within a conflict in which his or her idea or position is involved and displays a willingness to come halfway to move the group toward a mutually satisfying solution.

4. The *gatekeeper and expediter* maintains the flow of communication by keeping communication channels open and encouraging or facilitating the participation of others.

5. The *standard setter* expresses standards for the group to achieve in its functioning or applies standards in evaluating the quality of group processes.

6. The *group observer and commentator* keeps records of various aspects of the group process and, along with proposed interpretations, feeds such data back into the group's evaluation of its own procedures.

7. The *follower* goes along with the movement of the group, more or less passively accepting the ideas of others.

DeBono's Six Hats

(A thinking strategy developed by Dr. Edward DeBono of the International Center for Creative Thinking)
By Sheila Wright

To become a better thinker, try to separate positive from negative thoughts and recognize that maybe you are limited in your expression of certain thoughts based on your previous categorization.

Example: In a meeting environment do you suppress certain creative ideas because you have the reputation of being strictly a left-brained practical thinker?

Dr. DeBono has assigned 6 imaginary hats, each a different color, to the different types of thoughts we are capable of entertaining.

Here's how it works: You are conducting a meeting and would like to have everyone's total participation. By assigning the entire group a particular color hat, you can then solicit a specific type of thought on one project.

Once you are familiar with each color hat and what each represents, you can orchestrate your meeting with confidence. For example, you might say, "Regarding the cookware project, let's all put on a green hat and think of as many creative food combinations as possible." Or, "Now let's switch to a white hat."

If you use the hats from time to time while conducting meetings, your attendees will become familiar with each color hat and will know immediately what response you are soliciting without your reminder.

White hat: objective thinking. *White—neutral, objective.*

While wearing the white hat, you concentrate on the facts. You can also point out any gaps in information presented. White-hat thinking does not involve arguments, views or opinions.

Red hat: feelings. *Red—fire, anger, emotions.*

While you wear the red hat, you can express hunches and intuitive feelings. You may not be able to explain your feelings as they may be based on experiences you can't put your finger on.

In many discussions, particularly in business, we're not supposed to include our feelings, but we put them in anyway disguised as logic. The red hat lets us express our feelings openly.

Black hat: caution. *Black—gloomy, negative, the color of a judge's robe.*

While wearing the black hat, you can think about logical negatives—why something is illegal, why it won't work, why it won't be profitable, why it doesn't fit the fact or experience. It is sometimes important to consider the negative outcomes of a particular project.

Wearing the black hat allows attendees to contribute along those lines without being viewed personally as negative.

Yellow hat: logical, positive thoughts. *Yellow—sunny, positive.*

While you wear the yellow hat you must be logical. Here's an example. Your department is moving to another building. Yellow-hat thinking involves looking at logical considerations—plenty of electrical outlets for all the computers? Controlled thermostat? Proper distance between the shared printer and each workstation? Just saying that it would be nice to have a change is red-hat thinking.

Green hat: creativity. *Green—grass, fertile growth, energy.*
While wearing the green hat, you are free to generate new ideas, alternatives and possibilities. Right-brained creative folks thrive here.

Let's say you are conducting a marketing strategies meeting. You ask everyone to put on the green hat and contribute only wild, crazy, and off-the-wall ideas for new products. Could this be how the hula hoop was born?

In normal discussion it's very difficult to slip in creative ideas. Wearing the green hat is a way of making off-the-wall ideas acceptable.

Blue hat: objective overview. *Blue—cool, the color of a clear sky, which is above all else.*
The blue hat allows you as a meeting facilitator or an attendee to select one of the other five hats to wear. It's like controlling the direction of the conversation. A blue-hat statement would be, "We haven't gotten anywhere by being logical. Putting on my blue hat, I suggest we have some red-hat thinking to clear the air."

Wearing the blue hat lets you lay out your goals, evaluate how far you've gotten, summarize the results and reach a conclusion.

A tip for using the hats: Make sure that every idea that is brought up is analyzed under each hat. Once you've narrowed your options down to three or four, go back and do one more yellow- and black-hat check on each. At the end of this process you will have a well-thought-out plan of what you want to do.

Source: Sheila Wright, "DeBono's Six Hats," *Network Orange* (November/December 1991): 6.

Individual self-serving behaviors satisfy only personal needs and consequently inhibit task progress as well as group building and maintenance. These are dysfunctional activities that thwart group activity:

1. The *aggressor* expresses disapproval of the values, acts, or feelings of others and attacks the group or the problem it is tackling.

2. The *blocker* is pessimistic and stubbornly resistant.

3. The *recognition seeker* works in various ways to call attention to himself or herself by boasting, reporting on personal achievements, or acting in unusual ways. Often these people arrive 10 or 15 minutes late and make a grand entrance.

4. The *self-confessor* uses the opportunity that the group setting provides to express personal, non-group-oriented feelings, insights, or ideologies.

184 SKILLS FOR PROFESSIONAL DEVELOPMENT

5. The *clown* displays his or her lack of involvement in the group's process by disrupting the group and refusing to take ideas seriously.

6. The *dominator* tries to assert authority or superiority by manipulating the group or certain of its members.

7. The *help seeker* tries to call forth "sympathy" responses from other members or from the whole group.

8. The *special-interest pleader* speaks for the "small business-person," "the grassroots community," or some other specific interest, usually cloaking his or her own biases and prejudices in the stereotypes that best fit individual needs.

9. The *philosopher* focuses attention on his or her knowledge and persists in discussing abstract, theoretical issues.

10. The *storyteller* insists on relating personal experiences and uses the group situation to reminisce.

A number of additional obstructive roles have been identified and labeled. James McBumey and Kenneth Hance describe such role-players in discussion groups as "Mr. Pontifical," "Mr. Doom," "Mr. Smug," "Mr. Milquetoast," "Mr. Wordy," "Mr. Lunatic Fringe," and "Mr. Suspicious."[23] Also writing in the 1950s, William Sattler and Ed Miller add to the list such undesirable participants as "Mr. Orator," "Mr. Fearful," "Mr. Isolate," "Mr. Contrary," and "Mr. Emotional Antagonist."[24] you can probably further expand this list from your group experiences.

The recommendation should be clear: observe, identify, and analyze the task and maintenance roles, and expand your participatory flexibility. Practice a wide range of roles and choose those activities that are constructive rather than obstructive to the group process.

Group Networks

Group interaction may also be viewed from a network perspective. Networks are formal or informal communication patterns linking three or more members together. Network analysis is one of the best ways to examine the flow of messages within and throughout the organization and to assess the discussion effectiveness of small groups. Frequently used networks are the wheel, chain, Y, circle, and all-channel networks (see Exhibit 10–1).[25]

Looking at these visual representations, we immediately see the degree to which they are *centralized* or *decentralized*—the two principal characteristics of their design. Centrality refers to the degree to which all messages must flow through a single position or linkage in the network. In the wheel all messages must flow through the person occupying the middle position; he or she usually becomes the leader as a result of the

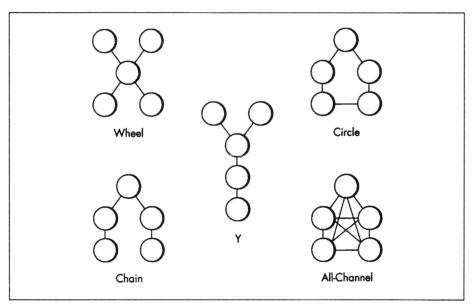

EXHIBIT 10–1: Group Networks

high degree of centrality. The Delphi technique, in which group members never meet face to face, would be an example of the centralized network, as would the Y or chain. In contrast, the circle has low centrality because each person sends and receives in either direction with no one person occupying the center, and in the all-channel network all communication lines are open. Most face-to-face problem-solving groups would represent one of these networks.

Research findings show that differences in the degree of interconnectedness or centrality in each of these networks result in different effects on the group process and product. Highly centralized networks inherently possess a greater propensity for leadership and organization, resulting in faster task performance with the fewest number of errors. Low-centrality communication networks, although seemingly more disorganized and unstable, reveal increases in group morale and prove most efficient when the group must solve complex rather than simple problems. Because organizations more frequently treat complex problems that require high group morale, it seems that decentralized, more fully connected networks would have certain advantages. Their open, sharing, and democratic procedures permit extensive message exchange and give them certain benefits that contemporary organizations are seeking. They enhance the exchange and management of information, contributing to a more cooperative environment and a more creative outcome.[26]

Functions of Groups in Organizations

Within any organization one usually finds a number of groups that exist to maintain and further the objectives of the larger organization. Organizations are composed of both formal groups and informal groups. Formally organized groups are those whose members have been assigned to permanent or temporary task groups to achieve some specific organizational goal(s). All organizations also have informal work groups that naturally emerge to satisfy individual needs not met by the formal networks. The former are primarily task oriented; the latter satisfy socioemotional needs. Gerald Goldhaber categorizes some small-group activities found in many different, complex organizations into two categories:

Formal Small-Group Activities
Quality circles
Brainstorming sessions
Decision-making meetings
Orientation session(s)
Training programs
Regular department meetings
Directors or executive meetings
Special purpose meetings (crisis, budget, safety)
Interdepartmental meetings
Roundtable discussions
Advisory councils
Committee meetings (regular and ad hoc)
Counseling groups
Transactional analysis groups
Conferences
Problem-solving sessions
Information-sharing meetings
Sales meetings
Labor and management negotiations

Informal Small-Group Activities
Informal meetings
Rap sessions
Luncheons
Coffee breaks
Grapevine
Retreats and informal conferences
Bowling and golf teams (or similar social groups)
Gripe sessions
Social events (picnics, meals, family nights)[27]

You will notice a preponderance of formal group activities and these do, by necessity, occupy more of one's time, but it would be a mistake to diminish the importance of informal group activities. Research indicates that an organization with strong informal groups will be more effective than an organization with weak ones. Moreover, needs not met by formal and informal groups will create frustration and disrupt organizational objectives,[28] so, rather than existing apart from the larger construct, these two types of groups are an integrated part of the total organizational system.

Researchers in group dynamics are in general agreement that every group serves one of two primary functions: it is either task-oriented or essentially socio-emotional/personal. This division is neither exhaustive nor mutually exclusive, but it does reflect the group process and serves as a helpful way of viewing the basic functions of groups in organizations.

Task Purposes

Task purposes are goal-centered, objective, and impersonal in nature. In organizations, group tasks are usually assigned by the larger organization. However, the origin of tasks may also be internal to the group, being created by the group's leadership or by the members of the group itself. Task functions in small groups include decision making and problem solving, informing, appraising, creating interest, and stimulating creativity.

Decision Making and Problem Solving. One of the most important and pervasive purposes of small-group activity is that of decision making and problem solving. All groups, regardless of specific purpose, must make a multitude of decisions involving the process of the group, the subject matter of the discussion, and the people in the group—decisions made by group members alone and in concert with one another. The solving of a problem requires that many, specific decisions be made relative to the nature of the problem, the criteria for a solution, possible solutions, the selection of a best solution, and its implementation. Problem solving requires that participants agree on a cause of action and make a number of decisions.

Informing. This purpose for discussion is also very prevalent. Almost all military staff meetings, many business and professional groups, and many student and faculty committees perceive themselves as essentially information or advisory groups. Such groups keep important people informed or consulted, and may also serve an orientation or learning purpose. Further, they can provide a public information service when an external audience is involved. These groups are distinguished from other task-oriented groups because of the peculiar forces operating on the members. They gather data, examine the nature of the problem, and may even generate and debate the merits of possible solutions, but they do not have the power to make any definitive decisions, although they are usually affected by any final decision. In effect, these groups recommend solutions to problems, and people at higher levels make the final decisions.

Appraising. Some groups are organized primarily for the purpose of examining a situation, such as fact-finding boards, committees of inquiry, investigating committees, and juries. Congressional investigating committees, a fact-finding commission charged to investigate a labor-management dispute or accident, management consultants called in to conduct a corporate survey, and grand juries are all representative of this group function. Appraisal may either take place before the fact, in which case it is proactive and a prelude to policy formation, or after the fact, in which case it is reactive and intended to set a value judgment on something that has happened. Appraisal groups recommend action(s) to be taken or decisions to be made as a result of their investigations and, like information groups, are not or are seldom directly responsible for the final decision. Moreover, group members often are not directly affected by the final decision(s).

Creating Interest. Public discussion is often used to stimulate interest and important timely questions or to activate others. In the first instance, experts present relevant information about a significant problem and discuss representative solutions. Although they may not agree on a final solution, the listeners become more aware of the problem and investigate it further. In the second instance, the group's task is primarily to recruit people and mobilize resources necessary for completing a particular project. Here, attention is given to persuading people to assume the necessary responsibilities and motivating them to act.

Stimulating Creativity. A final task function is to stimulate creativity and new ideas, with hope to deriving new solutions to specified problems. Advertising agencies, marketing departments, and sales divisions as well as legislative staffs, fundraising associations, and curriculum-development committees are typical examples of this group function.

Socio-emotional/Personal Purposes

Socio-emotional or *personal purposes* have their origins primarily within the individual and relating most directly to the satisfaction of self-centered needs or drives. People may also enter groups to seek personal satisfaction, to resolve personal need discrepancies, and to achieve a sense of psychological equilibrium. These groups are social, cathartic, consultative, educational, and therapeutic in nature.

Social. People in organizations engage in group discussion for what are primarily social purposes. Discussions over coffee, casual talk in the hall, and talk of sports in an elevator are examples of such discussions.

Individual goals may range from passing the time to deliberately trying to strengthen interpersonal relationships, promote status, or secure goodwill. The substance of most social discussions is of little moment, but such social discussion is often the prelude to considerations of more significant subjects.

Cathartic. This discussion function provides personal support through interpersonal dialogue. The intent is to allow people an opportunity to relieve their tensions, fears, gripes, apprehensions, and aspirations in a group. Bull sessions or counseling interviews are examples of such discussions. One should not dismiss cathartic discussion lightly because an invitation to "get things off your chest" is one which most people need and often seek.

Consultative. Employee counseling has come to occupy a very important function in today's organization. The current state of competition for attracting qualified personnel has resulted in an increased concern on the part of business to make every effort to reduce turnover and retain productive employees. It is in this capacity that counseling plays a major role. Employee counseling is a management function intended to satisfy personal needs and encourage individual growth and development through honest and rational discourse. Unlike cathartic discussions, employee counseling seeks to accomplish more than a reduction of frustration; it aims to increase individual potential and, in so doing, increase organizational productivity. Although counseling is most often a dyadic process, it can involve a number of people from a department or a number of line employees.

Educational. Certainly an important function performed by groups and one of the principal reasons for participating in groups is the opportunity to learn. Group members join together and participate in discussion intended to expand their thinking and develop new skills. Probably the class you are now taking uses discussion as a primary instrument for teaming. Orientation sessions and training workshops in many businesses may also be considered learning groups. Other examples include professional seminars or conferences and public symposia.

Therapeutic. The aim of the therapeutic discussion is to help alter people's attitudes, feelings, or behavior about some aspect of their lives. These discussions may be distinguished from cathartic and consultative group functions in that a highly skilled professional facilitator is needed to remedy the specific personal difficulties. Thus, this group function comes under the heading of psychotherapy or psychiatric treatment.

Common Work Groups

We have identified certain task and socio-emotional functions performed by groups. Earlier we said that organizations comprise many different formal and informal groups. Some of the specific work groups functioning in organizations include work teams, quality circles, study circles, management committees, focus groups, task force groups, and steering committees.

Work Teams. Organizational life, by necessity, involves us with work teams composed of a supervisor or director and our peers. Such teams vary in size and formality. Some work closely together, others meet infrequently to exchange information. Work teams may be long-standing with permanently defined responsibilities and few changes in membership, or project specific, formed around the technical specialties of other members of the organization. The latter are of short duration and must quickly clarify goals, roles, and responsibilities in order to establish effective working relationships.[29] Carl Larson and Frank LaFasto identify three features common to the members of effective work teams: (1) the possession of needed skills or abilities, (2) a desire to contribute, and (3) the capability of collaborating with others.[30]

Quality Circles. Probably no issue in contemporary American management is more prominent than that of worker participation as it relates to productivity. The success of the Japanese use of quality circles has led American managers to study the procedures in depth and implement such processes in American industry. Developed by W. Edwards Derning, quality circles are small groups of workers who voluntarily meet on a regular basis to discuss questions of quality, productivity, and output. Groups from the same general area select their own facilitator and meet on company time in a company location. The success of these groups requires considerable commitment throughout the organization so that managers and executives will be open to the recommended solutions from the groups and able to implement those solutions that can be effective in meeting problems. It is important that the workers not perceive quality circles as a management ploy to cut the workforce by increasing productivity.[31] General Electric, General Motors, Kaiser Aluminum, Westinghouse, and Motorola are only a few of the corporations that have documented increased productivity and worker satisfaction as a result of using quality circles.[32]

Study Circles. Developed in Scandinavia, some corporations use study circles in which personal as well as employers' needs and interests are discussed. Study circle participants decide what they will discuss, where to meet, the materials, the resources, the learning plans, and the problem-solving methods. In study circles there is a lack of structured discussion and no authority figure. The results, according to those who have observed study groups in operation, are well worth the investment of time, resources, and effort.[33]

Management Committees. Management committees use the talents of employees while building a strong spirit of cooperation and shared goals. The 8 to 15 members handle organization-wide concerns on a regular basis. For example, a computer/management committee may interact with automation vendors, prepare company-wide procedure manuals, and conduct computer training. The newsletter committee would be responsible for writing, designing, and printing the in-house newsletter. Other committees, such as a company committee and social planning committee, could also be formed. These are not business-planning committees nor do they play any part in managing the daily workflow. Rather, they have limited responsibilities and draw from across the organization. Committee assignments are rotated and no employee can serve on more than one committee. They represent a team effort that can "bring out the best in employees" and lead to the "development of a self-disciplined, self-motivated staff."[34]

Focus Groups. Focus groups bring people together at a central location to probe intensively for qualitative data related to specific problem areas or to react to proposed courses of action. Group members discuss problems openly and provide useful information. The interaction in focus groups is multiplicative, with each member becoming a richer source of information than he or she would be alone. To be successful, the facilitator must serve as a catalyst generating different viewpoints and uncovering reasons behind opinions rather than just discovering the opinions themselves.[35] Focus groups are frequently used by marketing and advertising professionals to gather information.

Task Force Groups. Task force groups bring diverse organizational members from the various operational divisions together for the purpose of strategic planning. They are study groups given specific responsibilities by management to make recommendations regarding organizational change. To be effective, group members must agree that change is needed and must work cooperatively toward the organization-wide objectives and projected vision.[36]

Steering Committees. Steering committees are similar to task force groups in their composition, but their charge is to implement organizational plans and processes for change. They direct, oversee, and evaluate the progress of plans, goals, programs, and mission. To be successful, steering committees must have the authority and power to strategically promote and manage change. Forward-looking companies proactively use task force groups and steering committees for organizational development (OD) or planned change.[37]

Regardless of the nature of the group or its purpose, it is only through the interaction of its members that groups can become effective. To encourage interaction, a number of discussion techniques have been devised and can be used in conjunction with the various types of groups.

Types of Groups in Organizations

The types of groups used in organizations and selected for conducting discussions vary with the group's purpose, the question being discussed, and the people involved (see Exhibit 10–2). Traditional discussion formats used in the organizational setting include the panel, roundtable, colloquy, symposium, brainstorming, case discussion, role-playing, and encounter self-development training.[38]

Panel

The panel is usually a public discussion in which a small group of experts or well-informed people examine some problem or issue in a free, direct exchange of ideas. The distinctive feature of the panel is the communication pattern. Participants engage in an open conversational interchange that can be lively and extemporaneous. Informality is the keynote and the members of the group can freely interrupt one another. This freedom can be both a virtue and a liability to the panel format. The panel is designed to solve problems, arrive at a consensus, and illuminate ideas. Panelists are usually chosen because they can supply needed information for well-informed discussion or because they represent views held by members of a larger group. The panel is also suitable for problem solving in less-public discussion situations.

Example: Economists, bankers, and government representatives meet to discuss the problem of a sluggish economy and, specifically, interest rates, mortgages, and the availability of money. There is an audience composed of the national press corps and interested people; additionally, the discussion is being carried on C-Span so the audience is significantly increased. Participants follow an agenda but engage in a

TYPE	PATTERN	PURPOSE
Panel	Open, direct, public or private exchange of ideas	Problem solving
Roundtable	Closed, investigative exploration of ideas	Understanding
Colloquy	Open, public exchange involving lay members and experts	Information sharing
Symposium	Controlled, public exchange of opinions of experts	Information gathering
Brainstorming	Noncritical, nonjudgmental generation of ideas	Creativity
Case discussion	Collaborative exploration of real/hypothetical situations	Teaching/learning
Role-playing	Participants enact varying roles in a "safe" environment	Attitude development
Encounter self-development	Intense awareness encounters with others	Self-improvement

EXHIBIT 10–2: Types, Patterns, and Purposes of Groups

free exchange of ideas. Although they disagree on a particular solution, they do reach an agreement on certain guidelines that might facilitate a solution. The discussion has been characterized by an active exchange or interchange.

Roundtable

The roundtable is usually a closed-group, enlightenment discussion in which participants with a common problem enter into a free exchange of ideas for the purpose of learning from each other. Said to have originated with King Arthur and the Knights of the Round Table (although whether this is fact or legend is uncertain), this type of discussion encourages a climate of equality and is used extensively in small decision-making groups and small learning groups. The purpose is to increase understanding about ways of approaching and investigating a problem that influences all of the involved members.

Example: The district supervisors of Southland Corporation meet to discuss a problem common to all Seven-Eleven stores in the area—the high rate of employee turnover. It is noted that the problem is not new and each describes current attempts to resolve it. Finally, solutions are advanced with the supervisors agreeing that increased attention should be given to applicant screening, working conditions, and job enrichment. Additionally, a study should be conducted relative to this problem. The discussion has been freewheeling and open, allowing all participants to voice their ideas.

Colloquy

The colloquy is an arrangement similar to the panel, intimately involving an audience and a platform of experts. Originally involving the reporting of information by experts and then questioning by an audience, an alternative format has evolved using a lay panel and a selected panel of experts. Although knowledgeable professionals formerly gave direction to the discussion, in the new format the lay panel prepares and directs the discussion with experts adding necessary information on request or as needed. This format was originally created to work out problems, but it has become essentially an information-sharing process.

Example: The area CETA planner, knowledgeable about minority training programs, meets with lay members of a Public Industrial Council representing a large midwestern city. The meeting is open to the public and addresses the allocation of training funds. The Council and members of business and industry developed the agenda, and the CETA planner serves as a resource person answering questions relative to career availability and governmental guidelines.

Symposium

The symposium also resembles the panel in that it is a public discussion, but participants present a prepared talk on one area or phase of the discussion question. Usually group members are chosen because they are acknowledged authorities in their fields, representing particular positions on a problem or possessing special competence, expertise, or information relative to the issue. Following the prepared presentations, the gathered experts may question one another or questions might be asked by another group of interrogators. The symposium is less spontaneous and more formal than other formats, but the questions and answers add a measure of spontaneity. The symposium is very much an information-gathering process rather than a problem-solving endeavor. It usually precedes problem solving.

Example: Experts from the Department of Agriculture, Soil Conservation Service and Agricultural Stabilization Agency, and the Army Corps of Engineers meet in west Texas to discuss the water shortage with county commissioners. The respective authorities in their fields give prepared presentations outlining the gravity of the problem and they advance potential remedies, given their specialized areas. During the ensuing discussion, there is general agreement that action must be taken soon to ensure an adequate water supply for the future. The county commissioners later meet to develop specific recommendations for their local jurisdiction based on the information gathered from the involved experts.

Brainstorming

Brainstorming is a type of small-group effort to encourage the free exchange of ideas and solutions leading to creativity and innovation. It is a creative problem-solving approach developed in the late 1930s by Alex F. Osborn, a New York advertising executive. The brainstorming procedure follows a definite structure intended to produce many ideas or alternatives by reducing some of the inhibitory influences normally associated with small groups. The basic premise is that a large list of potential alternatives increases the probability of achieving an effective solution.

Brainstorming, as a device for stimulating the production of ideas, involves two stages and is based on the observance of a few fundamental rules. During the first stage, the facilitator appoints a recorder to write down all ideas, then briefly explains the problem, which should be limited, specific, and restricted in scope. Members then suggest possible solutions. It is at this point that certain rules must be rigorously enforced to avoid some of the weaknesses of conventional problem-solving groups. The following rules permit creative idea generation without fear of censure.

1. No criticism! There is no such thing as a bad idea. Criticism contributes to a negative atmosphere that results in self-screening and inhibits the generation of ideas.

2. The more ideas the better. Be patient and push participants. Often the best ideas only emerge after the participants have been going for a time and are even slightly weary. Initially members are skimming the familiar and superficial ideas off the surface of their minds and only after these are listed do their brains really get busy and begin to think creatively.

3. The wilder, the better. Encourage free-wheeling and welcome the unconventional. Don't permit questions or discussion regarding ideas because this focuses the group's attention on a particular idea and prevents the exploration of other alternatives. Uninhibited thinking leads to unique solutions. Remember, it is easier to tame a wild idea than to energize a dull one.

4. Hitchhike on each other's ideas. Build on the thoughts of others to produce even better ideas. Everyone is to present new con-

---

Brainstorming Really Can Work

At my previous employment, I had the opportunity to attend brainstorming sessions. My first one was a three-day event, held in a remote location with approximately one-fourth of the company attending. We were seated in a large conference room at a horseshoe-shaped table. In the middle of the room, one of the vice presidents conducted the session.

Using a flip-chart and markers, he would write the heading of the topic to discuss. We were to spurt off any idea that came to mind. Each piece of paper would then be hung on the outer walls. At first, people were quite afraid of saying anything for fear of humiliation. The president and owner of the company was present, which had a way of intimidating you. However, around mid-day of the first day, people had forgotten who was there and were spilling off anything that came to mind. Many unique answers were given. Of course, no answer was considered bad, but you could always tell when the group didn't like it—there was dead silence. On the other hand, when an approving answer was given, you could hear the group members chatter, "Oh, that's pretty good."

By the end of the third day, we were all pretty burned-out with ideas and creativity. My only thoughts were how much longer would we go on with this. However, after it was over, seeing how this type of session is performed was an enlightening experience; a very unique style of group meeting for problem solving. The advantage with using this form was that it allowed for some interesting ideas to be generated. I guess brainstorming really can work.

Source: Student journal entry, Hamilton Holt School of Rollins College, Winter Park, FL, Fall 1991

cepts or variations on a theme, even if the original idea was presented by someone else.

5. Employ "plus-ing." Continually add to an idea to make it better. Ask, "What could be altered or added?" Your idea + my idea = WOW!

The second stage of brainstorming examines the list of ideas and the merits of each one's possible implementation. Other ideas may be added to the list during this stage and prior to any critical examination of the relative feasibility of solutions. It is advisable that a different group of people perform this essentially evaluative function because they would be in a better position to analyze ideas objectively and without personal biases or prejudices. Creative decision making and problem solving is necessary for the growth, development, and prosperity of any institution or organization.

Example: Akio Morita and his partners wanted a new name for their developing enterprise that could be recognized anywhere in the world and one that could be pronounced the same in any language. The brainstorming path they took led from "sonus," meaning "sound," to "sunny" and "sonny-bay." "Sonny" (pronounced "sohnnee" in Japanese) means "to lose money" and so was discarded. But take away one letter and you have "Sony," the name carried by the world's number-one brand in a host of products since the introduction of the first transistor radio in 1957.[39]

Case Discussion

The case discussion, popularized by the Harvard School of Business, consists of presenting a discussion group with a description of a situation requiring members to research, analyze, suggest potential solutions, and present final resolutions. Applicable to a wide variety of problems, this format serves principally as a learning device.

Example: A professor in the MBA program at New York University lectures on varying managerial styles. A specific situation involving a superior-subordinate interaction is then outlined. Students are asked to research the problem collaboratively and propose recommendations. Their analysis will be compared with actual solutions to similar situations and used to assess their understanding of basic concepts.

Role-Playing

Role-playing presents a problem situation, assigns appropriate roles, and asks the participants to act out in impromptu fashion the implications of the situation. Members in role-playing assume roles different from and possibly even contradictory to those normally played out in routine daily activity. Because role-playing can be more informal, flexible, and permissive, group members are more relaxed, openly communicating feelings, attitudes, and beliefs that might otherwise be masked. Today it is frequently used as a learning device in education and a training procedure in business and industry. Role-playing helps participants to better understand themselves, to see problems more clearly, and to develop empathy—that is, to gain insight into the ways other people view the world. It can be effective if the situations are clearly presented, a safe environment is created, and the participants understand the objective(s).

Example: Sarah Miles, a mid-level manager for Delta Corporation, is participating in a power-negotiation seminar recommended by her supervisor. During the course of the seminar, she is asked to assume the role of a union representative in a contract negotiation situation. While playing this role, Sarah gains an understanding of the pressures experienced by a union representative and an increased awareness of her own behavior. This non-threatening environment permitted an open disclosure of opinions, attitudes, and beliefs.

Encounter Self-Development Training

Finally, the encounter self-development training group functions in various settings. It may focus on specific training in human relations skills, or on the exploration of past experiences and the dynamics of personal development, or on creative expression. Although the focus may vary, there are certain similar external characteristics. The group, in almost every instance, is small, relatively unstructured, and chooses its own goals and personal directions. The leader's responsibility is primarily to facilitate the expression of both feelings and thoughts on the part of the group members. The dynamics of this type of group are such that it moves from confusion and discontinuity to a climate of trust and support. Group members eventually drop some of their defenses and facades, and relate more directly on a feeling basis with other members of the group. This is an intensive, personally revealing group experience that can contribute to a better understanding of oneself and one's relationships with others. Currently, a number of intensive training programs are being conducted by industries, universities, and churches and synagogues. A word of caution: encounter groups can be dangerous if the facilitators are not trained professionals.

Example: Raymond Thomas, an aspiring manager, is concerned about his lack of assertiveness when dealing with others. He decides to participate in an assertiveness-training program sponsored by the local community college to correct this perceived weakness. The seminar is conducted by a trained psychologist who places Ray and a small group of participants in a number of hypothetical situations requiring them to act assertively. These experiences are then transferred to Ray's work situation.

Group Techniques and Methods

"Technique" is defined as the systematic procedure by which a complex or scientific task is accomplished. Synonyms include "skill," "style," "routine," "plan," and "mode." Here we will explore selected interactional modes that can improve group discussion when skillfully applied. These specialized techniques include PERT, buzz groups/Phillips 66 technique, nominal group technique, Delphi procedure, and teleconferencing techniques.

PERT

Problem-solving discussions are a means of working toward a program end that can be evaluated in terms of how closely it meets desired goals. The worth and merit of the discussion process are measured against the desirability of the program. A quasi mathematical procedure called PERT offers a framework for problem solving, program planning, and implementation.[40] This procedure diminishes interpersonal conflict and encourages cooperation and the accomplishment of program goals. PERT (program evaluation and review technique) was introduced by the U.S. Navy in 1958 as a response to some of the problems arising in coordinating activities involved in the Polaris Missile program. It has subsequently been adopted by numerous other government agencies as well as private business concerns because it is well suited to large-scale program planning and management control.

The PERT procedure consists of a group working together to plot a network of the activities that necessarily precede a specific desired outcome or goal. The completed network defines and coordinates what must be done to accomplish the desired goal and reveals weaknesses in the implementation of the plan. PERT enables a planning group to identify potential bottlenecks, to appropriately allocate personnel, to estimate times for operations, to determine starting points for procedures, and to test the total logic of a plan or procedure. Based on the concept of probabilities, the logical structure of a proposed program can be tested in advance, and faulty or unfeasible steps revised or eliminated.[41] The PERT procedure, then, is based on a computer logic providing a step-by-step approach for program development involving the listing, ordering, diagramming, and statistical analysis of necessary events.

Buzz Groups/Phillips 66 Technique

A constant problem when working with large public groups is generating necessary participation. Buzz groups, or the Phillips 66 technique, are devices frequently used with success in resolving this difficulty. If a group of 20, 40, or more people, for example, is discussing a complex question, a small number of people usually dominate the group activity. But if the audience is divided into small buzz groups that discuss an aspect of the problem for a limited period of time and then report their findings to the whole assembly, involvement is increased. This procedure invites participation and allows all an opportunity to express their ideas.

The Phillips 66 method, originally developed by J. Donald Phillips, requires that the audience be divided into groups of six members and that each group discuss a specific topic for six minutes. This technique differs from buzz groups in that members both discuss a topic or problem and develop pertinent questions. The individual groups raise questions relevant to the discussion topic and the chairperson presents them to the primary discussion group, which then addresses these questions in the presence of the audience. Although buzz groups and the Phillips 66 technique can encourage involvement, they better serve to point out problems than to solve them.[42]

Nominal Group Technique

The nominal group technique, developed by Andre L. Delbecq and Andrew H. Vande Ven in 1968, has been used by organizations in health, social service, education, industry, and government. It is both a problem-solving and idea-generating technique emphasizing the private generation and ranking of solutions according to a rather rigid procedure. The group leader initially presents a statement of the problem to the assembled group and, using this statement as a basis, the group members follow the steps outlined below:

1. Members, individually, write down ideas, options, alternatives, and solutions without any open discussion.

2. Without discussion, members present their ideas to the group in a round-robin fashion and these ideas are recorded on large sheets of paper or a chalkboard for everyone to see.

3. Members may ask another person for clarification of an idea or proposal, but there should be no evaluative discussion or debate for the purpose of arriving at a sense of agreement or disagreement. At this point proposals may be combined or integrated to avoid overlap and reduce the number of possibilities.

4. Members individually rank the various proposed solutions and the results are tallied to determine the relative support for each solution.

5. Members individually vote on the higher-priority ideas until a convergence occurs.

The leadership role is critical to the success of the nominal group technique, for the leader must ensure that the behaviors vital to each step are observed–discouragement of talking, discussion of ideas, and critical observations. This technique permits a high degree of social and emotional involvement among members who might otherwise experience considerable communication anxiety. The nominal group technique has been referred to as "a group in name only."[43]

Delphi Procedure

The Delphi procedure, developed by Norman Dalkey and his associates at the Rand Corporation, was originally devised to help make long-range forecasts under conditions of uncertainties. The procedure as adapted to group problem solving provides an interesting approach because the group members do not have to meet face-to-face. The success of the Delphi process depends on the coordinator(s) and the selection of qualified participants in the problem area. Five basic steps are involved:

1. A question or problem statement is determined and sent to each of the selected participants who write down possible solutions, ideas, and suggestions that are forwarded to the group coordinators.

2. Individual ideas are collated and sent to each participant who must then combine and integrate the ideas in a way that seems to make sense and return the results to the group coordinators.

3. The proposals are further synthesized and integrated by the group coordinator(s) and then developed into a questionnaire that is sent to all participants.

4. The participants rank-order or rate the proposed solutions and return the questionnaire to the group coordinators.

5. Another questionnaire based on the averaged rankings or ratings is sent to all participants for reranking or rating, and this procedure continues until convergence occurs and a solution emerges.

The role of the group coordinators is obvious. Those who collect and distribute the information have a high degree of control over the process and its outcome. Still, the Delphi technique has its advantages: (1) it can involve a large number of participants in diverse geographical locations; (2) it prevents social conformity effects in the evaluation of proposals; (3) it circumvents the politics of cliques and subgroups; and (4) it incorporates mathematical group techniques to reach a group judgment, thus reducing the chances for errors in group decision making.[44]

Teleconferencing Techniques

It is estimated that 20 million meetings are held everyday in the U. S. and 80 percent of all meetings last less than 30 minutes.[45] This proliferation of meetings has prompted an increasing interest by business in teleconferencing techniques. Teleconferencing encompasses any form of electronically assisted communication, including: (1) audio-conferences where groups of three or more people participate simultaneously by voice alone over a telephone line; (2) videoconferences that use cable, satellite, or microwaves to transmit freeze-frame or full-motion color images of the participants; and (3) computer conferences that connect computer terminals so that participants in all locations can transmit information for immediate access or later retrieval.[46]

Teleconferencing obviously reduces travel costs and improves productivity through reduced travel time, but it also promotes faster decision making, which results in shorter and better-organized meetings than those that are held face-to-face.[47] However, is teleconferencing appropriate for problem solving? Are good, quality group decisions made via the teleconference? Research comparing decision quality under conditions of face-to-face and technologically mediated conferences indicates no substantial differences in the quality of decisions. In addition, communication styles were found not to be significantly altered by the presence of teleconferencing. The initial conclusions, then, are that supervisors and subordinates can be involved in decision making via telecommunications rather than being physically present in the same location with no changes occurring in decision quality, communication style, or participant satisfaction.[48] As one teleconferencing participant put it, "If I say something that makes the vice-president mad, at least I've got a 3,000-mile head start."[49]

Many of the guidelines for face-to-face meetings apply to teleconferencing, but there are some that are unique to electronic meetings:[50]

- ◆ Speakers should be close enough to the microphones to be easily heard.

- ◆ Participants should be careful to control noise of papers, tapping on tables, nervous coughing, clearing of the throat, and other distracting habits that the microphones will pick up. For the same reason, don't engage in side conversations with others because these will trigger the voice-activated microphones and disrupt the audio transmission.

- ◆ High-quality graphics must be prepared that fit the television format when using videoconferencing.

- ◆ Handouts should be sent early enough to be available for an audioconference.

- ◆ Dress for the camera's eye during videoconferencing and avoid strong patterns that may cause a wavy movement or light colors that bleed into a light-colored background. Neutral tones are preferable.

- ◆ Participants should be introduced at the start of the meeting and continue to identify themselves as they proceed through the teleconference.

- Departures and entrances should be announced.

- Participants, especially in videoconferencing, will have to wait until the cameras are turned to them before they participate.

- Keep a friendly expression, especially for a freeze-frame setup, because your picture will be transmitted only intermittently and you wouldn't want to be caught with a frown or in the midst of some nervous gesture. Also, try to look both at the camera and at others in your location to avoid glassy-eyed stares.

- Limit the agenda because people tire more easily during teleconferencing than they do in face-to-face meetings. The conference should be limited to no more than an hour; if longer, a break should take place.

Decision Making and Problem Solving

We previously defined small groups, identified the functions performed by groups and the reasons why individuals form groups, and explored various group types. We further examined selected techniques that may enhance group performance. And, throughout our discussion, problem solving was singled out as the most prevalent reason for group activity. It deserves even closer attention. Here we address some basic questions pertaining to effective decision making and problem solving: Just what is a problem? How can a problem best be resolved? What are some of the possible outcomes of group problem solving?

Problems and Questions for Discussion

A problem exists when there is a difference between what is currently happening and what the group or organization wants to happen; a difference between actual and desired conditions. Any charge, goal, or mission, whether externally imposed on the group or internally derived, can be viewed as a problem to be solved.

Problem-solving discussions usually begin with a question that expresses the problem. The question should be carefully formulated and frequently reexamined. The following criteria can be useful in formulating the problem-solving question:

- The problem should be stated as a question. Problem-solving involves answer seeking, so when presented in the form of a question discussion rather than debate can take place.

- The question should focus on the real problem. All too often discussion questions focus attention on some symptom of a problem; but good problem solving demands questions that focus attention on the causes of the problem. For example, if John, a usually productive employee, is constantly showing up late for work, a group of immediate supervisors might consider discussing the question of "should we fire John?" A better question, getting at the possible causes of the problem, would be "what can be done to motivate John to be prompt and responsible?" The former question limits discussion to a single solution resulting from the group's reacting to symptoms. The latter question permits the group to examine causes and alternative solutions.

◆ The scope of the question should be limited. It should specify whose behavior is subject to change. The question should focus attention on the problem and specify the group(s) whose behavior is to be directly affected by the solution. For example, the marketing department may work with production if the question is mutually contiguous, if both groups are directly affected by the solution. This has given rise to teambuilding and many of the common types of work groups previously described.

◆ The question should be stated impartially, not suggesting potential solutions. If the question is presented so that agreement or disagreement is asked for, the problem solving process is short-circuited. Such questions as "should the federal government require private industry to be more responsible to consumer interests?" or "should the federal government require that the closed-shop concept be abolished?" assume the dimensions of a national debate resolution and encourage conflict and polarization. The discussants enter the situation with a view toward accepting or rejecting a particular solution rather than creating a solution to the problem. Better questions for the purposes of problem solving would be "what can private industry do to be more responsive to consumer interest groups?" or "how can the problem of union membership versus no union membership be resolved?" These are open questions. Unfortunately, many questions that purport to stimulate problem solving are phrased so that they include solutions.

◆ The question should encompass both the problem and a solution. The question should call for more than a listing, and require a complete analysis and a solution to the problem. A problem-solving group should deal with the entirety of the problem.

Determining the question for discussion is a most critical process because of its influence on the nature of the goal(s) and consequently the quality of the solution(s). If the question is ambiguous, lacking definition, discussants will likewise be uncertain of their goal(s) and this uncertainty will be reflected in the end solution(s).

Standard Discussion Procedure

It is to be expected that people who get together as a group for the first time flounder for a while, trying to figure out how best to get the job done. Even established groups assigned new tasks may spend the first couple of meetings interpreting their task and deciding how to proceed. This was noted earlier when we identified the various stages groups inevitably go through. So, after the question for discussion has been appropriately phrased, the next step in small-group problem solving is determining a satisfactory and desirable problem-solving procedure. Procedures have been developed and perfected through use in literally thousands of groups in community, governmental, business, industrial, and educational settings. These procedures include agendas that can be intentionally and rationally used to systematically consider ideas as well as to encourage the maximum involvement of all group members.

The reflective thinking procedure, based on John Dewey's analysis of how people think and how they solve problems, is the most popular pattern for problem-solving discussion and one which is the basis for most alternative problem-solving procedures. In *How We Think* published in 1910, Dewey coined the term "reflective thinking" which he defined as "active, persistent, and careful consideration of any belief or supposed form of knowledge in the light of the grounds that support it, and further conclusions to which it tends."[51] Continuing to equate problem solving with reflective thinking, Dewey identifies five distinct steps: (1) a felt difficulty, (2) its location and definition, (3) suggestion of possible solutions, (4) rational development of the suggestions, and (5) further observation and experimentation leading to acceptance or rejection of a solution. The influence of Dewey's work is evidenced in the development by scholars in the field of the *standard discussion procedure*, which helps groups work through problems using the reflective thinking approach. Comprising the following steps, it outlines the course of productive group discussion:

1. *Problem*—statement of the question for discussion, clarification and definition of terms, possible delimiting of the question's scope.

2. *Analysis of the problem*—examination of the history and status quo relating to the problem. What is the background of the problem? Where are we today. Who's involved? Why? To what extent?

3. *Criteria*—establishment of general guidelines for any possible solution. To what ideals, values, principles, requirements must any solution we choose adhere or square?

4. *Possible solutions and evaluation*—solicit and list proposals, and evaluate each. What are the advantages of each proposed solu-

tion? What are the limitations or disadvantages of each proposal?

5. *Choosing the best solution*—through group consensus or majority vote, select a solution consistent with the criteria listed and decisions previously reached.

6. *Implementation*—operationalize the selected solution and evaluate its effectiveness.

The standard discussion procedure is particularly useful for ensuring that all people are operating from a common set of definitions and assumptions, have agreed on the nature and extent of the problem, and have established evaluative criteria to use in assessing solutions.

Rational Management Procedure

The rational management procedure, developed by C. H. Kepner and B. B. Tregoe, is one of several adaptations of the standard discussion procedure based on the Dewey model that is specifically designed for technical problems in business and industry.[52] Kepner and Tregoe define a problem as a deviation from a standard and identify the nature and extent of the problem by an elaborate set of step-by-step comparisons. The first comparison made is the "should" to the "actual"—that is, the ideal situation to actual conditions. Next, they compare the "musts" with the "wants" to determine those criteria that are required of an effective solution. The boundaries of the problem are located and a final solution arrived at by repeatedly measuring potential solutions against required criteria as well as against desirable criteria. This alternative procedure is particularly useful in arriving at an objective solution because the criteria are weighted by member ratings, thus giving any proposal a quantitative dimension. Often one solution emerges as clearly superior but, if not, the group can select from among equally rated solutions.

If problem solving is to be a rational process, rational procedures must be employed. The standard discussion and rational management procedures can serve as guides or process models to be followed to improve decision making and problem solving. Certainly, the more specific the wording of the question, and the more specific the goal or objective, the easier it is to select a suitable problem-solving mode.

Possible Outcomes of Group Problem Solving

Consensus is one of the most desirable outcomes of interaction in small groups. Consensus refers to a coming together of the minds of those in the group after a period of time, or it denotes general agreement or at least a "willingness to give it a try" among all members of a group concerning a given decision. If consensus can be genuinely achieved, it is valuable because member satisfaction and commitment to action are

The Standard Agenda Can Yield Results

By Sherry L. Knight

As the litigation legal assistant supervisor, I have many diversified duties. I am responsible for the operation of several different litigation procedures, as well as supervising the three paralegals in my department. One of my duties includes making sure that our docket and case list procedures are working and that the procedures are being followed by everyone in the litigation department. The individuals, two litigation paralegals and the librarian, who are responsible for the day-to-day activity of the case list and docket, came to me complaining of problems with these procedures. They indicated that there was a great potential for information to fall through the cracks because of the poor communication between these individuals and others in the litigation department. It is very important that all cases being worked in litigation are included on the case list, for one reason so that when pleadings or other documents with deadlines come in, the docketing person will know who is assigned to the case and who should receive reminders about the deadline.

We four worked as a group and discussed the various problems with the two systems and how those problems could be resolved. We came to a consensus and developed new forms to be implemented into the system. These forms would help the secretaries, and would make the two procedures operate more efficiently, more accurately and with less time than is presently being consumed.

We prepared our agenda to discuss the new procedures to be implemented; and developed and prepared the forms to be explained and distributed at the next meeting. I set the meeting well in advance, at a time recommended by the personnel director, and I provided doughnuts and coffee.

All but one secretary, who was on vacation, attended the meeting and all of the litigation paralegals were there. We began with my expanding the purpose for the meeting and giving some information about the new changes. I then turned the meeting over to the individuals who work with the two systems to explain the particular problems they are experiencing with communication breakdown among the departments. Initially, the secretaries did not visually appear to be very interested in our problems or proposed solutions but as they became more actively involved in the discussion, their interest increased. I personally tried to emphasize to the group that this had to be a team effort. I tried to help them identify with the problem and realize that they are an integral part of these particular organizational processes.

The secretaries asked questions and received clarification on the new procedures. They also voiced their opinions and made their own suggestions as to how these two departments could operate more efficiently and these suggestions and opinions were addressed and discussed at our meeting. After the meeting, we all felt that the communication in the meeting was excellent. There was a very positive climate and we all worked together and agreed to implement the new procedures. We also agreed to all work towards making these new procedures as well as the existing procedure run more smoothly.

It was very interesting to watch my group and the participants at the meeting work through the group problem-solving process. Whether intentional or unintentional, our group followed the Standard Discussion agenda based on Dewey's reflective thinking procedure. It worked!

Sherry L. Knight is a legal assistant supervisor for an Orlando, Florida, law firm.

likely to be stronger than when sharp differences remain. This is important because often the people who help make a decision are those who are also expected to carry it out.

Consensus is not always possible to achieve. The majority vote, where the solution with the greatest support is adopted, represents a frequently used alternative method of decision making. Rupert Cortwright and George Hinds observe that "the ideal outcome of discussion, theoretically, may be consensus, the common high ground of unanimous agreement. This, however, is never to be sought at the price of the slightest coercion of even one member. When discussion does not lead to unanimity within the time limits which are practical, the democratic process calls for decision or action by majority rule. Discussion ought not to become an instrument of endless delay foisted on a majority by a willful minority."[53] Consensus is preferred, but the majority vote is often necessary. It gives members an opportunity to voice their disagreement and allows the group to proceed.

Certainly, the least-desirable methods of arriving at a decision are those involving manipulation. Selected members within a group may form a coalition of interest in order to overpower other members. Although coalitions may be quite successful, they can have disastrous effects on group morale. Also, groups may be railroaded when one or a few influential group members force their will on the entire group. This, of course, is most likely to produce resentment and resistance.

Lastly, there may be no real outcome. Sometimes a group becomes hopelessly and bitterly split; the members see no way to resolve differences and produce a decision that comes close to representing a reasonable majority point of view. The group may have to abandon the project or resort to using outside third parties in mediation and/or arbitration.

Mediation is a method of resolving disputes and conflicts. It requires the participation of a mediator who tries to promote agreement. The mediator has no authority to impose a settlement on the parties, nor can the parties be forced to enter into mediation or to reach an agreement. Mediation will be successful if the mediator can help the disputants to compromise and reach agreement on their own. Compromise is at the heart of a successfully mediated dispute and the end result of a mediation session is that there are neither winners nor losers but rather, it is hoped, generally satisfied individuals.[54]

Arbitration is used when participants mutually agree that a neutral third person is needed to solve their conflict. Arbitration has some distinct features that make it useful as a form of third-party intervention. First, both parties enter into arbitration voluntarily, with neither party forcing the other into the process, and neither party feeling coerced into a settlement situation. Second, it keeps one party from using passive-aggressive or impasse tactics on the other—sooner or later the issue will be resolved for the arbitrator will ultimately make a binding judgment. Third, in many cases the arbitrator has special training in the content area of the dispute, such as contract arbitration. When the arbitrator has such special expertise, he or she can offer creative solutions. Fourth, arbitration is readily available for use in situations in which the participants experience a communication breakdown and are no longer able to solve their own problems. Finally, arbitration is a process that can be used for a wide variety of content areas, ranging from contract disputes to conflicts in domestic relations.[55]

The output in discussion is less inclusive, more refined, and more focused than the input. Martin Andersen has developed an elaborate model of group discussion that assumes a systems perspective and identifies six output characteristics[56]:

1. The purpose of every discussion is twofold: (a) to ensure group goal achievement and (b) to provide some member satisfaction.

2. Under conditions of maximum productivity, the component of content should be characterized by a cognitive-affective balance.

3. The output characteristics of the thought pattern are that the decisions and understandings reached should be based on the highest level of logic and evidence and optimum suasion— sound reasoning, well-supported facts and opinions, a proper inquiry-advocacy relationship, and sufficient motivating relevancy to ensure that decisions made will be supported.

4. Two qualities should characterize the group under conditions of maximum productivity, analytical maturity, and socio-emotional balance.

5. When a discussion group is functioning at its peak, there should be optimum opportunity for leadership development.

6. Finally, at its best the communication component should be characterized by clarity and acceptability.

This model focuses on fundamental constructs and can serve as an operational guide for practice and prediction in effective discussion.

Conference Techniques and Meeting Dynamics

The term "conference" is used most frequently to designate two types of activities. One type of conference is typical of a committee meeting; the group is usually small and the discussion is a closed group with members tackling a mutual problem. A second meaning of the word designates a large, more public meeting that may also be referred to as a convention or seminar. Conferences are types of formal discussions. Almost all conferences use discussion methods and evidence the group processes previously described. Our concern will primarily be with outlining ways in which conferences and meetings can be made more effective.

Survey after survey have indicated two prevalent attitudes or preconceptions on the part of managers about conferences. First, there are too many meetings. Second, too much time is wasted during the course of these sessions. These negative attitudes prevail despite the fact that conferences and meetings are essential to effective communication and information management within an organization. Why, then, are meetings so often considered boring, unproductive, and almost always too long? Some reasons offered are:

- No specific, clear-cut objective for the meeting, its leaders, or its participants
- No meeting agenda
- Too many or the wrong choice of participants
- No consideration for allies or antagonists
- Failure to prepare properly
- Inability to present ideas concisely
- Lack of sound leadership and control
- Improper use of visual aids
- Too many digressions and interruptions
- Time wasted on "why" rather than "how"
- Mixed final decisions[57]

However, meetings don't have to be long and unproductive. Careful planning and following of basic guidelines represent another, more dynamic way.

Initially, one's planning must address the question of group problem solving versus individual decision making. Is a conference or meeting the best and most desirable way to achieve your objective? It should be quite obvious that under certain conditions groups may not prove particularly useful. The following are important aspects to consider in deciding whether to use a group to solve a particular problem or to act singly. Depending on the particular circumstances, some aspects will be more important than others and so may require group activity. A "yes" response to several of the following questions indicates that an individual would probably have difficulty solving the problem alone and a group should be used:

1. Are many steps required to solve the problem?
2. Are there many parts to the problem?
3. Will the solution be difficult to verify?
4. Are the individuals involved likely to perceive the problem as an impersonal one?

5. Will the problem be of moderate difficulty for the individuals who constitute the group?

6. Is a great deal of information required to solve the problem? Would a single individual be unlikely to possess it?

7. Does the problem demand a division of labor?

8. Are many solutions desired?

9. Are many hours required for the problem's solution?

10. Will individuals have to assume a great deal of responsibility for the solution?

11. Are the proposed solutions likely to be diverse?

12. Are the attitudes concerning the problem likely to be diverse?

13. Does the problem immediately affect a number of people; will the solution immediately affect a number of people?

14. Is it unlikely that group members will engage in non-task-oriented behavior?

15. Does the problem lend itself to group methods? Are potential group members familiar with group activity?

If group problem solving is selected, careful planning must precede the conference or meeting.

When should meetings be called? When shouldn't they be called? Despite the time they take away from other work and the poor way in which they are often handled, business meetings are almost always unavoidable. There is no way to conduct business without occasionally participating in or leading meetings. Meetings may center on coordinating activities among departments or among the members of a department. The discussion might focus on how well everyone in a department or in a company is doing in meeting organizational goals. Different companies have different needs for charting their progress and coordinating efforts, so these meetings may occur quarterly, monthly, weekly, or daily. Business people also have meetings whenever changes arise, such as market changes, internal company changes, or external changes in suppliers. The best way to find out how to handle these changes is to have all people affected by the changes meet to discuss them. Such meetings may include clients and suppliers who could benefit from the information shared.

Before you call or attend any meetings, make sure you know the objective of that meeting. To find your objective, ask yourself

◆ Why am I holding the meeting?

◆ Why am I going to participate in the meeting?

- ◆ What do I want to achieve at the meeting?
- ◆ What do I want to achieve after the meeting is over?

A meeting without a specific objective is certain to achieve nothing specific. And that's a waste of time.

Once you have determined the value of having a meeting, look again at any alternatives. Perhaps you can achieve your objective by phone calls to some of the potential participants. Maybe you can ask for a written response to a memo you will send or use e-mail and then handle the problem yourself. Ask yourself the following questions to determine if you should hold a meeting:

- ◆ Is a meeting the *only* means of fulfilling my objective?
- ◆ If not, what are the alternatives?
- ◆ How effective are the alternatives?
- ◆ Is a meeting the *best* means of fulfilling my objective?
- ◆ Will a meeting use my time and my colleagues' time to the best advantage?

Once the value of the best alternative is assessed, you can decide which of the two, the meeting or the alternative, is better. You can then act accordingly.

When meetings prove necessary, what's the proper way to call a meeting? How should agenda be prepared? Use a memo or agenda as both a blueprint and a plan of action for every meeting. A written memo or agenda is the best means of giving and securing information and, if properly put together, will focus everyone on the objective and the means to achieve it. During the meeting it can also be used as a guide and reference, and after the meeting it can serve as a reminder of what was to be accomplished and a means of checking on follow-up actions. Time spent preparing a memo or agenda will be saved during the meeting.

A good memo or agenda should state the objective of the meeting, the issues to be discussed, the time the meeting will begin and end, the place, the participants involved, and what is expected of them in the way of preparation before the meeting. Certainly, asking yourself the right questions will help you find, formulate, and focus your ideas as well as assist the participants in their preparation for the meeting. Questions can stimulate thinking and motivate others into coming up with new and imaginative ideas. Above all, however, keep the memo or agenda to no more than one page with any supporting materials, charts, or graphs stapled or paper clipped to it. Careful preparation is the best way to keep any meeting on target and on time.

Milo O. Frank notes that "unfocused exploratory meetings are like trying to find your way out of a labyrinth in the dark."[58] Members planning a conference would be wise to use the following checklist as a guide. The conference or meeting can then serve as an effective channel of communication and information management

1. What is the purpose of the meeting?

2. What outcomes are to emerge from the meeting? When should these goals be reached?

3. What type of format will best achieve the meeting's purpose?

4. Who will participate? Have you left out someone who should be invited? Have you included someone who need not be involved?

5. Who will serve as leader, chairperson, moderator, or facilitator?

6. What is the best place to hold the meeting? What is a good time? How long should the meeting last?

7. How and when will the participants be briefed on the meeting and given directions for preparing to take part?

8. Who will prepare the agenda? Will it be circulated in advance?

9. What physical details need to be taken care of? Seating arrangements? Sound system? Ventilation and heating? Audiovisual aids and equipment? Other?

10. How will the proceedings and results be recorded?

11. How will the conference or meeting be evaluated?

12. What will be done to follow up?

Certainly, planning and attention to detail contribute to constructive meetings. However, they do not guarantee meeting success. What, then, is the difference between stimulating discussions and a productive meeting? Results! The following guidelines for effective group participation can be helpful in accomplishing results.

1. *Come to the meeting with questions.* If the meeting has been well planned, you will know the topic(s) of discussion in advance. Do some preliminary thinking, read, ask questions, and make notes of the points you want to raise during the discussion.

2. *Speak your mind freely.* Everyone's ideas are important. Your opinions and remarks are the substance of effective group activity; they can provide directions or energize others.

3. *Listen thoughtfully to others.* The hardest part of discussion is to concentrate on what is being said and not on what you plan to say as soon as you get a chance. Let yourself be stimulated by the thinking of others. Be an involved, critically active listener.

4. *Address your remarks to everyone.* Don't just talk to the discussion leader or chair, or any single individual. Address the whole group, even when replying to a specific remark by another par-

ticipant. This helps curb arguments or two-way conversations. It further serves to energize the involvement of the entire group.

5. *Don't monopolize the discussion.* The goal is group productivity, so make frequent but brief remarks—a minute or two is long enough to speak at any one time. If you like to talk, you'll have to watch yourself very closely because time seems to goes by twice as fast when you are talking.

6. *Assume diverse, positive role activities.* Involve yourself in a variety of communication roles—task and social maintenance roles. Don't allow self-centered or ego-enhancing behaviors to intrude and disrupt group activities. This may require that you refrain from describing at length interesting but unrelated personal experiences. Before you tell a story or joke, satisfy yourself that it will contribute to participation.

7. *Help the discussion leader.* Always be alert for the need to summarize or clarify the points under discussion. Help keep the discussion on track by being certain that everyone understands what's going on.

8. *Appreciate diversity.* Be sensitive to the individual personal characteristics, attitudes, and values of others. Our increased contact with other cultures makes it imperative for you to make a concerted effort to get along with and to try to understand people whose beliefs and backgrounds may be vastly different from your own. Remember, if you try to understand diversity, appreciation follows.

9. *Be friendly when you disagree* Conflict can be productive and friendly disagreement is a good way to stimulate sound thinking when agreement has been too hasty. Study ways to be tactful and then *be* tactful. Remember, there are at least three sides to most questions—yours, mine, and the right one.

10. *Be friendly when others disagree with you.* Be flexible and open to constructive criticism. The test of intelligence is how quickly you see what is right, not how often you are right to begin with. Critical thinking needs to be encouraged.

11. *Don't let silence embarrass you.* Silence often occurs and provides time to collect your thoughts. Patience is necessary if productive results are desired.

12. *Build group pride.* Be supportive of others and celebrate in the decisions made and progress achieved. Praise collaborative efforts and team membership.

13. *Welcome criticism of your discussion technique.* Discussion groups can often enhance their performance by using part of

their time for self-analysis. Assessing group effectiveness can contribute to future productivity.

14. *Reach decisions.* Act, try to reach agreement or a common understanding on the problems and topics of discussion. When meetings are successful, understanding, agreement, compromise, and concession will take place. Be willing to take responsibility for group outcomes.

15. *Follow through after the meeting.* Be clear on your own responsibility for future action(s).

Even if participants follow the above guidelines, meetings can run astray if not properly managed. How can participation at meetings be managed effectively? The four elements that will make a meeting successful are: time constraints, preparation, proper presentation, and control. Set time limits in advance and stick to them. This may include limiting the length of time that a speaker has the floor—ten minutes, five minutes, two minutes—whatever length of time seems appropriate to the length of the meeting and the number of attendees. Additionally, consider limiting to two the number of times a speaker may speak on any given question or issue. (This does not mean twice in the meeting, but on a specific point of discussion.) Finally, once a question or issue has been discussed, ask for a motion and vote—take action.

If the leader points the way, participants will follow. This means being prepared for the meeting and providing the needed direction. It is the leader's responsibility to maintain a focus and keep the meeting on track.

Each participant is expected to present his or her viewpoint in a clear, concise, and interesting manner within the prescribed length of time. A most-important consideration here is to discuss only one question or issue at a time. If a question or issue requires extended discussion, consider creating a subcommittee of interested participants; this can maintain the momentum of the meeting and prevent it from becoming interminable.

The leader or director controls the meeting and each person's participation. Priorities should be set and a firm but polite attitude should prevail. This may mean interrupting when you want to take the floor and gain control. Judiciously interrupting is a meeting tool to achieve a purpose—to cut off a digression and save time. The leader or director should also end a meeting when the objective has been accomplished. Know when to say, "Thank you for attending this meeting."

It is vital to determine the value of any meeting. At every meeting's end, restate the objective and summarize the results. Also restate any assignments that have been made and the follow-up actions required. To evaluate further, ask each participant to submit in writing brief answers to the following questions:

The Kennedy Space Center Thumb Twiddler

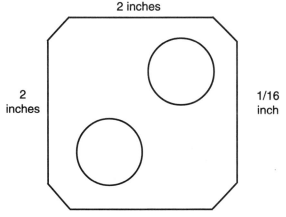

2 inches

2 inches

1/16 inch

Bill Brett runs a major operation at the Kennedy Space Center and has developed a high-tech device to focus, tighten, and shorten meetings. It is a thin, flat plywood square with two holes in it—"The Kennedy Space Center Thumb Twiddler." When meetings wander off track, and lose sight of their objectives, a participant places his or her right thumb in one hole and left thumb in the other hole from the opposite side, intertwines the fingers, and rotates the twiddler. Those watching get the point and soon the meeting is back on track.

If you're curious to try it out, it takes only a minute or two to manufacture this ingenious high-tech object out of a piece of cardboard or even a narrow strip of plywood. It will save many minutes when you determine its use the next time one of your meetings begins to wander. It works. It may not get you into space, but it will keep your meetings on track.

Source: Milo O. Frank, *How to Run a Successful Meeting in Half the Time* (New York: Pocket Books, 1989): 156–157. Copyright © 1989 by Milo O. Frank. Reprinted by permission of Simon & Schuster, Inc.

◆ Did we achieve the meeting's objective as stated in the agenda? If not, why not?

◆ What three positive things can we do to improve the next meeting?

◆ What are the two most important things the leader can do to improve the meeting?

◆ What are the two most important things the participants can do to improve the meeting?

◆ Could we have done without this meeting? If so, how?

The answers to these questions can provide an assessment of meeting effectiveness and promote the increased involvement and responsibility of all participants. The net result will be better and briefer meetings.

Meetings are a fact of organizational life. Whether it's a gathering of ten people or a conference with hundreds in attendance, no meeting has to be boring, time-wasting, or unproductive.

Summary

Group activity is a way of life, with each of us simultaneously a member of many kinds of groups. And people in organizations spend a good part of their time as members of various small groups—social, informational, educational, and problem-solving or task groups.

Numerous factors influence the outcome of small-group efforts. Small-group communication can be viewed as a subsystem operating within an organization to achieve organizational goals. There are inputs, outputs, and feedback.

A small group is a collection of individuals in face-to-face relation that makes them interdependent to some degree. A group is not just any collection or aggregate of people, but rather a collection of individuals who develop a certain dynamic over a period of time. Group dynamics encompasses group types, functions, norms, roles, and networks.

The groups we operate in may be formal or informal in nature. They develop norms that outline and direct member behavior. Normative group development melds individual members into a cohesive unit that often proves productive, but may produce a risky or groupthink outcome. A variety of role behaviors are played out within any group. Members may assume task, group maintenance, or self-serving behaviors. Although role flexibility is desirable, most people interpret the role of group member rather narrowly, performing only a few of the behaviors described. These are, it is hoped, constructive rather than destructive behaviors. Finally, group networks also influence the end product of group activity. Highly centralized networks (wheel, chain, Y) make the fewest errors and take less time; decentralized networks (circle, all-channel) better handle complex tasks, generate more messages, and produce a higher sense of morale or member commitment.

Functionally, groups are essentially task-oriented while at the same time addressing socio-emotional purposes. In addition to being goal centered, group activity satisfies personal needs. Among the different types of groups are panel, roundtable, colloquy, symposium, brainstorming, case discussion, role-playing, and encounter self-development training sessions. A variety of techniques can be employed to promote the effective functioning of groups, including PERT, the buzz Group/Phillips 66 technique, the nominal group technique, the Delphi procedure, and teleconferencing techniques.

Problem solving is the most prevalent of group activities. A problem exists when there is a difference between what is currently happening and what the group wants to happen. Although a number of solution procedures may be used, John Dewey's reflective thinking process generally serves as a basic foundation for most problem solving.

The problem is defined, clarified, analyzed, placed in relation to a standard set of criteria with solutions being advanced and discussed, and finally a best solution is adopted and implemented. The optimum outcome of the problem-solving process will be group consensus—general agreement among all members of a group concerning a given decision—but in its absence, other alternatives for arriving at a decision range from majority rule to withdrawal and disbanding in response to unreasonable conflicts.

Group activity is most closely associated with conferences and meetings—facts of everyday business life. Many of us perceive them as a useless waste of time, but they can be dynamic and stimulating interchanges that yield productive results.

Throughout this chapter, emphasis has been given to the significance of small-group activity—a position supported by Dorwin Cartwright and Alvin Zander who wrote in 1968:

> A democratic society derives its strength from the effective functioning of the multitude of groups which it contains. Its most valuable resources are the groups of people found in its homes, communities, churches, business concerns, union halls, and various branches of government. Now, more than ever before, it is recognized that these units must perform their functions well if the larger system is to work.[59]

Questions for Discussion and Skill Development

1. Why are groups necessary and valuable in society? How do groups function in the organizational setting? What kinds of groups do you belong to?

2. Your boss is trying to decide if it would be worthwhile to set up an interdepartmental small group to discuss employee grievances. What would be the advantages and disadvantages to using such a group? Also, make suggestions that would help in planning a meeting of the group.

3. What types of groups have you participated in? Panel? Roundtable? Colloquy? Symposium? Brainstorming? Case discussion? Role-playing? Encounter self-development training? Was the outcome satisfying and rewarding? Why or why not?

4. Think of the last group meeting you attended. What norms or rules can you identify? Did most members observe them? How did the group handle deviants? What role(s) did you play? Did anyone display self-serving behaviors? How were most decisions made? How was conflict resolved? Were most members satisfied with the outcome(s)?

5. What do you consider to be the major problems inhibiting productive conferences or meetings? How can conferences and meetings be made more productive?

Notes

1. Rollie Tillman, Jr., "Problems in Review: Committees on Trial," *Harvard Business Review* 21 (May–June 1960): 6–12.

2. M. Kriesberg, "Executives Evaluate Administrative Conferences," *Advanced Management* 15 (1950): 15–17; and E. Lawler and S. Mohrman, "Quality Circles After the Fad," *Harvard Business Review* (January-February 1985): 65–71.

3. Michael Doyle and David Straus, *How to Make Meetings Work* (New York: Wyden Books, 1976).

4. Norman Maier, *Problem-Solving Discussions and Conferences* (New York: McGraw-Hill, 1963): v.

5. E. K. Clemons and F. W. McFarlan, "Telecom: Hook Up or Lose Out," *Harvard Business Review* 64 (1986): 91.

6. Ernest Bormann, *Discussion and Group Methods.* (New York: Harper and Row, 1969): 3–4.

7. Stewart L. Tubbs and Sylvia Moss, *Human Communication,* 2nd ed. (New York: Random House, 1987): 251–252.

8. H. Lloyd Goodall, Jr., *Small Group Communication in Organizations* (Dubuque, IA: Wm. C. Brown, 1985); R. Y. Hirokawa, "Discussion Procedures and Decision-Making Performance," *Human Communication Research* 12 (1985): 203–224; and R. W. Napier and M. K. Gershenfeld, *Groups: Theory and Experience* (Boston: Houghton Mifflin, 1989).

9. R. Y. Hirokawa, "Group Communication and Decision-Making Performance," *Human Communication Research* 14 (1988): 487–515; Patrick Laughlin and Richard McGlynn, "Collective Induction: Mutual Group and Individual Influence by Exchange of Hypotheses and Evidence," *Journal of Experimental Social Psychology* 22 (1986): 567–589; and D. G. Leather, "Quality of Group Communication as a Determinant of Group Product," *Speech Monographs* 39 (1972): 166–173.

10. John K. Brilhart, *Effective Group Discussion,* 2nd ed. (Debuque, IA: Wm. C. Brown, 1974): 17.

11. Marvin Shaw, *Group Dynamics: The Psychology of Small Group Behavior,* 3rd ed. (New York: McGraw-Hill, 1981): 11.

12. B. Aubrey Fisher and Leonard C. Hawes, "An Interact System Model: Generating a Grounded Theory of Small Groups," *Quarterly Journal of Speech* 57 (1971): 445.

13. B. Aubrey Fisher, "Decision Emergence: Phrases in Group Decision Making," *Speech Monographs* 37 (1970): 53–66; and B. Aubrey Fisher, "The Process of Decision Modification in Small Discussion Groups," *Journal of Communication* 20 (1970): 51–64.

14. Bruce W. Tuckman and Mary Ann Jensen, "Stages of Small-Group Development Revisited," *Group and Organization Studies* 2 (1977): 419–427.

15. Kenneth Cessna, "Phases in Group Development: The Negative Evidence," *Small Group Behavior* 15 (1984): 3–32; Marshall Scott Poole, "Decision Development in Small Groups I: A Comparison of Two Models," *Communication Monographs* 48 (1981): 1–20; Marshall Scott Poole, "Decision Development in Small Groups II: A Study of Multiple Sequences in Decision Making," *Communication Monographs*

50 (1983): 206–226; and Marshall Scott Poole, "Decision Development in Small Groups III: A Multiple Sequence Model of Group Decision Development," *Communication Monographs* 50 (1983): 321–341.

16. Edgar Schein, *Process Consultation* (Reading, MA: Addison-Wesley, 1969): 41.

17. Muzofer Sherif, *An Outline of Social Psychology* (New York: Harper and Brothers, 1948): 59.

18. John Wenburg and William Wilmot, *The Personal Communication Process* (New York: John Wiley & Sons, 1973): 256.

19. Irving Janis, *Victims of Groupthink* (Boston: Houghton Mifflin, 1972): 9.

20. Donald Harvey and Donald Brown, *An Experimental Approach to Organization Development* (Englewood Cliffs, NJ: Prentice Hall, 1988): 256.

21. Irving Janis, *Groupthink*, 2nd ed. (New York: Houghton Mifflin, 1982). Copyright © 1982 by Houghton Mifflin Company. Used with permission.

22. Kenneth Benne and Paul Sheats, "Functional Roles of Group Members," *Journal of Social Issues* 4 (1948): 41–49.

23. James H. McBurney and Kenneth G. Hance, *Discussion in Human Affairs* (New York: Harper and Row, 1950).

24. William M. Sattler and Ed N. Miller, *Discussion and Conference* (New York: Prentice Hall, 1954).

25. Everett M. Rogers and Redkha Agarwala-Rogers, *Communication in Organizations* (New York: The Free Press, 1976); and Raymond Ross, *Small Groups in Organizational Settings* (Englewood Cliffs, NJ: Prentice Hall, 1989).

26. Norman Gilroy and Jim Swan, *Building Networks: Cooperation as a Strategy for Success in a Changing World* (Dubuque, IA: Kendall/Hunt, 1983).

27. Gerald M. Goldhaber, *Organizational Communication*, 4th ed. (Dubuque, IA: Wm. C. Brown, 1986): 281.

28. C. Hendrick, *Group Processes and Intergroup Relations* (Newbury Park, CA: Sage, 1987).

29. John Cragan and David Wright, *Communication in Small Group Discussions* (St. Paul, MN: West Publishing, 1986).

30. Carl Larson and Frank LaFasto, *Teamwork: What Must Go Right/What Can Go Wrong* (Newbury Park, CA: Sage, 1989).

31. Berkeley Rise, "Square Holes for Quality Circles," *Psychology Today* (February 1984): 17–18.

32. Arnold Kanarick, "The Far Side of Quality Circle," *Management Review* 70 (1981): 16–17; and Hobart Rowan, "The Japanese Advantage," *Washington Post*, October 7, 1981, G2.

33. Roy Berko, Andrew Wolvin, and Ray Curtis, *This Business of Communicating* (Dubuque, IA: Wm. C. Brown, 1986).

34. Bob Rush, "Making Use of Management Committees," *American Agent and Broker* (March 1991): 24–28.

35. Jane Farley Templeton, *Focus Groups* (Chicago, IL: Probus Publishing, 1987).

36. Pamela Shockley-Zalabak, *Fundamentals of Organizational Communication*, 2nd ed. (New York: Longman Publishing, 1991).

37. Stephen Stumpf and Thomas Mullen, *Taking Charge* (Englewood Cliffs, NJ: Prentice Hall, 1992).

38. John K. Brilhart and Gloria Galanes, *Effective Group Discussion*, 6th ed. (Dubuque, IA: Wm. C. Brown, 1989); Bobby R. Patton, Kim Griffen, and Eleanor Patton, *Decision-Making Group Interaction*, 3rd ed. (New York: Harper and Row, 1989);

and Beatrice Schultz, *Communicating in the Small Group: Theory and Practice* (New York: Harper and Row, 1989).

39. Akio Morita, *Made in Japan: Akio Morita and Sony* (New York: E. P. Dutton, 1986).

40. Gerald M. Phillips, "PERT as a Logical Adjunct to the Discussion Process," *Journal of Communication* 15 (June 1965): 89–99.

41. Harry F. Evarts, *Introduction to PERT* (Boston: Allyn and Bacon, 1964); and K. R. MacCremmon and C. A. Ryavec, *An Analytical Study of PERT Assumptions* (Santa Monica, CA: Rand Corporation, 1962).

42. Ronald L. Applbaum, Edward M. Bodaken, Kenneth K. Sereno, and Karl W. E. Anatol, *The Process of Group Communication,* 2nd ed. (Chicago: Science Research Associates, 1979).

43. Andre L. Delbecq, Andrew H. Vande Ven, and David H. Gustafson, *Group Techniques for Program Planning* (Glenview, IL: Scott Foresman, 1975); and Andrew H. Vande Ven and Andre L. Delbecq, "The Effectiveness of Nominal, Delphi, and Interacting Group Decision Making Processes," *Academy of Management Journal* 17 (1974): 605–621.

44. Gerald Wilson, H. Lloyd Goodal, and Christopher Waagen, *Organizational Communication* (New York: Harper and Row, 1986); and J. T. Wood, G. M. Phillips, and D. J. Pedersen, *Group Discussion: A Practical Guide to Participation and Leadership,* 2nd ed. (New York: Harper and Row, 1986).

45. Kathleen Wagoner and Mary Ruprecht, *Office Automation: A Management Approach* (New York: John Wiley & Sons, 1984).

46. J. Fulk and C. Steinfield, *Organizations and Communication Technology* (Newbury Park, CA: Sage, 1990).

47. Eleanor Tedesco and Robert Mitchell, *Administrative Office Management—The Electronic Office* (New York: John Wiley & Sons, 1984).

48. L. E. Albertson, *The Effectiveness of Communication Across Media* (Melbourne, Australia: Australia Research Laboratories, 1991); A. Chapanis, R. N. Parrish, R. B. Oshman, and G. D. Weeks, "Studies in Interactive Communication II: The Effects of Four Communication Modes on the Linguistic Performance of Teams During Cooperative Problem Solving," *Human Factors* 19 (1977): 101–126; R. S. Hiltz, K. Johnson, and M. Turoff, "Experiments in Group Decision Making," *Human Communication Research* 13 (1986): 225–252; M. Moss, *Telecommunications and Productivity* (Reading, MA: Addison-Wesley, 1981); and Larry R. Smeltzer, "Supervisory-Subordinate Communication when Mediated by Audio-Graphics Teleconferencing," *Journal of Business Communication* 29 (1992): 161–178.

49. Marya Holcombe and Judith Stein, *Presentations for Decision Makers* (New York: Van Nostrand, 1990): 181.

50. Bonnie Roe White, "Teleconferencing: Its Potential in the Modern Office," *Century 21 Reporting* (Fall 1984): 5.

51. John Dewey, *How We Think* (Boston: D. C. Heath, 1910): 68–78.

52. C. H. Kepner and B. B Tregoe, *The Rational Manager: A Systematic Approach to Problem Solving and Decision Making* (New York: McGraw-Hill, 1965).

53. Rupert Cortwright and George Hinds, *Creative Discussion* (New York: Macmillan, 1959): 14.

54. John W. Keltner, *Mediation: Toward a Civilized System of Dispute Resolution* (Annandale, VA: Speech Communication Association, 1987); and J. A. Wall, "Mediation: An Analysis, Review, and Proposed Research," *Journal of Conflict Resolution* 25 (1981): 157–180.

55. R. T. Clark, *Coping with Mediation, Fact Finding, and Forms of Arbitration* (Chicago, IL: International Personnel Management Association, 1974); M. A. Rahim,

Managing Conflict in Organizations (New York: Praeger, 1986); and B. H. Sheppard, "Third Party Conflict Intervention: A Procedural Model," *Research in Organizational Behavior* 6 (1984): 141–190.

56. Martin P. Andersen, "A Model of Group Discussion," *Southern Speech Journal* 30 (1965): 279–293.

57. Milo Frank, *How to Run a Successful Meeting in Half the Time* (New York: Pocket Books, 1989): 18.

58. Frank, *How to Run a Successful Meeting*, 39.

59. Dorwin Cartwright and Alvin Zandler, *Group Dynamics* (New York: Harper and Row, 1968): ix.

Public Communication— Message Preparation and Delivery ◆ ◆ ◆ ◆

Learning Objectives

◆ To indicate the importance of public communication to the organization.

◆ To describe different types of presentations.

◆ To explain communication anxiety and ways to control your fear when making public presentations.

◆ To select a proper topic for a presentation.

◆ To analyze the audience you will address.

◆ To gather interesting examples, statistics, quotations, and stories for your presentation.

◆ To organize your presentation for the greatest impact.

◆ To explain the functions and types of visual aids.

◆ To deliver your presentation with power.

One afternoon a Roman emperor was entertaining himself at the Coliseum by feeding Christians to the lions. Several Christians were sacrificed and the crowd screamed for more. The next martyr entered the arena and said something to the lion. The beast cowered away. Then a second lion approached, with the same result: and then a third. The amazed throng began to shift its sympathies to the Christians. The emperor announced that the Christian's life would be spared, and that the would-be martyr should appear before him.

"I am sparing your life," said the emperor, "but before I release you, I demand to know what it was you said to those beasts."

"I merely said to each lion: After dinner, of course, you'll be expected to say a few words."

Again and again throughout our lifetimes each of us is called upon to "say a few words." A knowledge of public communication is critical to your success in today's organization because it is very likely that you will be called upon to deliver a number of presentations at work. How well you succeed in these presentations will determine, in part, how far and quickly you advance in your particular organization. Preparing public presentations and delivering them to audiences are skills you need to master.

Tom Parker, in his book, *In One Day*, writes about the many and varied activities in which Americans engage every day. One of the most important of the activities he chronicles, especially for Americans in the workplace, is speaking in public. He writes that "in one day Americans make 100,000 presentations. If they were all waiting their turn at the same lectern, the speakers would form a line 28 miles long. It would take the last speaker nine hours just to walk to that lectern."[1]

Public Communication in the Organization

Whatever your occupation, you will find yourself presenting information about your work to others. After he studied public communication in a number of organizations, Ernest Bormann concluded that "you will be giving presentations to offer yourself, a sales proposal, a program, an important budget or organizational change to others who have the power to accept or reject the substance of your message."[2] Speaking in public has become increasingly common and especially important in organizations. In her essay on training twenty-first century managers, Elizabeth M. Fowler observes that they must be skilled in public communication and, citing a report on the qualifications needed by top managers in the year 2000, she observes, "it was found that our corporate leaders will have to be accomplished public speakers who have learned the art of addressing small and large groups as well as the news media."[3] Management understands that a lack of public speaking skills affects the company in many ways—including the bottom line. Roger E. Flax, president and CEO of Motivational Systems, a management and sales training firm that trains over 50,000 people a year in communication skills, observes that "companies are finally saying it's costing us billions of dollars a year because employees don't know how to stand up and give speeches."[4]

In the past, corporate administrators, board directors, and public relations practitioners did most of the speaking for the corporation, and it is still true today that highly placed personnel do a lot of speaking in representing their organizations. Western Electric Company has over 100 speakers who make some 2,000 presentations each year. Standard Oil has between 50 and 100 representatives delivering some 500 speeches annually. Dow Chemical employees face 1,000 audiences each year, and 300 Georgia Pacific speakers make approximately 1,500 presentations every year. In the 1990s, however, it seems that nearly every employee of every corporation has a responsibility to present information to others. One study found that 50 percent of a group of blue-collar workers reported giving at least one public presentation within the past year, and 31 percent said they gave more than three speeches.[5] It is now common practice for corporations to encourage all of their employees to participate in the delivery of presentations. For example, over

90 percent of the 2,200 presentations given by General Motors' employees each year are delivered by middle managers, and 2,000 mid-level personnel of Phillips Petroleum Company deliver almost 10,000 presentations annually.[6]

It has become axiomatic that if you work, you will speak. When you first begin your career, many of these presentations will be in-house in front of coworkers. However, as you grow within your organization, you will also be expected to give speeches to listeners outside your workplace. Consider these examples: the vice president of marketing for a cable television company presents a new marketing strategy to the division heads of the company; the company president addresses the local Rotary group about the economic future of the area; the accounting manager for a large development firm explains zero-based budgeting to a group of department managers; and the corporate trainer for a bank speaks to a group of new tellers about their duties. These employees are representative of all kinds of workers in all sorts of businesses in all parts of the country, and they understand that being skilled in public communication enables them to perform better at work and to move up the corporate ladder.

Differences Between Public and Written Communication

That public communication is now common in America's organizations doesn't mean that written communication is unimportant. There are times when writing a memorandum, a written report, or a letter is absolutely necessary to communicate your message. However, you need to be aware that at times there are clear benefits to the use of oral public communication. Efficiency, effectiveness, and influence are some of the critical factors you must consider.

Efficiency. Oral communication often saves time because written forms of communication can be lost or buried under other materials on a desk or a conference table. No doubt there have been times when you have misplaced important files or reports. The result can be minimal if the written communication is quickly found, but it can be disastrous if it is found too late or never found at all. Furthermore, responding to a written communication can be put off for any number of reasons, and important feedback can be postponed. With oral communication, however, feedback is much more immediate because people hear the presentation and respond to it at once. Even if the audience members wait to respond for hours or days after the presentation, the speaker knows that the audience has received the message, and that may not be true with written communication.

Effectiveness. Oral communication is often more efficient than written communication because of its face-to-face nature. When you give a speech or make a report, you are able to see how your audience reacts to your ideas immediately because of the nonverbal and verbal communication that takes place. You can clarify your message on the fly if you see confused looks on listeners' faces, or you can begin to wrap it up if the audience looks bored or restless. Similarly, you can increase your enthusiasm while presenting your message when you see that the audience is excited about what you are saying. And oral communication gives you the chance to answer the questions of the audience and clear up issues immediately—both during and after the presentation.

Influence. Oral communication can be much more persuasive than written communication. The charisma, appearance, and knowledge of the speaker cast an influence over the members of an audience that a written memorandum simply cannot achieve. Think back to the last time you heard a really persuasive speaker and try to remember how you felt. You probably were moved to put into action what the speaker was requesting. This is a common response when the spoken word persuades us. Another reason that oral communication is more influential is that it is difficult to turn someone down or to say no face to face—the immediacy of the situation often calls out for interaction and rebuttal.

There is also more variety possible in spoken than in written language. Some of the differences between oral and written presentational styles are the following:

- Sentence length should be shorter in oral style.
- Oral style permits a greater variety in sentence structure: imperative and explanatory sentences are better suited to oral style, emphasizing the personal elements and relationships of face-to-face communication.
- Sentences are structurally less involved in oral style.
- Personal pronouns are more numerous in oral style.
- Fragmentary sentences may be used in oral style.
- Contractions are used more often in oral style.
- Repetition is necessary in oral style because speech is a linear temporal act.

A speech or report is not an essay, and it is imperative that your language and phrasing communicate your concern and involvement. The most effective oral presentations are those that communicate, linguistically and nonlinguistically, a sense of commitment.

Public Communication Defined

What comes to mind when you hear the term "public communication"? Many people imagine a public speaker standing behind a lectern and reading a prepared speech to an audience of hundreds or thousands of strangers. Others conjure up thoughts of a manager using visual aids and handouts as she talks to a group of a dozen coworkers in a company boardroom. You also might think public communication refers to a company president addressing the board of directors or stockholders about the company's strategic plans. Actually, all of these speakers are engaging in public communication, which we define as face-to-face communication in which a speaker has control of the speaking situation and the primary responsibility of presenting a message to one or more people.

Let's examine our definition of public communication in more detail so you can comprehend its parameters.

First, public communication is face-to-face with one or more people, i.e., it involves a speaker talking directly to an audience of other people. There may be a secondary external audience that doesn't actually see the speaker (such as people listening to a speech over a radio), but there must be a primary audience located proximally and listening to the speaker.

Second, the speaker has control of the speaking situation in public communication. By this, we mean that it is the speaker, no one else, who controls what is happening during the occasion. In other communication situations, such as an interpersonal encounter or a selection interview or a small-group discussion, the control of the situation is shared with other people.

Third, in public communication the speaker's primary responsibility is to present a message. Here, it is the speaker who assumes the role of being responsible for getting the message across to the listeners. In other forms of communication, certain responsibilities may be more important than the delivery of a message. For example, in interpersonal communication the development of the relationships between and among people is often more important than the messages they exchange. In other settings, this responsibility of getting a message across is shared with the other participants in the situation.

Finally, the number of listeners may be only a few or even just one other person. It isn't the size of the audience that determines whether public communication has happened; the audience can be any size. You are engaging in public communication when you attempt to persuade your boss that you deserve a salary raise or when you inform your manager about the recent disagreement between two people in your department.

Forms of Public Communication

There are a number of different forms or types of public communication that commonly occur in organizations. You have probably used or even seen and heard a number of the following examples of public communication:

- ◆ research and technical reports
- ◆ briefing announcements
- ◆ orientation sessions
- ◆ question-and-answer sessions
- ◆ informational reports
- ◆ training and development programs
- ◆ conference presentations
- ◆ introductions of speakers
- ◆ convention programs
- ◆ sales presentations
- ◆ after-dinner speeches
- ◆ special project proposals
- ◆ progress reports
- ◆ award ceremonies
- ◆ press conferences

Throughout the chapters on public communication, we will be using the general term "presentations" to refer to these many and varied forms of public communication. These presentations fall into two groups—formal speeches and reports. Although all speeches and reports meet the criteria of our definition of public communication, they differ in some important ways. Frank E. X. Dance explains that the differences between speeches and reports are "not of the genre but of the situation or setting."[7] Dance recognizes that speeches and reports are inherently similar in nature and in certain respects overlapping, but let's examine a few of the more explicit distinctions between them.

First, formal speeches generally are designated for larger and more heterogeneous audiences than are reports. These public speeches are often delivered to a larger number of people and these people may not have a lot in common. The audience members may be attending the speech voluntarily or they may have been assigned to attend the speech. On the other hand, reports are usually delivered to smaller and more homogeneous groups of people. These presentations can be delivered to a few people seated around a board table or to only one person in an office. The listener in these smaller audiences is most likely to be there because her or his job requires attendance.

Second, the places where formal speeches and reports are delivered can also vary. Speeches are sometimes delivered in business settings,

Speech Writers in the Thick of It
By Jeannette Spalding

President Steve Ewing of Michigan Consolidated Gas company (MichCon) often drops by and makes himself at home in the office of Ed Stanulis, seemingly a nobody. Then the two men hash over some weighty issues of the Detroit-based gas utility. At other times, Stanulis talks turkey with Al Glancy III, Chairman and CEO.

Where does a non-management professional like Stanulis get off being such a casual acquaintance with the president?

Why does he get in to see the chairman and CEO?

He's the speech writer.

"There's clout, prestige, and power in being a speech writer," Stanulis says. "The speech writer becomes a confidant and an adviser."

The clout, power and prestige of speech writing should make business communicators stand up and take notice. Business communicators sit in ideal positions to gain speech writing skills and to become speech writers. When the clout is added to a potential $100,000-a-year plus income, no business communicator can afford to overlook the possibilities.

But while prestigious, speech writing can be thorny.

Speech writers circulate among the company's movers and shakers and get in the thick of company decisions.

"We are at the forefront of what's happening," Stanulis says. "Often, I know what will happen way ahead of some of the vice presidents."

Speech writers publicize the company's policies by preparing speeches for top management. Speech writers intimately observe policy in the making a policy carried out. In this process, speech writers can't help but learn the top-level management skill of policy formation. It's a skill that can boost business communicators into the executive suite.

"Speech writing is a valuable arrow to have in your quiver if you want to be vice president of communication," says Steve Hallmark, an independent speech writing consultant based in Chicago and a former American Bar Association speech writer.

Stanulis' speeches go through an elaborate approval system to avoid inaccuracies. Top executives and appropriate technical people put their eagle eyes to these speeches. This approval process seems laborious at times because everyone feels a need to make changes, whether or not those changes are really warranted.

Negotiating copy changes and working with top management join responsibilities that speech writers and other business communicators share. These common skills give business communicators some savvy to give speech writing a try.

Floyd Walker suggests ways corporate writers can get speech writing experience. These writers should put themselves in positions of writing for the spoken word—newscasts or video scripts, says the administrator of Community Relations and Media Services for Allied Signal Aerospace Co., based in Kansas City, MO. Such writing gives the writer experience about what works and what doesn't work for the spoken word. Also, writers should seek out opportunities to write speeches.

Aspiring speech writers should watch people speak, listen to speech content, read speeches, know the speakers, and know the company, Walker says. By observation, the writer learns some dos and don'ts of speech writing and how specific people talk. The writer's knowledge and tenure with the company give the powers-that-be confidence to let the novice speech writer have a go at it.

As the corporate writer adds a growing number of speeches to a portfolio, who knows where opportunity will lead?

Stanulis, for example, eased into speech writing from a technical writing and technical training background. He worked for the Federal Reserve Bank addressing audiences about the bank and its monetary policy. Later, he wrote speeches on the same topic for other speakers, a chore that turned into a full-time speech writing job. He hired on as company speech writer at MichCon. Speech writers like Stanulis learn speech writing on the job. In fact, many middle to upper-level managers get conscripted into speech writing service without particularly asking. Not only do these managers come from business communication, but they also come from law, operations, human resources and strategic planning.

Hallmark knows one such draftee. The chairman needed a speech about strategic planning, so the strategic planner wrote the speech. The chairman loved it. The next time the chairman needed a speech, the strategic planner received the assignment, even though the speech had no connection to strategic planning. Thus, a speech writer was born.

"The Chicago Speech Writers Forum has 70 writers and not a single one of us set out to be a speech writer," Hallmark says. Stanulis says the same things about the 45-member Detroit Speech Writers Forum.

It's no accident that upper managers are well-versed in the intricacies of corporate policy making. They work and negotiate on the same level with the CEO, which is what the speech writer must do.

"Speech writers are seasoned observers and participants in the corporate environment," Hallmark says. "They have made major management decisions. They have made policy. They have been there."

Speech writers also have a temperament and willingness to set aside their egos to allow the speaker's ego to shine forth—not a universal trait in everyone, Hallmark says.

His speech writing experience over the years has led him to a point where he now writes 50 speeches a year and draws top dollar for each one. A speech writer's income in the U.S. ranges from the median $56,000 a year to the top end income of $115,000 a year, according to an informal survey by Ragan Communications published in its November 17, 1989 *Speech Writer's Newsletter.*

The speech writing demand these days is as good as the money. Hallmark says that Peggy Noonan's popular book, *What I Saw at the Revolution,* spurred an interest in speech giving among entrepreneurs, a field ripe for the harvest by independent speech writers. Also, the Chicago speech writer says that CEOs talk more to audiences in-house to motivate them on issues such as customer service, an opportunity for speech writers who prefer the inside corporate scene.

And speech writers really get inside the inside corporate scene. How much more on the inside can a professional get than someone like speech writer Stanulis? He has frequent visits to his office by one of the company's top officers, and he is one of the first to know what will happen in his company. Being this much "in the know" is something business communicators thrive on.

Source: Jeannette Spalding, "Speech Writers in the Thick of It," *Communication world* (October 1990): 23–25.

but they can also be delivered in convention halls, stadiums, and auditoriums that accommodate larger audiences. Reports, however, are more frequently presented in business settings such as boardrooms, conference and meeting rooms, and other general business environments. These smaller places are appropriate for reports because the audiences usually comprise a small number of listeners.

Third, the topic and manner of its choosing is different in most formal speeches and reports. In speeches, the topic is quite often left up to the speaker—at least, the speaker is given a general topic area and is allowed to provide the focus. Listeners will generally accept a slight variation from the announced topic. In reports, however, the topic is usually assigned to the presenter by a corporate superior, often a manager or department head, and the purpose is quite specific.

Public communication, then, is commonly associated with the term "presentations" and is marked by its face-to-face nature, the control the speaker exerts over the situation, and its purpose of extending a message to one or more people. Presentations comprise formal speeches and reports that are similar in nature, but which differ in certain specific ways including the types of audiences, the places where the presentations are delivered, and the choice and orientation of the topics presented.

Speaker Apprehension

One of the major concerns of employees who make presentations is the fear of speaking before other people. This fear is known by many names—stage fright, nervousness, anxiety, or speaker apprehension— and it is very common among people who make presentations.

For years, a number of surveys have indicated that Americans fear speaking in public more than anything else and, in *The Book of Lists*, David Wallechinsky, Irving Wallace, and Amy Wallace cite one survey in which 3,000 Americans listed fear of speaking before a group ahead of such other fear-provokers as heights, snakes, sickness, financial distress, and death.[8] About 20 percent of Americans suffer so significantly from communication apprehension that their presentations are adversely affected.[9] James McCroskey and Lawrence Wheeless further note that "communication apprehension is probably the most common handicap suffered by people in contemporary American society."[10] Exhibit 11–1 presents some of the behaviors characteristic of excessively frightened people.[11]

Everyone has some apprehension about making a presentation before other people. You can never eliminate your fear of speaking before others, nor should you. Some anxiety is good because you need the adrenaline produced by your body in stressful situations to push you to your peak performance. Just as athletes get "psyched up" before an im-

Voice	quivering or tense speech too fast speech too slow monotonous; lack of emphasis
Verbal fluency	nonfluencies; stammering; halting speech vocal pauses hunts for words; speech blocks
Mouth and throat	swallowing clearing throat breathing heavily
Facial expression	lack of eye contact; extraneous eye movements tense face muscles; grimaces; twitches deadpan facial expression
Arms and hands	rigid or tense fidgeting; extraneous movements motionless; lack of appropriate gestures
Gross body movement	sways; paces; shuffles feet

EXHIBIT 11–1: Physical Signs of Anxiety and Fright

portant game or meet, you also need to be somewhat tense before you make your presentations.

Now, it's important for you to begin the process of understanding your own personal anxiety so you can learn to control it and not allow it to control you. Everyone has a different degree of anxiety and, if it's within certain limits, it's considered normal. Here's an opportunity to measure your speaker apprehension:

How Apprehensive Are You in Making Presentations?[12]

This instrument consists of six statements about your feelings on giving a presentation. Indicate the degree to which each statement applies to you by marking whether you (1) strongly agree, (2) agree, (3) are undecided, (4) disagree, or (5) strongly disagree with each statement. There are no right or wrong answers. Don't be concerned that some of the statements are similar to others. Work quickly and just record your first impression.

___ 1. I have no fear of making a presentation.

___ 2. Certain parts of my body feel very tense and rigid while making a presentation.

___ 3. I feel relaxed while making a presentation.

___ 4. My thoughts become confused and jumbled when I am making a presentation.

___ 5. I face the prospect of making a presentation with confidence.

___ 6. While making a presentation, I get so nervous that I forget facts I really know.

Scoring: To obtain your presentation apprehension score, use the following formula—To a base of 18 add your scores for items 1, 3, and 5; then subtract your scores for items 2, 4, and 6. A score above 18 shows some degree of apprehension, and places you in the company of the vast majority of people.

Now that you have a better idea about your own personal degree of speaker apprehension, we offer you the following suggestions for controlling your fear of speaking before others.

Understand What Causes Your Fear. To control your anxiety, you need to understand what causes your fear. Raymond Beatty identifies five contributing factors that influence presentational anxiety.[13] An understanding of these factors will give you a better idea of your own fear and how to best control it. First is perceived novelty. Most of us show some anxiety when we face new situations. When your boss first asks you to make a presentation to the rest of the managers, you will probably be influenced by the newness of speaking in this particular situation. To minimize this factor, it is important that you gain as much experience as possible in making oral presentations. Volunteer to make presentations at work, join your local Toastmasters organizations, or speak in your civic and church groups. Do anything you can to gain the experience necessary to become a veteran at speaking because then the novelty of making presentations won't be a factor in making you apprehensive.

Second is a potential sense of subordinate status. You can also become apprehensive when you believe that certain people in your audience are better speakers than you or that they know more about your subject than you do. This feeling of inadequacy can damage your self-esteem and prove personally demoralizing, so it's important that you bolster your self-confidence when you enter speaking situations and realize that speaking isn't a contest against others. Keep focused on your message and not on what you believe others may be thinking about you. You must know as much as you can about your subject and be well prepared. This should help to quell otherwise subordinate feelings.

Third is a feeling of conspicuousness. Your nervousness increases if you believe everyone is looking at you. Have you ever noticed how much easier it is to speak when you are at your seat instead of standing behind a lectern in the middle of the room? Again, this is a common feeling among all people who make presentations. Many of us don't like to be in the limelight and become more anxious if we believe we look conspicuous. To reduce this factor, think of the audience as a small group of colleagues who only want the best for you—this is probably true anyway. And again, concentrate on the message you are presenting and not on yourself as the presenter.

Fourth is the factor of dissimilarity. People feel more nervous when they think they have little in common with their listeners. This factor doesn't have as much impact when you present reports because you usually know the members of these audiences. However, dissimilarity is common when you give speeches because you may not know very

Taking the Terror out of Talk
By Michael T. Motley

Surveys show that what Americans fear most—more than snakes, heights, disease, financial problems, or even death—is speaking before a group. This is surprising, in a way, since even a dreadful speech isn't as serious as illness, poverty, or the grave. Yet about 85% of us feel uncomfortably anxious speaking in public. Even professionals, evangelists, and entertainers suffer extreme stage fright, or, to use its more formal label, "speech anxiety."

While it's comforting to realize that such anxiety is almost universal, a magic formula to dispel it would be even more comforting. There is no such formula, but recent research that helps us understand speech anxiety better also suggests ways to control it.

The most familiar aspects of speech anxiety are its physical symptoms. Most people report some combination of sweaty palms, dry mouth, increased heart rate, shaky hands, weak knees, shortness of breath and butterflies in the stomach. Laboratory measurements add increased blood pressure and muscles tension to the list of symptoms. With all of this going on, it's no wonder the experience is unpleasant—for some, so unpleasant that they avoid public speaking completely, whatever the cost. I have treated attorneys, ministers, and public-relations executives who were ready to quit their professions to avoid public speaking. Other clients were losing chances for advancement by passing off speaking assignments to colleagues.

Physical symptoms are just one component of speech anxiety. More important is how people interpret the symptoms. A few speakers, the confident ones, see their physical reaction as a positive sign that they are emotionally ready for the speech. Most of us, however, interpret the feelings as fear. To justify this fear, we need something to be afraid of, so we begin to imagine what will happen if our speech is less than perfect. These imagined consequences are usually exaggerated and irrational. People say, for example, "The audience will ridicule me if I make a mistake. I'll be embarrassed to death," when in fact audiences usually ignore errors and awkwardness as long as they get something out of the speech. These irrational fears and physiological symptoms often feed on each other—the fears increase the symptoms, which in turn increase the fears—until extreme physiological arousal combines with thoughts of catastrophe. Heart rates can approach 200 beats per minute in speakers convinced that they will make fools of themselves.

Excessive anxiety is especially common among people who view speeches as performances, in which they must satisfy an audience of critics who will carefully evaluate gestures, language and everything else they do. Though they can't describe precisely what these critics expect, people with a performance orientation assume that formal, artificial behavior is somehow better than the way they usually talk. Research has shown that expecting to be evaluated or being uncertain about the proper way to behave arouses anxiety in almost any situation. A much more useful orientation, and a more accurate one, is to view speeches as communication rather than performance. The speakers' role is to share ideas with an audience more interested in hearing what they have to say than in analyzing or criticizing how they say it—a situation not very different, at least in this regard, from everyday conversation.

A number of techniques are being used successfully to control anxiety. One popular approach, systematic desensitization, is aimed specifically at lessening physiological arousal. The technique involves training in muscular relaxation, coupled with visual imagery. People are taught to relax as they imagine giving a speech, the assumption being that psychological anxiety doesn't go with physical relaxation. Typically, people start by imagining an event fairly remote from the planned speech, such as being in the audience for someone else's speech. Once they achieve relaxation with that image, they repeat the process while imagining events closer to giving the speech, until they finally visualize their own speech, still feeling relaxed.

Another popular approach, rational emotive therapy (RET), works on irrational thoughts that contribute to anxiety. RET and its variations try, in particular, to get speakers to realize that many of their fears are ill-founded. After people explain precisely what they fear, the therapist points out flaws in the reasoning and helps them adopt a more realistic attitude.

In my public speaking courses, for example, students will often say that what they are afraid of is getting a bad grade on the impending speech. If this were the real problem, my offer to leave the room and allow the speech to remain ungraded would eliminate the anxiety. It doesn't, of course, since their fear of audience evaluation remains.

Other speakers will mention some more generalized fear, such as "I just never seem to speak well," or make self-fulfilling prophecies, such as "I'm going to bore them to death." The therapist helps them replace such statements with more positive and reasonable ones, such as "Since this information is interesting to me I can make it interesting to others."

Another approach I find effective shifts the speaker's orientation away from performance and toward communication. "Communicative pragmatics orienting" works to persuade people that effective public speaking is more like ordinary communication than like a public performance. Once people genuinely view making a speech as communication, they can think of it in terms of their normal, everyday conversation rather than in terms of past anxiety-ridden performances. I have found that with this approach, speech anxiety almost always subsides and the speeches improve.

There is an exercise I use to demonstrate the point: as the speaker approaches the podium, I dismiss the audience temporarily and begin a "one-way conversation" with the speaker. I tell him or her to forget about giving a speech and simply talk spontaneously to me, using the speech-outline notes as a guide. In this situation, most people feel rather silly orating, so they start to speak conversationally, using natural language, inflections and gestures. I ask the speaker to maintain this conversational style while the audience gradually returns, a few people at a time.

The speakers usually do this successfully as the audience returns. When they don't, the transition from talk to speech is invariable identified later by the audience as the point when effectiveness began to decrease and by the speaker as the point when anxiety began to increase.

All the speech-anxiety therapies I've mentioned involve more than I have described here, of course, and require qualified therapists. For most of us, giving a speech is an important and novel event. It's natural and appropriate to feel some anxiety. A speaker's aim should be to keep this natural nervousness from cycling out of control; not to get rid of the butterflies but to make them fly in formation.

Source: Michael T. Motley, "Taking the Terror Out of Talk," *Psychology Today* (January 1988): 46–49. Reprinted with permission from *Psychology Today* magazine, copyright © 1988 (Sussex Publishers, Inc.).

many, if any, of the listeners. In these situations, you need to find similarities between you and the listeners and stress them in the preparation and delivery of your speeches.

Finally, one's prior experience may be a contributing factor to speaker apprehension. You will exhibit apprehensive behaviors more often if you've felt such nervousness before. Unfortunately it is true that communication apprehension feeds on the past. More importantly, even if your listeners don't perceive you to be nervous but you felt nervous, it is your perception of anxiety that will influence you the next time you speak. To minimize this factor, gain positive experience by participating in successful speaking situations. If your memories are positive, you will feel much less apprehension when you make your presentations.

Correct Your Misconceptions About Making Presentations. Misconceptions, myths, or misplaced beliefs about speaking in public contribute to our feelings of anxiety. These ideas have arisen over the years and become near-truths to many people. But, realizing that they are *not* true, you can further control your speaker apprehension.

Myth One: Good Speakers Are Born, Not Made. This myth assumes that certain people are born with an innate ability to speak well and others aren't, i.e., you either have it or you don't. People who accept this myth believe that actively working to improve your presentational ability is a waste of time if you aren't one of the gifted. Actually, all good speakers are made through hard work and practice. Socrates, the progenitor of Greek eloquence, observed that effective speakers required some natural talent, much training, and considerable courage. By volunteering for more speaking opportunities and working hard on your speeches and reports, you can develop the skills necessary to deliver a solid presentation.

Myth Two: Presentational Speaking Is Unnatural. People who accept this myth believe that public communication is totally different from the everyday, conversational communication in which we all engage. They see people who make speeches or reports as stiff speakers standing behind a lectern droning on to uninterested listeners, or they see glib, silver-tongued orators persuading others with slick visuals, fancy words, and smooth delivery. In both situations, presentational speaking is seen as different from everyday speaking. Presenting speeches and reports, however, is really very similar to the conversational speaking you do all the time. Think about the similarities: both forms have the essential components of speaker, listener, message, and channel; they both involve and depend upon feedback between speaker and listener; they both use verbal and nonverbal symbols; and they both depend upon clarity of expression and sound logic. In fact, you aren't a novice at presentational speaking because you have already had considerable experience speaking to other people. James Fallows, President Jimmy

Carter's chief speech writer, further notes that traditional public speaking has been replaced by a less ritualized, less formal type of speaking when he observes that "fifteen years ago, the public responded to the graceful artifice of noble speech. . . . Now it's more important to people to hear a rough approximation of how the person actually speaks than to have something glamorous. It's reassuring to feel that you are seeing a slice of the real person."[14]

Myth Three: Presentational Speaking Just Means Sounding Good. To the believers of this myth, the delivery of the message is everything, and content counts for nothing. This is the dangerous assumption that the public speaker should be concerned primarily with technique. Here a speaker is effective if she has a dynamic delivery, meaningful gestures, direct eye contact with the audience, and an attractive appearance. The purpose of speaking becomes the management and maneuvering of people rather than a responsible act. It is this kind of thinking that has led to the phrase "mere rhetoric." This myth is symbolized by the stereotypical used-car salesman and the slick politician who try to con us into buying or believing something. Actually, content—your message—is the reason for speaking, and the delivery of that message is the way it gets to the audience. Speakers should be well informed, speak with the best knowledge possible, respect the responses of others even when contrary, and make clear personal commitments. By hard work in your practice sessions and by concentrating on your message and not on yourself, you can both sound good and say something meaningful.

Visualize Yourself Being Successful. When you are apprehensive about your upcoming presentation, you are visualizing a negative outcome. If you have an especially powerful imagination, your mind can create frightening scenarios in which you see yourself forgetting your message, failing to answer a difficult question, stumbling over your words, and even blushing when the audience laughs at what you have just said.

Instead, use visualization to your benefit. Professional athletes and actors have used positive visualization for years to preview their success, and effective presenters use visualization as well. When you practice your speech or report, try to see the audience applauding your effort, picture your boss congratulating you on your successful presentation. As you prepare, try to replace negative thoughts with positive ones by turning them around. For example, instead of thinking, "I'm going to forget what to say," think to yourself, "I've practiced so much I know what to say"; and instead of thinking, "Someone will ask me a question I won't know how to answer," think, "I know this subject, and I'm prepared."

Lately, presenters have adopted scripts to use before they make their speeches or reports to prompt their visualizing a successful performance. We have provided you with the following script to use before you make presentations.[15] The best way to use a visualization script is to read it several times before your presentation or tape record it and listen to it again and again. Business executives and other presenters believe these scripts allow them to change their negative thoughts to positive ones.

Try this exercise:

Close your eyes. Allow your body to get comfortable in your chair. Take a deep breath and hold it ... now slowly release it through your nose. Now take another deep breath and make certain you are breathing from the diaphragm ... hold it ... now slowly release it and note how you feel while doing this ... feel the relaxation flow throughout your body. Now take one more really deep breath ... pattern. Shift around in your chair so you are comfortable.

Now you see yourself at the beginning of the day when you are going to give your presentation. See yourself getting up in the morning, full of energy and confidence, and looking forward to the day's opportunities. You are putting on just the right clothes for your presentation that day. As you are going to work, you note how clear and confident you feel and how others around you comment positively on your appearance and demeanor. You feel completely prepared for the task at hand. Your preparation has been exceptionally thorough, and you have really researched the topic you will be presenting today.

Now you see yourself in the room where you will make your presentation, and you are talking very comfortably and confidently with others in the room. The people to whom you will be presenting your message appear to be quite friendly and are very cordial in their greetings and subsequent conversation. You feel absolutely sure of your material and of your ability to present the information in a convincing and positive manner. Now you see yourself approaching the area where you will make your presentation. You are feeling very good about yourself, and you see yourself moving forward eagerly.

You now see yourself delivering your presentation. It is really very good and you have all the finesse of a polished speaker. You are aware that your audience is giving you head nods, smiles, and other positive responses that clearly give you the message that you are truly on target. You are now through the introduction and the body of the presentation and are heading into a brilliant summation of your position on the topic. You now see yourself fielding audience questions with the same confidence and energy that you exhibited in the presentation itself. You see yourself receiving the congratulations of people around you. You see yourself as relaxed, pleased with your presentation, and ready for the next task you need to accomplish that day. You feel filled with purpose, energy, and a sense of general well-being. You silently congratulate yourself on a job well done!

Now ... you have returned to this time and place. Take a deep breath and hold it ... and let it go. Do this once more and feel yourself comfortably back where you began. Take as much time as you need before you leave the room.

Practice Thoroughly. This final suggestion is one that we can't empha-size enough. A legitimate reason for speakers to feel nervousness and low confidence is inadequate preparation. Prepare and practice thor-oughly—preparation without practice is sure to doom even the best pre-senter. Speech practice must be undertaken systematically. Practice time will vary from presentation to presentation. For example, there will be times when your employer will ask you to present the next day, and your time to get ready and practice will be very short. For more elabo-rate presentations, especially speeches, you'll have a longer time frame in which to practice. Even if you're asked to speak in one or two days, the following three-step schedule will allow you to properly practice most of your presentations:

Step One: Read Your Speaking Outline Aloud. After you have researched your topic and transferred your information to notecards or another similar aid, you need to begin your practice sessions by going through the presentation aloud several times. You'll want to explain your ex-amples and state fully all quotations and statistics. Try to complete the presentation even if you stumble or make a mistake.

Step Two: Polish and Refine the Presentation. This is the time to check on physical movement, eye contact, gestures, and distracting aspects of your delivery such as vocalized pauses ("uh ... ah ... um"). You should also smooth out your delivery and speak as much as possible without using your notes. This second step is also an excellent opportunity to ask other people—coworkers, your boss, friends, and family—to listen to you and make suggestions. If these people aren't available, you can use a full-length mirror to get a visual idea about how you will look to your listeners.

Use a tape recorder during rehearsal to make you conscious of slang expressions and annoying repetitions that creep into your speech. Vid-eotaping provides even more specific feedback—your gestures and movements can be very revealing. You may initially be somewhat un-certain about videotaping, but once you've adjusted to seeing yourself as others see you, you'll find videotaping a terrific bonus. Seeing what patterns you fall into when you are nervous will make it easier to correct them—you can't change something you don't know you do.

Step Three: Have a Dress Rehearsal. This is the last opportunity to prac-tice before you speak, and this session should take place under condi-tions closely approximating your real speaking situation. Go through the entire presentation, making the final changes you need for the pre-sentation to be as solid as possible. When this session is over, you should feel confident and be looking forward to your presentation.

Remember, presentational success comes from earning the right to the time. You earn that right by knowing the topic. You earn that right by research and careful reflection. And, you earn that right by careful preparation and speaking—practice, practice, practice. A reporter asked the world-famous pianist Arthur Rubinstein, near the end of his life, "Are you the greatest musician who ever lived, as some people have said?" The wise old maestro responded, "Music is an art, not a science and no one ever becomes the greatest at an art—they could always be greater!" We can say the same about the art of public speaking. No amount of practice will make you perfect, but it will make you consistently good, and sometimes great.

Steps in Preparation and Delivery

Perhaps before analyzing the specifics of preparing the presentation—selecting a topic, defining the purpose, analyzing your audience, researching the topic, organizing the body, planning your introduction and conclusion, delivering the presentation and evaluating your presentation—it is important to ask: What is an effective speech? This is a difficult question to answer. You can learn all the proper techniques and still not give an effective speech; and even if it is effective, there may be no concrete evidence of the results; and even if the results are immediately apparent, there may be considerable disagreement about whether they are desirable. This doesn't mean that there are no standards for distinguishing an effective speech from an ineffective one. It means that the results depend not so much on how well you apply the techniques as on the use to which you put them. The answer to our question ultimately rests with the qualities that characterize an effective speaker:

1. The effective speaker has developed the capacity for observation, has sharpened senses, and has learned to use them accurately and fully. He or she is sensitive.

2. The effective speaker has built up a broad background of knowledge in the area(s) in which she or he wishes to communicate. The speaker is knowledgeable.

3. The effective speaker not only understands the subject matter but also his or her own capabilities and limitations. Closely connected here is an ability for self-criticism.

4. The effective speaker has developed the capacity for thinking purposefully and logically.

5. The effective speaker will have a generally accurate image of the audience.

6. The effective speaker will use every opportunity for practice.

7. The effective speaker will keep in mind his or her ethical responsibilities. Two thousand years ago the great Roman teacher,

Quintilian, defined the orator as a "good man skilled in speaking."

On November 19, 1863, two men spoke at the dedication of a national cemetery in a small Pennsylvania town. The first speaker was Edward Everett. He was considered a genius and heralded as a brilliant speaker. He stepped to the platform and for more than an hour his powerful, carefully organized remarks and eloquent oratory held the attention of his audience. The second speaker was a man so awkward in appearance that one of his critics called him "the big baboon." This man had been too busy to do much preparation, only jotting down a few notes on the brief train ride from Washington that day. When he strolled to the podium, he had no smile for the audience, no humorous stories, no heartwarming illustrations. His speech contained only 266 words and lasted less than five minutes. "Fourscore and seven years ago, ... " he began, and the rest is history. The second speaker was Abraham Lincoln and his message was the famous Gettysburg Address. His speech effectively touched the hearts of the people; it spoke to their needs, their dreams, their fears, their sufferings. So, an effective speech fits the speaker, the audience, its purpose, and the occasion. To borrow from the Gettysburg Address, it is "altogether fitting and proper."

What are the steps in preparing and delivering a speech? How do you determine your topic, your purpose? How do you organize the material? What are the functions of the introduction and the conclusion? What can be used as supporting material? What about style and delivery? How can you be effective? Business presentations being delivered in today's corporate world are all different. A briefing by the company president may be succinct and limited to one issue while a speech to the company's stockholders may be lengthy and cover many diverse topics. A sales presentation may have two listeners and be interrupted constantly by questions, and a slide presentation in a 50-person department may have all questions delayed until the end. Although these presentations differ in a variety of ways, the preparation for them is very similar. Effective speakers generally follow the same steps in planning and developing any presentation. All of your presentations will make use of each of the following stages of preparation. As we discuss these stages, it is well to keep in mind the advance of Dionysius: "Let thy speech be better than silence, or be silent."

Step One: Select and Narrow Your Topic

The first step in preparing your presentation is to select and narrow your topic. Rarely will you find a situation in which topic selection is a function solely of your choice. Oral reports require that you address a specific subject and, even when speaking to outside audiences, general parameters are usually suggested. Your subject matter is fairly rigidly dictated when you are asked to present an orientation session to new employees about company benefits or to inform the members of the department about the current new software package; choice is equally limited when you're asked to respond to citizen concerns about a new runway proposed by the local airport authority or address the local Chamber of Commerce about your company's role in the community during the next decade. But there will be times when you'll have the opportunity to choose your own subject for an upcoming presentation or be allowed to specify the exact nature of the general topic suggested to you. At these times, you need to make wise decisions about topic selection.

Certainly, your personal knowledge, experiences, attitudes, and beliefs will be reflected in your approach to any topic. Although speeches may vary in purpose, each is essentially a personal statement from you as a speaker to others who choose or are asked to listen. Regardless of attempts at objectivity, you cannot totally divorce yourself from the personal history that has shaped your perceptions, so your frame of reference helps determine the focus you adopt on any particular topic. The following criteria can also be used when you make your topic selection.

The topic should interest you because you'll give more of your time to preparing a presentation if the topic interests you. If you're enthusiastic about the topic, or if you could become excited about it, you'll probably research, organize, and practice your presentation with more vigor. It is also true that you'll have more fun with your topic if you find it interesting, and having fun is a part of presenting well.

The topic should be important to your listeners. Topics of import to you may not seem so to your audience, and topics perceived to be unimportant aren't listened to enthusiastically. A legitimate question for any listener to ask is: why is this topic important to me? The effective presenter always addresses the timeliness and significance of the topic early in the presentation before the listener asks.

Narrow the topic so it is appropriate for the speaking situation. This requires you to analyze the topic in relation to the time allotted. There may be elements of your presentation that could better be handled in forms other than the oral presentation. For example, certain parts might be better communicated by a written memo to specific listeners. This analysis can also reveal those parts of the subject with which you feel comfortable and which you may choose to ignore.

The length of time you'll be given to speak depends on a number of variables, over most of which you'll have little control. The length can be from a very few minutes to well over an hour for many reports and speeches. You do, however, have control over your rate of speaking. The average speaker says approximately 125 words per minute. The typical journalistic paragraph of simple sentences also runs about 125 words. Thus, a very general rule is that an average speaker speaks about one short paragraph per minute. Of course, if the material is highly technical or statistical, or if you speak slowly, the time can stretch to almost two minutes per paragraph.

Another way to determine the number of ideas you can present is to section the presentation. If you have ten minutes to inform your staff about a new corporate smoking policy, then you'll usually devote one to two minutes to introduce the policy and about one minute to conclude the presentation. That leaves seven to eight minutes to discuss the core information. If you decide to cover three or four main issues, you'll only be able to devote a couple of minutes to each and that may not be enough time to fully develop any of them. Therefore, you may decide to narrow your topic to two or three main issues, thus giving you more time for each. The important point here is that your topic needs to be well chosen and narrowed to fit the speaking situation. Note: Let the rambler beware! No one likes someone who exceeds the time limit.

Step Two: Define Your Purpose

An effective speaker must assume a purpose and a structure. Your task as a public speaker is to determine why you are going to speak to a particular audience. You should determine what your stated purpose is, what your audience thinks your purpose is, and what your real purpose is. It's important to have the purpose clearly defined in your mind because your purpose will influence what you say, how you say it, and what responses you want.

Traditionally, presentations are divided into three major categories: informative, persuasive, and entertaining. The informative presentation is designed to educate your audience by expanding their knowledge or teaching them specific facts. Here you explain, instruct, define, clarify, or demonstrate new information. Your goal is to help your listeners understand your topic, not to change their attitudes or behavior. Your purpose is to produce clear ideas in the minds of your listeners. This necessitates identifying what knowledge your hearers already have about the subject, and using what they already know in constructing the new meanings you want them to grasp. Instructing the staff about the basic principles of zero-based budgeting, demonstrating the operation of the video camera to the interns, and training the new sales representative are typical examples of the presentation to inform.

The persuasive presentation is intended to influence audience members to change their opinions, attitudes, or actions. In persuasive presentations you wish to influence, convince, motivate, sell, or stimulate your listeners to alter their beliefs or to act. You go beyond giving information to actually espousing a position. The difference between informing and persuading is the difference between "explaining" and "exhorting."[16] The persuasive effort attempts to solidify, to modify, or to change the audience's attitudes and behaviors; the speaker chooses to stimulate, convince, or actuate the audience. Persuading the vice president of marketing to try a new marketing strategy, convincing the CEO that new markets need to be opened, and selling a computer system to a new client are examples of persuasive presentations.

The entertaining presentation provides pleasure and enjoyment with little serious intent to disseminate information or prompt change. This speech, built around a kind of theme often involving the recounting of a series of personal experiences or humorous anecdotes, is no small task because people's notions of what is humorous and what they find to be entertaining vary widely. After-dinner speakers and those participating in "roast and toasts" often speak to entertain, with varied success.

However, because the purpose of communication is so complex and multileveled today, these traditional labels can be confining and misleading. A less-traditional approach to presentational content is more accurately reflective of the modern business and professional arena. The purpose of a presentation is determined not by its content, but by the motivation of the person sending the message. Why are you giving this presentation? What rewards do you hope to achieve as a result of it? What punishments do you wish to avoid by engaging in this speech making? What do you want the audience to do, to feel, or to believe as a result of hearing your presentation? For example:

- The professor lectures. Why does he? Perhaps he wants his students to have information he thinks is valuable. Maybe he wants his students to achieve good grades as evidence to his peers that he's a good teacher. Perhaps he wants his students to see the world from a particular perspective. He may be motivated by any number of factors.

- The corporation treasurer reports. Why? She wants the stockholders to know the state of affairs. Why? Perhaps she wants them to continue holding stock or to buy additional stock certificates. Maybe she wants them to support the current board of directors— or to withdraw their support from the board.

Thus, the determining question is: Why are you giving a speech or report? The answer to the *why* influences what information you will include and exclude from a presentation. Your motivation also influences how you present the material.

Moreover, the purpose of any presentation is also dependent upon the members of the audience. Some may see the presentation as providing only information; others may be persuaded by it. Given the nature of the communication process, the audience plays a significant role in the perception of purpose. Audience members do not determine the purpose for you, but they do determine the purpose they perceive. Communication is a receiver-based phenomenon; the receivers' perception of your purpose will influence their subsequent behavior. Naive receivers may perceive a presentation as purely informational. A cynical audience may perceive your planned informational approach as information control, attempted manipulation, or attempted opinion modification. A contented, self-satisfied audience may perceive a witty and humorous presentation as purely entertaining in purpose, when, in fact, you might have been trying to inform, to attack, or to prompt action. Consequently, the three traditional presentational modes—to inform, to persuade, and to entertain—can more properly be viewed as devices used for achieving objectives. In a sense, all presentations seek to control a listener's attention and they all request his or her understanding. But, depending on a speaker's goals, a particular presentation may be primarily informative, more persuasive, or little more than entertaining.

When you determine your purpose, you must narrow your choices and decide specifically what you want to accomplish, what you wish your listeners to understand, or the attitudes and behavior you want the audience to change. The following suggestions can prove useful when framing your specific purpose statement. First, express your purpose statement as an infinitive phrase, not as a fragment. You might use a few words or fragments of a sentence to tell others what your subject will be, but when you begin working on your presentation you need to state it in the form of an infinitive phrase. This will clarify your purpose and your goal for you.

Not: My purpose is work clothes.

But: My purpose is to have you understand how to dress appropriately for your job.

Not: My purpose is union dues.

But: My purpose is to persuade you that union dues should be increased by ten percent this year.

Second, express your purpose as a statement, not a question. Questions may make good titles for presentations, but they are usually too vague to service as a working purpose statement. Moreover, questions don't show the direction the presentation is headed.

Not: Is buying IBM stock a good idea?

But: To persuade you to buy IBM stock today.

Not: Should you start your own childcare business?

But: To persuade you that you can establish a childcare business on your own.

Third, identify exactly what you wish to accomplish in the presentation. This requires your limiting the purpose statement and phrasing it with your listeners in mind. Less-accomplished speakers believe they, rather than the audience, are at the center of the speaking situation. When this happens, you lose sight of whether your desired goal is accomplished. But, limiting your purpose statement and relating it to listener concerns, you improve your chances of reaching and accomplishing your goal.

Not: To sell you this product.

But: To convince you to purchase the Panasonic KX-P1524 computer printer.

Not: To explain the telephone answering system.

But: To have you understand the operating advantages of our newly installed telephone answering system.

Determining your topic and narrowing, focusing, and adapting it to your purpose and audience are probably your most difficult tasks. Completing these steps successfully is essential to developing an effective presentation. Rarely will a presentation have the power and give the satisfaction you desire if you do these initial steps hastily or haphazardly.

Step Three: Analyze Your Audience

Audience analysis is essential because all oral presentations are transactions between a speaker and listeners. Your central concern as speaker is, therefore, twofold: your interest and their interest. Ralph Waldo Emerson said it well when he observed that the key to successful communication is to "translate a truth into language perfectly intelligible to the person to whom you speak."[17] Every topic must, then, be approached with equal concern for personal and audience needs and values. Both speaker and listener must be "alive" to the topic if the communication exchange is to be meaningful and reciprocal. Jo Sprague and Douglas Stuart describe the relationship between speaker and listener this way: "When you ask an audience to listen to your ideas, you are asking them to come part way into your experience. It is your obligation to go part way into theirs."[18]

There are a number of audience-related dimensions to be considered. The purpose of analyzing an audience is to help the speaker better understand the target listeners and, consequently, to design and deliver a message that will be understood and given fair consideration. The most crucial problems of choice facing the speaker arise from his or her estimation of the nature of the audience and the accommodations to be made. The speaker addresses a group and the purposes, positions, attitudes, and expectations of that group. So the speaker's knowledge of the audience reflects certain assumptions about those assembled and about the ways in which they will think about the substance of the discourse. Effective speakers often use an audience analysis that identifies the demographic features of the audience and estimates which of these factors are important to the situation. The following are some of the demographic factors you may choose to consider:

◆ *Age.* What is the average age of the audience? What is the range of ages? Does the audience include different age groups? Is age an important factor to members of this group?

Putting More Oomph in Your Oratory
By Dick Janssen

Robert Burns once wrote of the yearning to see ourselves as others see us. Today, thanks to the camcorder, the poet could see himself, hear himself—and then be critiqued. How would he like that? I think I know.

I found out, as many managers do, by taking a crash course in communicating. Much of the time, I felt like a butterfly under a magnifying glass. By the time I was released, though, I had confronted some dismaying habits and had a headful of pointers on how to handle any audience.

A number of image gurus run such programs for corporate clients. Among the largest firms are New York's Communispond (212-687-8084), Atlanta's Speakeasy (404-261-4029), and Chicago's Executive Technique (312-266-0001). Decker Communications, based in San Francisco (415-546-6100), taught my one-day senior executive course, which costs $2,500. Pricey—but the limit is six students; a two-day session for 15 costs less.

Our instructor, Bert Decker, displays all the empathy of a drill sergeant: "I've trained over 32,000 people, and there isn't anyone who comes here who really wants to be here," says Decker, a former documentary filmmaker. Yet, the motivation to rough it out is strong: managers spend 94% of their time communicating, "giving off cues about ourselves dozens of times a day."

I soon found out what sort of cues. After taking my turn standing up and telling the class about my job and family, I am whisked off to watch a video replay. There I am, in living color, looking at the floor and occasionally heavenward. Staring longingly at the (off-limits) shelter of the lectern. Clutching my prop, a ball-point pen, and using it to make feeble gestures. Rocking backward, with my voice a guarded monotone. And, sin of sins, I often stall with a meaningless "uh."

The tape ends. I am shaken and don't believe that I will be redeemed as a speaker in just one day. But my coach finds glimmers of hope. After the first minute, I had let a smile break through, and I had even said something mildly amusing. (Personal and audience-tailored anecdotes are in; jokes are out.) And, while I didn't use my hands expansively enough, I never put them in my pockets. It is time for one of Decker's upbeat generalizations: "We are all better than we think we are."

My peers, meanwhile, display flaws of their own. An advertising exec fails to leave room in her speech for the commas or periods that would let listeners keep up with her rapid-fire thoughts. A manufacturing honcho's delivery is so wooden that he might have been reading aloud from a physics text.

Soon, Decker tosses us some surprise ad-lib topics. Mine is "feet," and what counts here is not accuracy but free association and enthusiasm. ("They're vital to the shoe industry," I offer). Later, in pursuit of persuasion, we have to outline and deliver a speech on a real-life situation, such as urging a skeptical sales force to push low-end merchandise.

In between, we absorb Decker's mini lectures on principles. A speech, he proclaims, should convey an overall impression rather than just facts and figures: "You have to reach people emotionally, not mechanically, if you want to cause change." Our words are only a small part of the message we convey and are easily undercut by visual cues such as poor posture or darting eyes.

To avoid such a problem, he reminds us of things our mothers probably taught us, plus some finishing touches. Like not slouching. We learn to stand with our knees flexed, tilting slightly forward, a nuance of body language meant to serve us as well at a cocktail party as on the speaker's platform. Instead of averting our eyes from one amorphous glob of an audience, we learn to seek eye contact with an individual—for three to six seconds, max, that is. We find we do gain encouragement from this fleeting but intimate human contact. Then we move on to nurture rapport with another listener.

More videotapes show we are improving. And we are made privy to some of the subtler secrets of well-coached CEOs and pols. Never say: "That's a good question." (It reflects poorly on other questions.) Look away fast from a hostile questioner, so you don't get locked into a counter-productive debate. When you avoid making a direct reply, use the question as a bridge to a point you wish to make. To make the most of a crash course, follow up on your own later. All it takes is a videocamera or just a mirror and a sample cassette tape recorder. When will I start finding the time for this? Well, uh…

Source: Dick Janssen, "Putting More Oomph in Your Oratory," *Business Week* (June 4, 1990): 165. Copyright © 1990 by McGraw-Hill, Inc.

- ◆ *Size.* How many people will be listening to you? Is this group a part of a larger group?

- ◆ *Gender.* What is the distribution of men and women? Is the audience predominantly one sex? Do these men and women view this topic differently? Would certain statements be seen as offensive to parts of the audience?

- ◆ *Education.* What is the average educational level? What percentage of the audience has some college education? Have the listeners attended primarily one school or one type of school?

- ◆ *Religion.* What religions are represented in the audience? Is there a dominant religion? What is the strength of their beliefs? Is religion an important factor in this situation?

- ◆ *Culture.* What is the audience's racial and ethnic background? Is one race or culture dominant in the audience? In what ways might culture be affected by this topic? Will the audience see you as an outsider to their race or ethnicity? Would certain issues be seen as insensitive?

- ◆ *Occupation and Income.* What are the major occupations of the listeners? Is one occupation more dominant than others? What is the general status of the occupations of the audience? What is their income level? What is the range of incomes in the audience? Does occupation and/or income have a bearing on this topic?

- ◆ *Knowledge and Experience.* How much does the audience know about this topic? What don't they know? Are certain of the members likely to be experts on the subject? What biases or prejudices might they have about this topic? What does the audience know about me as the speaker? Will they be hostile, indifferent, or friendly toward me?

Much of the information needed to answer these questions will be unknown to you, so it's vital that you seek a number of different sources for help. First, you may be able to observe the group directly. Second, you might use your contact person. Whether giving a speech or a report, you'll usually be approached by another person who may know more about your audience than you do. Ask this person as many specific questions as necessary to make you feel comfortable. Third, you may be able to speak with a few members of the group before your presentation. This will permit some immediate information which might prompt adaptations to your presentation. Finally, even if you know nothing of your audience, don't despair—use your own intuition and experience. At these times, draw upon your own knowledge of communication, human behavior, and groups.

In a sense, the groups with which any person seeks affiliation become his or her reference groups; the individual "refers" to the positions, values, and attitudes of some group in choosing his or her own personal positions, values, and attitudes. In short, you need to be audience-centered in your approach to making presentations. Public communication, including oral reports, occurs primarily not as the product of the autonomous needs of individuals, but as the product of efforts to organize, sustain, and shape the lives of groups or social institutions.

Other than demographic information, there are three additional components involved in an audience analysis: (1) the listeners' interest level, (2) their relationship to the speaker, and (3) their measure of identification with the speaker.

The interest level may range from concerned, to moderately interested, to apathetic, to hostile. What determines the interest "set" of an individual? What is it that makes one attend to specific portions of his or her surroundings and ignore others? Research in this area suggests that two factors are especially important: self-interest and familiarity. Anything that affects us vitally is interesting to us. Matters associated with the satisfaction of our deep physiological needs or with fundamental psychological concerns command attention. The power of the familiar as a factor probably results from its giving specific meaning to the situation that confronts us. There is, of course, a point where this factor ceases to function as a means of gaining and holding interest. When situations have become completely familiar and offer no further challenge, we choose to be disinterested in them. Thus, the message must adapt to that level of interest present in the audience. For example, consider Eliot Asinof's vivid description of Dick Gregory's 1968 M.I.T. address:

The scene is the Massachusetts Institute of Technology—the spacious Kresge Auditorium packed with students waiting for the guest lecturer. He is not a leading world scientist or engineer, nor is his subject matter of any technological concern. He is Dick Gregory, the ubiquitous Negro comedian, author, actor, Presidential candidate (without a party) and crusader for human rights who—to emphasize his commitment—has virtually given up comfortable nightclub engagements to tour college campuses.

Since Gregory has been tied up in traffic driving down from Portsmouth, New Hampshire, where he lectured earlier in the day, the audience grows good-humorously restless, tossing paper airplanes with a technical artistry befitting M.I.T. In time, there is a rhythmic clapping and foot stamping in the classic undergraduate appeal for action.

"What brings you here?" I ask a few students seated around me. "Well, I hear he's very funny," replies a very serious-looking boy with horn-rimmed glasses. There are more young men wearing glasses than not. A small percentage are long-haired, and it is difficult to find one without a necktie and a jacket. It is almost impossible to find a Negro.

Finally, an hour late, Gregory strides on stage to an extremely warm greeting. He is wearing blue coveralls—with uncut hair and a six-week-old beard—and he is far leaner than I remember him, especially around the face, after his recent 40-day fast. He stands there for a long moment in the anticipatory silence, looking them over. Finally, he walks to the front of the huge stage and takes an even closer look. "Why, you're normal. You're just a bunch of cats like anywhere else.... Man, it's M.I.T. and I expected robots!"

They roar with laughter and he is off and running.[19]

Here, Gregory immediately secures and holds the interest of his audience by gaining their attention, addressing their expectations, and adapting to the situation.

The relationship between you, the speaker, and the immediate audience may be that of (a) superior to subordinate, the reverse of that, or as an equal; (b) politically or socially obligated; or (c) obligation free. Relationships within a structure influence how a message will be received. The speaker must candidly assess whether he or she is a member of the group which that audience represents, is in the decision-making circle, on the fringes or, possibly in a competing group. Then, the speaker must determine how he or she would like to be thought of by that audience, and the construction of the message, whether directly or subtly, ought to provide answers to the relationship desired by the speaker.

Finally, an audience analysis should measure the degree of identification existing between the speaker and the audience. Identification is vital to achieving effectiveness. Kenneth Burke succinctly describes the proximity between identification, persuasion, and communication: "As for the relation between 'identification' and 'persuasion' we might well keep in mind that a speaker persuades an audience by the use of stylistic identifications.... So, there is no chance of your keeping apart the meanings of persuasion, identification, and communication."[20] In short, regardless of form, public communication is a matter of understanding another's reasoning; comprehending another's beliefs, attitudes, and values; and sympathizing with another's verbal and nonverbal codes. Identification is a process of becoming more alike. As Burke puts it, "You persuade a man only insofar as you can talk his language by speech, gestures, tonality, order, image, attitude, idea, *identifying* your ways with his."[21] In practical terms, then, you are attempting to discover commonalties.

Step Four: Research Your Topic

It is not enough to believe something is the case. When delivering a speech or report, you must be fortified with information. For certain presentations, the information you'll need is obvious. If you're informing the members of your firm's board of directors about last month's banking activity, your information will include the receipts and disbursements from that month. If you're demonstrating a new piece of equipment recently purchased by your office, your information will be the operating instructions for the machinery. Most of your presentations, however, will require you to research your topic, and the information available for most topics can seem overwhelming. This year, more than 50,000 books will be published in the U.S.[22] Add to this the millions of pages of information printed in newspapers, magazines, and other periodicals; volumes of public and private agencies' reports, hearings, and pamphlets; and hours of news and opinions broadcast via television and radio.[23] It is clear that a wealth of information exists for your presentations. Not all the information you acquire will appear in the text of your speech or report, but you'll need it all to select the materials you'll include. Furthermore, you'll need extra information to respond successfully to questions and challenges arising as a result of your presentation.

When gathering information, you're responsible for determining the accuracy of the material, the plausibility of stated or implied conclusions, and the expertise of the author. You are not a mindless collector of other people's verbiage, but must function as a thoughtful, inquisitive, critical investigator. Not everything in print is true, reasonable, or acceptable, and it's your task to make discriminating and knowledgeable choices. You must seek and gather and think. You can help yourself immensely in this critical process by making a habit of cross-checking all significant information. Newspapers have been mistaken, books have contained erroneous material, and people have lied. Don't be caught in this web of potential falsehood. Double- and cross-check.

Look for the information you need in personal experiences, interviews, general references, and specific references. Personal experiences and knowledge acquired through the years offer good starting points for your research, but don't generalize too broadly from your personal experiences. Your personal information needs support from other information to give it a broader perspective.

As a rule of thumb, most presentations should use independent primary references. Independent references are not connected with each other. For example, three books written by the same author are not independent, nor are a series of pamphlets published by the same organization. Some of your references may be interrelated or interdependent, but at least three should be independent. Consult the complete texts of pertinent material, avoiding abridgments.

General references such as dictionaries and encyclopedias, and specific references such as books, newspapers, television and radio broadcasts, records, magazines, and scholarly journals are excellent information sources. Also, most of the research for your business presentations will be provided by the company for which you work. Among the types of materials you are seeking are quotations or expert testimony, statistics, examples, comparisons, analogies, and interesting descriptive stories.

Quotations. Quotations are the word-for-word or the paraphrased use of an expert's statement on your topic. They are used to support an assertion you've made in your presentation. You need to indicate the source of the quotation in your speech or report to enhance the credibility of the evidence, and you need to be sure that the source is unbiased. Additionally, you need to be sure that the quotation applies directly to your assertion, is appropriate to the situation and to the audience, and is neither too long nor too short. When using expert testimony:

1. Be sure that testimony comes from a reasonable authority in the subject area of the presentation. Verify the competency of the source.

2. Be sure that the testimony is reflective of current opinions; date the testimony.

3. Be sure the testimony is used in the proper and intended context.

4. Keep quotations brief.

5. Identify for the audience both the credibility of the source of testimony and the place that the quotation was located.

Statistics. Statistics are data collected in the form of numbers and are especially useful in business presentations because so much of business is concerned with numbers. Statistics, essentially, are used to give your ideas numerical precision. They're especially powerful in bringing your topic alive and dramatizing it. Your statistics need to be current, understandable, representative of what they claim to measure, and from a credible source. When using statistics, you should answer the following questions:

1. Are the statistics dependable?

2. Are the statistics current?

3. Are the statistics valid?

4. Can the statistics be simplified to round numbers?

5. Are statistics so copious that the audience will be overwhelmed and lose interest?

Examples. Examples are single instances that develop a general statement, and they can be very persuasive. In fact, research has shown that vivid examples have more impact on the beliefs and actions of the audience than any other kind of supporting material.[24] Examples can be about real or hypothetical circumstances and can be brief, such as a single specific instance, or extended, such as illustrations, narratives, or anecdotes.

Comparisons. Comparisons relate the known to the unknown by fusing already familiar material with unfamiliar material. Accepted ideas are integrated with new concepts, permitting greater identification with the audience, so ideas take on greater clarity and more acceptable dimensions when related to those already understood.

Analogies. Analogies present parallel situations for purposes of illustration and clarification. However, the parallel is indirect or implied and the instances are only figuratively similar. For example, our earlier comparison of communication to the lifeblood of a human organism was an analogy. Analogies are useful as a means of illustration and can make a presentation memorable.

Stories. Stories are very detailed examples and can be used to expand an idea you've made in the presentation. This form of research is especially powerful because it can build suspense and keep the attention of the audience focused on the speaker. For this reason, stories are especially valuable in the introduction and the conclusion. They must be relevant to the point you're making, neither too long nor too short, and appropriate to the situation and the audience.

Research of the materials discussed isn't done randomly. You need to have a plan. The following research strategy will optimize your efforts: First, fit your research to the time allotted. If you have considerable time to peruse materials, you can go to a variety of sources and use a number of different sources for the speech or report. But when time is at a premium, you will be limited to using a few sources and less materials. Second, approach the topic so that you progress from the general to the specific. You need to start from the largest data base possible—research summaries or state-of-the-art books and articles that synthesize current thought on the subject—then move to more specific sources of information. Third, develop important questions to be answered from your initial analysis. If you're preparing a speech to persuade the audience to join the teacher's union, the following questions will probably surface from your initial research efforts: What are the benefits of unionization? What are the disadvantages of joining a union? How many school districts are currently unionized? Why hasn't this district joined the union in the past? How much does it cost to join the union? Once these questions are answered, your information gathering can address other more specific questions. Throughout the process, remember your responsibility to interpret the information you collect.

Research is at the heart of the speech preparation process and should be undertaken with care and diligence. Effective research will provide proof for your arguments, vividness for your speaking, and credibility for you in the eyes of the audience.

Step Five: Organize Your Presentation

Plato observed centuries ago, in the *Phaedrus*, that "every discourse ought to be a living creature, having a body of its own and a head and feet; there should be a middle, beginning, and end adapted to one another and to the whole."[25] Every presentation must be well organized if it is to be effective. All of us seem to realize intuitively that organized essays, articles, and oral presentations are more understandable than those that are not organized. Moreover, a number of research studies verify that a presentation is more effective when it is well structured. One study tested the comprehension of two audiences hearing the same message; as you might expect, the group hearing the organized presentation scored higher on the post-comprehension test.[26] Other studies have also indicated that effectively organized messages help listeners learn and retain material during informative presentations.[27] Finally, a clear and specific method of organization increases the speaker's confidence and the ability to fluently deliver the message.[28]

There is no set formula for the meaningful arrangement of one's presentation, but you may profitably think of organization in terms of the following sample diagram:

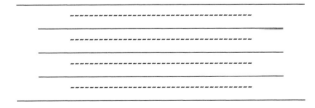

The longer first line represents the central idea. If the presentation has unity, it should have a single main theme, thesis, controlling purpose, or thrust (the first long line). Then this central idea should be based systematically on appropriate main headings, here represented by the three shorter, solid lines. The main headings are further developed by the use of supporting materials or information gathered during research. Lastly, the presentation provides a summary of ideas, stimulates action, and challenges the audience, as represented by the final long line. The short, broken lines in the diagram represent transitions from one part to another. If you think of your speech or oral report as a series of linked ideas, some more important than others, you should begin to understand the principle of subordination that underlies the theory of speech organization. The specific purpose or thesis states the goal of the presentation; the main points divide the specific purpose into its key parts; and the rest of the body of the presentation develops, explains, or proves the main points. The following guidelines should be useful as you organize the body of your presentation.

The central idea should describe your thesis and be phrased as a full, declarative sentence. The thesis statement, or central idea, encapsulates what the presentation is about and expands and clarifies the specific purpose statement. In an informative presentation, the central idea is a statement of what you want the audience to learn; in a persuasive presentation, it is a statement of what you want the audience to believe or how you want them to act. It should be limited to one clear idea and be phrased in a single, declarative, full sentence. Phrasing it as a question or a sentence fragment doesn't provide the precision necessary for this important aspect of the presentation.

The body of your presentation should contain no more than five main points. As you begin to phrase prospective main points, you may find your list growing to five, seven, or even ten. If you remember, however, that every main point must be developed in some detail and that your goal is to help the audience retain the subject matter of each main point, you will see the impracticality of more than five main points. You should be able to organize your presentation around a few main points that develop the thesis. Moreover, these main points need to be mutually exclusive, i.e., the ideas in your main points must be inherently different. Thus, having more than five main ideas usually is a sign that your purpose needs to be limited, or that like ideas need to be grouped under a single heading.

Main points should correspond exactly to your thesis statement, being phrased as complete sentences using a parallel style. As a rule, main points are complete sentences that best develop the specific purpose. Your analysis of the topic will allow you to use the thesis statement as the standard against which to measure the main points. Vague, meaningless main points will have the same effect on the development of your presentation as a vague purpose. Using parallel wording when phrasing your main points will further help you and the audience to recall the main points. Consider the following thesis statement and main points:

Thesis: Changing our company's hiring policy to assure more diversity will increase the quality of our workforce.

    I. Our present hiring practice doesn't consider diversity when seeking prospective candidates.

    II. The company is very homogeneous, with many employees having similar skills and experimental backgrounds.

    III. We can hire a more diverse workforce this year, given the current turnover in positions.

Certainly the main points presented are important because they suggest a possible violation of EEO guidelines and a failure to have an operative Affirmative Action program. However, they do not address the issue of "diversity and a quality workforce." Without this relationship, the thesis statement is wanting. More appropriate main points supporting the thesis and conforming to a parallel style would be:

Thesis: Changing our company's hiring policy to assure more diversity will increase the quality of our workforce.

    I. A diverse workforce will encourage a multiplicity of perspectives, given company issues.

    II. A diverse workforce will enlarge our current skill-base.

    III. A diverse workforce will enhance our customer service and relationship with the community.

Here, the main points directly support the thesis and the parallel wording improves audience retention. Your main points anchor the structure of the presentation and should be carefully selected, phrased, and arranged.

Logically arrange your main points in an order appropriate to your subject and stated purpose or thesis. Effective speakers have found that their ideas blend together better, will be more easily phrased, and will be more easily understood if they follow one of several common presentational patterns: chronological, spatial, cause-and-effect, problem-solution, pro-con, or topical. The particular pattern that is best for your presentation depends on your purpose and the effect you want to achieve. What is important is that the material be organized.

Chronological Pattern. This pattern follows a time sequence where information is arranged from a beginning point to an ending point. Presentations using the chronological pattern present events in the order in which they occur. If the focus of the presentation is "how" or "when," this type of pattern can be effective. For example, a report on how to prepare a financial statement according to the accounting cycle might be arranged this way:

    I. The first step in preparing a financial statement is to journalize the entries.

    II. The second step is to post the entries.

III. The third step is to prepare a trial balance.

IV. The fourth step is to prepare the adjustments.

V. The fifth step in preparing the statement is to prepare the adjusted trial balance.

Or, you might present the history of your corporation using a chronological order:

I. The Abbott Corporation began in the 1970s as a small, family-owned business.

II. It grew steadily in the 1980s into a medium-sized company.

III. It emerged in the 1990s as a large, international corporation.

Spatial Pattern. This pattern organizes ideas according to physical properties, location, or geographical relationships. Space and direction become your ordering principles—from left to right, east to west, top to bottom, or inside to outside. This pattern is often appropriate with problems focusing on area. A presentation that explains a new marketing strategy using flyers for a pizza company might use the following spatial pattern:

I. The first area where the flyers will be distributed is in zip codes 32570–32579.

II. The second area is in zip codes 32580–32589.

III. The third area is in zip codes 32590–32599.

Cause-and-Effect Pattern. This pattern is used to show events that are causally related. Causal analysis determines whether one factor caused another factor to occur—an effect. The key word is "caused." A cause-and-effect arrangement tries to show that an incident or series of incidents contributed to or triggered a related event or series of events. Determining such relationships is particularly difficult because of the complex nature of human affairs. A chronological relationship does not necessarily equal a causal relationship. One event following another may as easily be chance as cause. Although two factors often appear together with regularity, this is not evidence that one causes the other. For example, when it rains the sidewalks are wet, but wet sidewalks do not necessarily mean it rained. Moreover, confusion can also arise from a misunderstanding of *necessary* and *sufficient* conditions. The presence of oxygen is a necessary condition for fire to burn, but fire does not occur whenever there is oxygen; the presence of oxygen alone is not sufficient to cause fire. The cause-and-effect pattern can be very effective, but you must be careful not to confuse relationship and correlation with causation. In an informative report to the company about recent layoffs, the CEO might arrange the issues as follows:

I. The layoffs were caused by recessionary pressures and a large reduction in orders from our major buyers.

II. The layoffs have resulted in a 10 percent reduction in the company workforce.

Problem-Solution Pattern. The problem solution pattern is often used in persuasive presentations and is divided into two main points. The first describes the existence and seriousness of a problem; the second develops an acceptable and workable solution to that problem. Such an arrangement should (a) define relevant terms, (b) analyze the problem historically and in terms of the status quo, and (c) offer a desirable solution that the audience is willing to adopt. In explaining the new company drug-testing policy, the director of human resources might organize the main points of the presentation like this:

I. The number of company employees who use drugs that impair their work has increased to an intolerable level.

II. Drug testing will better guarantee that company employees remain drug-free.

Pro-Con Pattern. This pattern discusses the positive side of the situation and then the negative side of the situation, or presents your arguments and your opponents' arguments. The pro-con approach can be useful when the audience is well informed on the issue(s) and familiar with opposing arguments, or when a speaker for the opposition precedes or follows you. It may also be used when, as a result of your research, a preferred solution does not naturally emerge and you wish to leave the selection of a preferable alternative up to the audience. The vice president of safety for a railroad line who is concerned about the number of older freight engines that may be unsafe could organize a presentation to colleagues as follows:

I. The older freight engines that pose safety hazards should be retired.

II. The older freight engines that pose safety hazards should be overhauled and retained.

Topical Pattern. This is the most common pattern and consists of selecting a limited number of equally important issues related to the stated purpose. The topical arrangement deals with types, forms, qualities, or aspects of the selected subject and collectively presents a particular perspective. It can be useful to present familiar ideas first and then progress to the unfamiliar, or to present the easiest material first and then move on to the more-difficult material. The topical pattern is well suited to both informative and persuasive communications. A presentation intended to persuade an audience that company benefits need to be increased might argue from the following topical pattern:

I. The company's medical benefits have a very high deductible payment.

II. The company has no dental policy benefit.

III. The company has no tuition payment policy for higher education.

Taken collectively, your main points outline the structure of your presentation. Whether your audience understands, believes, or appreciates what you have to say will depend on your development of these main points. They cannot stand alone; you have to support them with examples, illustrations, statistics, comparisons, analogies, testimony, and the use of visual aids.

Use transitions between major parts of your presentation. Transitions are words or phrases that form a bridge from one section of your presentation to the next. These connectives are similar to ligaments and tendons in the human body. Without connectives, a presentation is disjointed and uncoordinated. When building transitions between thoughts consider the following words and their use.

These expressions indicate that what follows is supplementary to what precedes. They link matters of like kind and grammatical form:

also	*and*	*moreover*	*furthermore*
likewise	*again*	*in addition*	

These expressions indicate that what follows is the result of what precedes:

therefore	*and so*	*so*
consequently	*subsequently*	*as a result*

These words indicate a change in direction. They suggest conflict and sometimes imply concession:

but	*however*	*yet*	*on the other hand*
still	*nevertheless*	*notwithstanding*	*nonetheless*

These words indicate concession:

although	*even though*	*though*

These words indicate a reason for a subsequent sentence:

because	*for*

These words show cause or relationship in time:

then	*since*	*as*

These words restrict or enlarge:

so that	*in order that*	*for this reason*	*of course*
in other words	*in fact*	*for example*	

Transitions are usually necessary between the introduction and the first main point, between main points, and between the last main point and the conclusion. They summarize one idea and preview the next.

An ordered presentation has an introduction, a body, and a conclusion. The introduction gains our attention; the body develops major ideas that support the stated purpose; and the conclusion provides a summary and a forceful, positive close. This organizational pattern is much like the saying you've probably heard, "Tell them what you're going to tell them. Tell them. Tell them what you told them." Having discussed the body of the presentation, you're ready to prepare the introduction and conclusion.

Step Six: Plan Your Introduction and Conclusion

On the evening of October 9, 1986, a conductor stepped to the podium at Her Majesty's Theatre in London, tapped his baton, raised his arms, and signaled the orchestra to play. Moments later the audience heard the dramatic opening chords of "The Phantom of the Opera." Several hours later the theatre rang with applause while the curtain descended and the orchestra played Andrew Lloyd Weber's dramatic finale. Like most musical stage plays, *Phantom of the Opera* begins with an overture—an orchestral introduction that captures the audience's attention and gives them a preview of the music they are going to hear—and closes with a musical climax. Similarly, you must set the stage, introduce the theme, focus the audience's attention, tap their interests, and then provide a powerful close. Just as musicals need an effective beginning and ending, your presentations need a solid introduction and conclusion. Without them, the body of your speech or report will be incomplete, and you won't effectively achieve your purpose.

Introduction. This portion should (a) capture the attention of your audience, (b) provide a clearly stated and fully qualified statement of purpose, (c) establish your credibility, and (d) forecast the focus of your presentation. The introduction should cause your audience to feel that they have a reason for listening to your speech or report. These first two minutes of your presentation are the most crucial for it is now that the audience will decide either to sit up and listen or drift off into their own thoughts.

The introduction is the time to figuratively grab the audience and make them want to listen to you. Remember that some members of your audience may be ambivalent, believing they already know what you have to say or feeling that they can't afford the time to listen to you. If you don't capture their attention at the outset, you'll probably lose them for the entire speech or report. By motivating them to listen during the first minute or so, you can be reasonably certain that they are psychologically prepared to listen to the heart of the presentation. How you go about gaining audience attention and focusing that attention on your specific purpose can vary. Commonly used techniques include: the rhetorical question; the startling statement; the quotation; the anecdote, narrative, or illustration; and humor.

The *rhetorical question* plants an idea for consideration and immediately involves the thinking processes of the audience. Next you pause and then proceed to answer this question, or series of questions, in the body of the presentation. Rhetorical questions do not seek an outward verbal or behavioral response from the audience, but rather are meant to stimulate thought and pique curiosity. Questions should be pertinent to the topic and meaningful to the audience.

The *startling statement* is a headline technique that serves the same function in a presentation as large print does in a newspaper. You present certain bold statements or startling statistics intended to arouse attention and interests. Shocking, unusual, or dramatic statements should be evaluated for their potential effectiveness, their reflection of good taste, and their indication of good sense. Avoid opening statements that are trite, boring, or distracting.

A *quotation* can provide a challenging thought and prepare the audience for the presentation to follow. It can enhance your personal credibility by association, so take care to choose a quotation from a source the audience will respect and trust.

The *anecdote, narrative,* or *illustration* can provide detail and personalize your subject for the audience. These devices may focus on a personal experience or they may recall an example or event read or remembered. They may be true or hypothetical, literary or historical. Because we all like to hear stories, they can vividly set a tone to your remarks and draw the audience into your presentation.

Humor must be selectively and carefully used. There is always the risk that using humor in the introduction may detract from the seriousness of your subject. And there is probably no worse way to begin a presentation than by telling a joke that flops; the pitfall is being corny or trite. When tastefully chosen and told well, a funny story that is relevant to the topic and the occasion is extremely effective.

These and other techniques may be used to gain the attention of your audience. In selecting an attention-getting strategy, keep in mind the need for appropriateness. Your approach should be in harmony with the nature and tone of the presentation, with your talents and personality, and with the tastes and expectations of the audience. Rarely is your only choice the dull and unimaginative opening clichés, "Today I am going to talk about ..." or "I am pleased to be here to talk about...."

In these first several moments you reveal your purpose and state your central thesis. This may seem elementary, but many speakers are unclear in the beginning, leaving the audience no defined path to follow the subsequent development of ideas. So the rambler should beware, heeding the expectations and demands of the audience.

It is also in the introduction that your audience will decide if they want to listen to you, if they like you, and if they find you credible. Therefore, at this point you must establish why you, in particular, are in a position to address this topic. What knowledge, skills, and experiences do you bring to the situation? How honest and trustworthy are your opinions, attitudes, and beliefs? You must, however, use subtlety and diplomacy in establishing your credibility—the line between seeming to brag and merely stating your qualification is narrow. Indicate your interest, express concern, display sensitivity, and gently tell your audience who you are. Abbreviate this if you are already familiar to your audience.

Finally, you want to forecast your main points for the audience. This preview will help your listeners follow your subsequent progression of ideas. A presentation is an immediate event and your audience is *listening* to you, not reading your speech or report; so if they lose your train of thought at some point, they can't go back and reread the material. Previewing the main points lets your listeners better understand your approach to the topic and your point of view.

Having noted what you should do in an introduction, let's briefly examine some introductory don'ts. *Don't apologize or discredit yourself.* Some speakers begin their presentations by saying: "I'm really nervous today, ..." or "I'm not very good at public speaking, but ... ," or "I don't know much about ... so bear with me as I speak...." They believe that a brief apology will endear them to the audience, but the opposite is true. Listeners generally reject speakers who begin with an apology or who discredit themselves. *Don't make the introduction too long.* The introduction should represent only 10 to 15 percent of the total presentation. Longer introductions will probably prompt listeners to ask, "When are you going to get to the point?" *Don't use a false start.* Some speakers begin with a false start by saying, "Before I begin, I'd like to say. . . ." Such unnecessary beginnings only detract from a more effective introduction.

The introduction is not going to make your speech or report an instant success, but an effective introduction will get an audience to look at you and listen to you. That's about as much as you can ask of an audience during the first few minutes of a presentation.

Conclusion. The conclusion of the speech or report is especially important. A presentation must have feet—it must have a conclusion. Speakers often mistakenly believe their presentation is over when they complete the body of the speech or report. As a result, they fail to close effectively, choosing instead to mumble, "That's all I have" or "Thank you," or simply walking from the lectern to their seat. The conclusion should succinctly bring your remarks to a close and leave a forceful, positive image with the listeners.

One of the most common ways of concluding a presentation is to summarize the main ideas you have chosen to communicate. In summarizing, you may reiterate the main points in a straightforward, almost literal manner, or you might restate them in a more concise fashion. Your summary may also include a quotation, illustrative anecdote, or narrative to make for a more memorable closing. Poems, lyrics, or striking memorable slogans can also be effective if carefully chosen and well integrated. The important issue is that the audience should hear one last time what you want them to remember.

The challenge is a call for action. You may challenge the audience to act, to believe, to meet a need, to demonstrate concern, or even to live a different kind of life. The challenge may be specific or general; it may be a direct plea for some type of action or a rhetorical question raised for the audience to answer in their lives. The anticipated result is an acceptance of the challenge issued—action.

The conclusion is also an excellent opportunity for you to leave a positive, strong, and lasting impression. End your presentation just as you started it—with strength and confidence. A too-short conclusion will deny you the chance to fulfill the important functions of the conclusion and will leave a weak impression with the audience. The way you conclude should leave your listeners in a particular frame of mind.

There is much you can do to make the conclusion effective, but there are also a number of pitfalls you should avoid. *Don't use concluding phrases in other parts of the presentation.* Phrases such as "in conclusion" or "to summarize" announce your intentions to close. You can confuse listeners when you use these phrases before your wrap-up and force them to reorient themselves to your ongoing presentation. *Don't end with an apology.* Concluding statements such as, "Well, I guess I've rambled on long enough," or "I hope I haven't bored you today," will only decrease your credibility and undo what you have accomplished in the presentation. *Don't introduce a new issue.* The conclusion is not the place to introduce new ideas into your speech or report. You may present new evidence and extensions of arguments made earlier, but completely new and different ideas should be avoided. Carolyn Planck, president of Communication for Professionals, observes: "Few things are as annoying as the speaker who behaves like a car with a faulty idle ... when the key is turned off, the engine continues to sputter, cough, and go on and on and on. When the speaker has summarized and created the proper mood, he/she should give a final, concluding statement and STOP."[29]

Conclusions, like introductions, cannot do much for a poor presentation, but they can heighten the effect of a good presentation. They tie the presentation together into a compact, concise package by summarizing the main points and providing direction, action, or visualization.

Step Seven: Select Your Visual Aids

We live in a society that places a premium on the visual. Toddlers are viewing computer screens in their preschools, adolescents are playing video games in arcades, adults are watching large-screen televisions in their living rooms, and renting videos has become commonplace. We see huge billboards with moving parts and blinking lights on our highways, and read books, magazines, and newspapers with visual images that inform us about news events and persuade us to buy new products. Our information age exists within the confines of an electronic age that is integrally related to visual imagery. Consequently, visual support is a critical component of most management presentations.

The last half of the 1980s witnessed major changes in audience expectations for quality visual support. Before desktop publishing, overheads were often difficult to read and time-consuming to create. Charts were handmade and text visuals were usually typed or carefully hand-printed. Thirty-five-millimeter slides were used occasionally at great expense, as were videotapes. Audiences understood these constraints and accepted the results. But now anyone with a personal computer can quickly create graphics or produce handouts, and inexpensive portable camcorders permit easy videotaping. Moreover, programmed and interactive computer presentations are playing an increasingly frequent role in conference room activity. Visual aids have become an expected part of most informative and persuasive speaking and, if used well, can powerfully increase the effectiveness of a presentation.

The purpose of any visual is to help the audience understand and believe you in the shortest possible time. Visuals should add value to the presentation, and to do this, they must be easy to see or read and easy to understand. Furthermore and, most importantly, their content must support your words. If an aid does not present the idea more clearly than it can be presented without the aid, or if it does not add a dimension of credibility or interest, then it becomes a distraction that will inhibit the interaction between speaker and audience. Speakers often want to use visual aids just because everyone else uses them. But when considering using visuals, you should ask yourself: "Do I *need* to use visual aids in this presentation?" If the answer is "yes" and you choose them carefully, they can enhance your presentation in a number of ways.

Visuals Create Interest. Visual aids can be helpful in gaining and maintaining the attention of your listeners. Words alone may seize attention and develop interest, but visuals can enhance your words significantly. An engineer speaking on the future of energy can increase interest by displaying a piece of oil shale or showing a model of a high-tech wind generator. A speaker on the environment could show samples of water or particles removed from the air. A corporate executive emphasizing the need for a crisis management plan might show a videoclip of the destruction left in the wake of Hurricane Andrew. The more abstract the ideas, the more a concrete demonstration, object, picture, or recording can hold acceptable levels of attention. Visuals can grab the audience's attention and create an interest in the presentation.

Visuals Aid Understanding. Listeners understand better if they both hear your words and see visual aids that reinforce your message. Some topics, especially those involving physical objects or processes, simply cannot be well explained with the oral message alone. William Seiler reports that even simple drawings enhance recall, and charts and photographs help listeners process and retain data.[30] Because we can only remember a limited number of thoughts and impressions, we remember only those things important to us, deeming the rest trivia and disregarding it. We tend to remember (a) what we pay close attention to, (b) what we clearly understand, and (c) what we vividly experience. Visual aids help listeners remember more of your speech and remember it for a longer period of time.[31] If receivers can watch a demonstration, see pictures, hear a tape recording, view a film, feel an object, or even do an activity along with the speaker, they will comprehend more and retain the message longer.

Visuals Boost Personal Impact. Visual aids also enhance your credibility and increase your personal impact. They add dynamism and sizzle to your presentation, and that transfers to you personally. There is a carryover effect to you as a speaker from visuals that are vibrant, exciting, and even artistic. So the effective use of visual materials often promotes a favorable audience response. They appreciate the noticeable time and attention given to careful preparation and the obvious concern for increased understanding. Listeners perceive you to be earnest, confident, and speaking with knowledge.

Speakers sometimes avoid using visual aids in presentations because they require more time, energy, and risk to develop and use. But they can be a crucial component of the public-speaking process, and they are consistent with our increasingly visual culture and with the norms or expectations of audiences in the business and professional setting.

Once you have decided that your presentation will be enhanced by visual support, you have two decisions to make: (1) the form of the visual, and (2) the substance of the visual. Visual aids may assume various forms, shapes, and sizes with the specific choice being determined by the nature of the presentation, the audience, and the occasion. Each form serves a particular purpose and has specific design guidelines that apply equally to any medium. Here we will examine those visuals common to informative and persuasive presentations—personal demonstration; physical objects; models; text visuals; conceptual visuals; tables, charts, or graphs; pictures or diagrams; maps; audio/videotapes; and on-screen computer displays.

Personal Demonstration. When speakers personally exhibit a particular behavior, like swinging a tennis racket, performing first aid techniques, or operating a machine, they become the visual support as well as the primary information source. The advantages are increased animation, adaptability, and realism. You can move around to appropriate positions and postures, change your behavior to meet unexpected situations, and actually show how a particular activity should be performed. Certain delivery problems to consider are the difficulty in using notes during the demonstration and the physical effort required. However, more critical is the danger of failing, or performing awkwardly and with embarrassment, distracting the audience and damaging your credibility.

The Role of Visual Aids in Presentations
By John J. Makay

In an attempt to discover whether visual support materials give presenters a persuasive edge, Douglas R. Vogal, Gary W. Dickson, and John A. Lehman, researchers at the Management Information Systems Research Center at the University of Minnesota and the 3M Corporation conducted the following study:

They gathered nine groups of thirty-five undergraduate business students each. The groups were shown a ten-minute speech to influence the audience to sign up for a series of time-management seminars. (The seminars involved two three-hour sessions at a cost of $15.) To make sure the quality of the speaker was consistent, each group watched the same presentation on videotape. The difference in the presentations was the use of visual support. While one group watched the presentation with no visual support, the other eight groups watched videotapes enhanced by some form of high quality visuals. (One of the researchers manually displayed the visual material for these presentations.) The variables in visual support treatments included color vs. black-and-white, plain text vs. text enhanced with "clip art" and graphs, and 35-mm slides vs. overhead transparencies.

At the conclusion of each videotape researchers surveyed the subjects to learn their degree of interest in the time-management seminars (a questionnaire had been administered before the videotapes to determine initial attitudes) and to assess their comprehension of the videotape. Ten days later, a final questionnaire was administered to test how much of the videotaped information the students retained.

According to the researchers, compared to their pre-speech attitudes, the groups who had seen a speech supported by visuals were willing to spend 43% more time and 26% more money on the seminars than those who had seen the presentation without visual support. In addition, the various components of persuasion were improved by the presence of visual support. Action (the commitment to sign up for the course) improved by 43%; positive comprehension by 7.5%; and agreement with the presenter's position by 5.5%. When the speeches were delivered with visual support, the audience perceived the presenter as more concise, clearer, making better use of supporting data, more professional, more persuasive, and more interesting.

Specific characteristics of the visuals also influenced the persuasive force of the presentation. Color overhead transparencies had the greatest positive impact on action. In addition, comprehension and retention improved with color vs. black-and-white visual support. The researchers also found that 35-mm slides increased the audience's perception of speaker professionalism.

These findings were in response to an "average" or "typical" speaker. To determine the impact of visual support on the persuasive ability of a superior speaker, the researchers videotaped a second speaker with better skills. Both speakers read identical remarks. The researchers found that "typical" speakers who integrated visuals into their speeches were as effective as "better" speakers who use no visuals. They also found that the better presenters were most persuasive when they used high quality—machine produced rather than hand-drawn—visual support. Audiences were less willing to commit their time or money to the seminar when the "better" speakers used inferior visual material.

These problems can be solved by careful preparation and practice.

Physical Objects. Audiences appreciate seeing appropriate physical objects that have the advantages of realism and exactness. There is obvious value in using physical objects, when the subject of your presentation is the real-life experience gained by the listeners. The sales representative for a carpet manufacturer can be much more effective if samples are shown to potential buyers, or a personnel supervisor can more effectively explain how to complete a medical form if employees can see a form at the same time. Objects are sometimes too big or too small to be practical for a particular speaking environment. If it is too large to take into the room (such as an airplane) or too small to be easily seen (such as a computer chip), use a reproduction such as a model airplane or an enlarged replica of the computer chip. Physical objects are particularly useful when your purpose is to develop the audience's skills in such activities as operating equipment or creating an arts-and-crafts project.

Models. Models can be replicas of the real thing or theoretical representations of a process and its relational components. Physicians often use plastic models of body parts that can be further disassembled to show the inner workings when describing particular procedures for patients. Genetic engineers have created theoretical molecular models, and communication scholars have designed various models of the communication process. Models are useful for instructional purposes and can help listeners organize and relate information. Moreover, theoretical models can serve to stimulate further research.

Text Visuals. Text visuals contain only words or phrases and serve to preview or summarize information. They can keep important information in front of the audience and help them follow the presentation. It's especially important that text visuals convey a readily understandable message and be simple in content and in design. You should use action or message phrases rather than topic words or complete sentences, and keep lists parallel and in the order you intend to follow. It can also be helpful to highlight the most important message on the visual. Your goal is to have an easy-to-read, esthetically pleasing visual.

Conceptual Visuals. Conceptual visuals are clip art or images to make a point by analogy or to show the relationship of ideas. Boxes, arrows, pyramids, or pictures are often used to convey a message. They clarify a point by putting it in a nonbusiness context that has meaning to the audience. It is critical that the analogies or pictured relationships show what you mean to show and are meaningful to your audience. Although relatively new, conceptual visuals permit a latitude of creativity that can capture and maintain the interest of your audience.

Tables, Charts, or Graphs. Tables, charts, or graphic representations of data show statistical or conceptual relationships among variables. They are the visuals most often used in business presentations. Computer software programs offer you a broad range of variations and combinations of chart forms, so it is important to understand the purpose of each form and how each can be used most effectively.

- *Tables* can give exact numbers for multiple variables and work well as backup visuals to provide details (e.g., a table showing the quantitative growth of selected product lines over a ten-year period of time).

- *Bar and column charts* are most useful for illustrating the relationship between two or more sets of figures, comparing several variables at one time, or one variable at discrete points in time (e.g., a bar graph comparing sales of different product lines or a column graph comparing the sales of one product line over time).

- *Gantt charts* focus attention on the parts of a process over time (e.g., a Gantt chart displaying the development and implementation of a management training program noting the time frame for each component in the process).

- *Pie charts* show the relationship of one or more parts to each other and to the whole by dividing a circle (or pie) into the representative portions (e.g., a pie chart can indicate the percentage of listeners in specific age groups who listen to a particular radio station).

- *Scatter charts* show the correlation or lack of correlation between two variables (e.g., a scatter chart can compare faculty salary to academic rank to assess the degree of equity or degree of compression).

- *Line graphs* indicate the changes over time of one or more variables (e.g., a line graph can indicate the turnover rate in a company over time or compare/contrast the turnover rate with similar companies over time).

Pictures or Diagrams. Photographs, paintings, and drawings improve a presentation by giving listeners a visual sense of what you are talking about. Topics involving particular places, people, or themes may rely more heavily on pictorial content. If you wanted to show your listeners the effects of smoking, contrasting pictures of lungs from a smoker and a nonsmoker would concretely and effectively make your point. Indeed, a picture can be worth a thousand words. Diagrams or drawings of actual objects can show three-dimensional views and concentrate on important features. It is important that pictures, drawings, and diagrams be simple, relevant, and large enough to be seen by the audience.

Maps. Maps show dimensions, distances, terrain, contrasts, and geographical relationships. They are often indispensable when speaking on the weather, international politics, travel, transportation, military activities, historical topics, and various business and government issues. To be effective, maps must be current, contain relevant detail, and be easy to read or see from a distance.

Audio/Videotapes. The electronic age makes audiovisual materials especially appealing and informative. Audio/videotape systems permit the audience to experience your topic. The strategic impact of carefully planned audiovisual materials can be significant, but the use of electronic media brings with it some possible problems: poor quality of sound or inadequate amplification, tape breakage or malfunction of equipment, and loss of electric power. Because such speakers as training officers, teachers, and sales representatives need to use these aids regularly, they develop ways to systematize their use and have experience in coping with these problems. For the rest of us, the use of electronic media requires practice.

On-Screen Computer Displays. Over the past few years, computers have become an increasingly useful tool for producing visuals before presentations and for developing visuals during presentations. Computer-generated graphics used before your presentation can increase the sophistication and clarity of your visuals if you follow a few simple guidelines. First, you can supplement your computer-generated graphics by providing the audience with computer-generated handouts to take with them when they leave the meeting. And, second, remember that the information presented by the graphics is most important. Edward R. Tufte offers this warning:

> Computers and their affiliated apparatus can do powerful things graphically.... But at least a few computer graphics only evoke the response, "Isn't it remarkable that the computer can be programmed to draw like that?" Instead of "My, what interesting data...." These graphics are really all non-data-ink or redundant data-ink, and it is often chart-junk. Graphical decoration ... comes cheaper than the hard work required to produce intriguing numbers and secure evidence."[32]

Computers can also be programmed for use during a speech to produce a series of visuals from memory, resulting in a presentation similar to one using slides but with an increased sense of forward movement. Programs such as "Freelance Plus," "Harvard Graphics," or "Show Partner" can add color, motion, and sizzle to your presentation. But maybe the most attractive use for computers in the presentation arena is the ability to play "what if?" games with a small number of participants. A graphic display can illustrate powerfully the effect that a small change in one variable can have on other variables. To use the computer this way, the presenter must decide which graphic form best displays the data, and what and how much data manipulation to use. Done effectively, these presentations can be both exciting and persuasive.

Currently, the use of computers in presentations requires considerable skill, training, and sophistication and a substantial investment in both software and hardware. Their use will undoubtedly increase as managers become more comfortable with computers and as cost-effective, user-friendly programs are developed.

The effective use of visual aids requires careful planning and preparation of materials, always with an eye to the purpose and main ideas of the presentation and the audience for which it's intended. And, no matter how well prepared, visual aids that are ineptly presented are at best useless, and at worst a distraction.

Prepare Well in Advance. Last-minute attempts to find appropriate pictures, draw charts, or arrange for demonstration equipment are not only hectic, but the audience usually senses the lack of careful preparation and is left with a negative impression of the speaker and the message. Making professional-looking visuals takes time and may require the help of artists, photographers, statisticians, drafters, audio/visual technicians, and computer programmers. Some presenters try to save money, cut corners, or rush production, and it doesn't work. Today's business and professional audiences *expect* high-quality, carefully crafted, and creative visuals that present information in a fresh and interesting form.

Consider the Medium and the Occasion. Make the visual aid and all its components suitable to the unique characteristics of the medium and relevant to the topic and occasion. Overheads, slides, and flip-charts require you attending to size of type, visual dimensions, and consistency as well as to artistic and mechanical concerns. Audiovisual materials demand that you consider production techniques, sound systems, and visual angles. And you must prepare your visuals for the audience—for what they know, what they don't know, and what they expect to know. The communications director explaining a new television advertising campaign will include a video because the audience will expect to see a sample advertisement. The corporate executive proposing a policy change will include a handout because the audience will want to see the policy itself. When you approach the use of visual materials from a receiver-centered perspective, the aids become a means of ensuring that receivers will understand and appreciate the intended message. Screen visual materials carefully, asking: Are these devices really necessary? What do I hope to achieve that cannot be gained without them? Have I selected appropriate visual forms to clarify ideas? Do they provide fresh and interesting information? Will I insult my audience's intelligence by using these aids? Too often, speakers toss in extra materials as an afterthought simply because the aid is available, looks good, and "might as well be shown."

Patricia Rowell, director of business and special projects at Seminole Community College, recommends using storyboards and visual imaging when developing a presentation with visual support.[33] These provide a mechanism for checking the flow of information and assessing the use of multiple channels or mediums to support your message. You write the key ideas of your presentation as headings at the top of each boxed storyboard. Next, note the selected visual form for support and sketch the visual. Finally, add a transition. The series of storyboards outlines your presentation and indicates where visuals might be inserted. Visual imaging is a method of diagramming that permits a broader view of the presentation and the multiple channels or mediums you might use. Each channel or medium is assigned a geometrical shape or image—for example, a square might represent lecturing, a circle an overhead or flip-chart, a triangle might indicate slides or videotape, a rectangle a discussion, and an octagon could stand for handouts. When the flow of a presentation is diagrammed using these shapes, you can better determine the appropriateness of each channel or medium, predict time requirements, and weigh potential impact:

Once you've diagrammed your presentation, you may want to reassess the use of certain channels to better break up the presentation and add interest as well as to invite more audience involvement. Or, you might gain additional speaking confidence by seeing that your presentation, as illustrated above, reflects an effective balance of channels and use of visual support. Certainly the visual dimension of your presentation can be a key factor in achieving your communication goals.

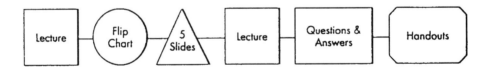

Keep Aids Clear, Simple, and Visible. Each visual should illustrate one idea with a clear point of focus. Guard against creating overly elaborate visuals with unnecessary information or extraneous lines and vibrating patterns that will only confuse and distract the audience. A series of simple charts, graphs, or pictures may be more useful than one large complicated one. Or a complex aid can gradually be built up with overlays as you guide the audience through the parts of the picture step by step. Remember: you want to focus attention on the message, not on the visual, and you do this by keeping it simple and ensuring that most of the ink on the page relates to the message. Visual aids must also be large enough to be easily seen, and using bold lines and dark or contrasting colors can help. It's very frustrating to try to see a visual that's too small. Avoid having to ad lib an embarrassed, "I know you can't see this clearly, but. . ." by making the message easy to read and eliminating unnecessary design details and text. Visuals should aid, not burden, your presentation.

Be Wary of Handouts. A common tactic of business and professional speaking today is to hand out duplicated materials so that everyone can read along while the speaker elaborates on the information. Although this procedure is productive in certain workshops, training, and conference settings, it can present a problem. George Grice and John Skinner describe this difficulty when they observe: "If you distribute handouts before your remarks, the audience is already ahead of you. Passing out information during a presentation can be distracting, especially if you stop talking as you do so. Disseminating material after the presentation eliminates distractions but does not allow the listener to refer to the printed information as you are explaining it."[34] Given the paradox, if a handout must be distributed, it usually should be made available at the end of the presentation. Increasingly, however, busy executives are demanding handouts in advance, allowing them an opportunity to review the ideas and make notes. When this is necessary, consider writing an executive summary that uses headings and summary pages to focus attention and highlight major ideas. Be careful not to provide so much information that people stop listening to you in order to read.

Introduce Visuals Effectively. The use of visual materials usually either leads to improved audience understanding and interest or distracts the audience from the speaker's message. A visual aid is only effective when you introduce it at the proper psychological point in the presentation. Visuals should be in view only when they help the audience understand the speaker's idea—introduced, used, then removed. Too many presenters speak to the audience with their visuals in full view when they aren't being used, thus deflecting attention away from themselves.

Speak to the audience and not to the visual aid. The audience should always be the speaker's primary concern. Few sights are more ludicrous than an adult standing before an audience but engaged in a serious discussion with a blackboard, a chart, or a slide. If you must turn your back to the group to write, don't speak while you write—the silence won't bother your audience because they'll be busy watching what you're writing. When you are well prepared, only an occasional glance at a visual to tell that everything is in order or to see where to point will be necessary. Because eye contact has such potency for maintaining audience attention, you cannot abandon this critical tool.

Certain delivery techniques with particular media can enhance their effectiveness. Standing close to a flip-chart, blackboard, or projection screen can prove helpful when pointing out information. But when you position yourself and use visual support, remember not to block anyone's view. Using a remote control for slides or videotape presentations gives you greater flexibility and movement. Using overheads, slides, films, and VCRs professionally means being certain that your equipment is in good working order and that you know how to use it correctly.

Practice Beforehand. This step in preparation and use is frequently overlooked. Speakers practice the verbal message orally and occasionally *think,* "At this point I'll pick up the object and show how it's used, or bring up a chart or graph." But thinking is not *doing,* and many speakers have been surprised by unexpected problems at crucial moments in their presentations. Perhaps the color slides are not in order; or a device won't work properly; or an important detail has been omitted from a diagram; or the aids are too bulky to hold, clumsy to manipulate, or difficult to set up. Practicing will not guarantee that unexpected problems never arise, but it can significantly reduce their likelihood and improve your speaking confidence. We especially encourage your rehearsing in the presence of a listener.

Step Eight: Deliver Your Presentation

A well-reasoned, well-supported, well-arranged collection of thoughts is only the skeleton of a presentation. The speech or report does not become a presentation until you deliver it. Delivery is the use of voice and body to convey the message; it is what we see and hear; it is the physical medium through which the ideas are perceived. That 40 percent of managers surveyed in a study admitted to falling asleep during a meeting or presentation suggests that presenters need to respond more effectively to the demand for exciting presentations.[35] Here we will discuss the common types of delivery and provide guidelines for the effective use of vocal and physical elements of delivery. Throughout our discussion, we will emphasize the concept of *enlarged conversation* as the method you should strive to emulate in your presentations. Conversation depends on verbs, nouns, and adverbs for impact—it is direct and straightforward.

Three common presentational formats are manuscript speaking, impromptu speaking, and extemporaneous speaking. Manuscript speaking, although difficult, permits the greatest control over the presentation. Impromptu speaking requires that the speaker construct the outline of the speech while speaking. Extemporaneous speaking requires a well-developed outline and the ability to conversationally present your ideas.

Manuscript Speaking. A manuscript speech or report is used when tight control of language, ideas, or time is necessary. Business and professional speakers frequently use the manuscript. Howard Haskett, Jr., professor of communication for the General Motors Institute, offers this rationale for manuscript delivery:

> If the apparent problems of preparation and delivery of a speech from manuscript are excessively involved, why do executives in large corporations make widespread use of it? The answer is in the *control*. Management feels that it must have control over the content put in speeches given by executives in company-related situations. This control is exercised through approval or disapproval of the prepared speech manuscript by an executive's superiors prior to its use. He commits himself to reading the approved manuscript word-for-word. The other control factor is time. In a tight time situation in a meeting a manuscript tends to assure that the time restrictions will be followed. Since these two factors are easy to measure and manipulate, manuscripts are used extensively. Also to a busy executive the temptation to delegate the writing of the speech manuscript is extremely hard to resist.[36]

Manuscripts are often required if the speaking occasion is especially important. It is excellent for such situations as upper-level corporate gatherings, meetings concerning technical and detailed material, or formal addresses to an external public.

Manuscript speaking requires skill at capturing the listener's interest and emotions, and maintaining a sense of involvement demands even greater skill. Especially useful is mastery of visualization and conversationality. A speaker must be listener-oriented during delivery, acknowledging the audience. Visualization creates, through voice, gesture, and movement, the images expressed in the presentation. And, by using a conversational style, the speaker recognizes the presence of the audience and personalizes an otherwise formal situation.

Manuscript speaking is not merely reading words; the audience needs to experience the ideas. Common problems associated with manuscript speaking include limited eye contact, word choice and sentence structure better suited to written works, difficulties associated with reading, and inflexibility. Good ideas alone do not make a presentation effective; the life of the ideas must be communicated. The following guidelines can be useful when preparing a manuscript:

1. Have the manuscript typed in capital letters with triple spaces between lines.

2. Don't attach the pages to each other. Loose pages enable you to move from page to page by merely slipping each completed page to the side and beginning the next page. You have faster, easier access to each page without the distraction of turning pages.

3. Practice delivering the speech or report orally. On the manuscript, underline or highlight the words and phrases you want to emphasize.

4. Become sufficiently familiar with the manuscript to deliver at least several lines from the presentation directly to the audience, without referring to the text. But, *don't memorize the speech or report.*

5. Don't practice so much that you become bored with the material.

When properly used, the manuscript speech or report represents a condition of maximum control and should foster an increased sense of confidence. When you use a manuscript, you can plan tangential elements more accurately, and use more vivid and precise language.

Impromptu Speaking. In 1789, the delegates to the United States Constitutional Convention, trying to create a workable government for the new country, were torn into angry factions by deep disagreements. They became so disheartened that many delegates wanted to patch together an easy compromise and go home. But their chairman, George Washington, rose and delivered one of the briefest speeches in the history of statesmanship. "If we offer to the people something of which we ourselves do not approve," he said, "how can we afterwards defend our work? Let us raise a standard to which the wise and honest may gladly repair. The event is in the hands of God." There was silence when he finished; then the members resumed their work with increased determination. They produced the U.S. Constitution, one of the greatest documents in history. Washington's direct, timely, and concise impromptu remarks, spoken with the confidence of a leader, had inspired them to action.

Impromptu speaking is informal and without prior preparation, planning, or intent. It requires you to think quickly, often planning while speaking. You may have a moment or two to prepare a few key ideas before speaking, but that's the maximum possible preparation time. Because you are usually formulating ideas and patterns of presentation while speaking, you need to help the audience follow the development of your thought patterns. The following guidelines can be useful when placed in an impromptu speaking situation:

1. Quickly select a theme around which to build your presentation. Try to link your topic to a subject you already know well.

2. Plan your first and last sentences. Concisely stated opening and closing summary statements allow you to avoid the aimless rambling so common with impromptu speaking. If possible, you might write these out along with a brief outline before speaking.

3. Select a simple organizational pattern. It's best to use a basic, logical arrangement of thoughts because you won't have the time to develop complex ideas associated with more complicated organizational patterns. Because of the free-flowing manner of this presentation, include summaries throughout to permit your listeners to fill in information they have missed, to clarify relationships among points, and to reinforce points you've already made.

4. Keep ideas direct, concise, and simple. Limit yourself to one, two, or three main points supported with personal knowledge or experience. Introduce these major points at a slow rate of speech and with pauses to permit the audience to digest each idea.

5. Maintain your composure and speak with confidence. Audience members understand the difficulty associated with impromptu speaking and don't expect a polished presentation.

Impromptu speaking is not easy because it excludes the opportunity for research, audience analysis, strategic planning, and practice. However, a recent survey of alumni at five universities ranked impromptu speaking as the most important mode of delivery in business situations.[37]

Impromptu speaking is a common occurrence in daily organizational life. There are situations when no realistic amount of preparation would lead you to believe that you would have to speak. Often impromptu speaking is a response to some question or a reaction to a statement during a business meeting. As a result, you have minimal control over critical communication variables.

Extemporaneous Speaking. An extemporaneous speech or report is planned, practiced, and well-outlined. Cal Downs and his associates observe that "by *extemporaneous* we mean a speech carefully prepared, thoroughly outlined, rehearsed but not memorized, and delivered from notes rather than manuscript."[38] Because the speaker is not committed to a manuscript, extemporaneous speaking can be modified during presentation permitting greater accommodation to audience needs, attitudes, and responses. The speaker is constantly creating, analyzing, adjusting, and searching as he or she "realizes" ideas in the presence of an audience. It is a challenging and demanding style of delivery. The following guidelines can be useful when speaking extemporaneously:

1. Carefully plan and prepare the presentation. Select and narrow your topic, define your purpose, analyze your audience, gather information, and organize the presentation. Your audience *expects* a well-developed and well-thought-out presentation.

2. Convert your full-sentence outline to speaking notes. A full-sentence outline is useful when preparing the presentation, but after that make notes on the key ideas and components of the outline for use during delivery. Quotations, statistics, and other technical data should be included, but keep your notes brief, legible, and not distracting to the audience. Some speakers use index cards; others prefer to type their notes in large print on letter-size paper so they can see the entire outline at a glance.

3. Rehearse your presentation. Practice thoroughly, but avoid memorization. Using your outlined notes, take each point and

talk about it. Notice here the verb "talk." A speaker *talks*. A speaker does not read. The outline guides ideas so that the speaker can establish and sustain contact with the audience, can share ideas with them. This is the hallmark of an enlarged conversational style.

The extemporaneous style of delivery is used for formal and semiformal planned occasions. Well suited for the oral report, it tends to be the preferred style of delivery and is most frequently recommended.

Regardless of the type of speaking format you choose, any presentation requires your attending to the vocal and physical elements of delivery. The best of ideas poorly delivered will have little chance with an audience. The following guidelines should enable you to acquire a powerful and compelling delivery.

Guidelines for Delivery: Vocal Elements

Develop a Skilled and Controlled Voice. Most of us have potentially effective speaking voices. We need only listen to our voices and concentrate on how we are using them. A good speaking voice should be balanced between extremes of volume, pitch, and rate, and have a pleasing sound quality. Nothing is more disconcerting to an audience than a speaker who cannot be heard. And your listeners won't fully understand your message if you don't project enough to be heard clearly. Volume should be varied to add emphasis or dramatic impact to your presentations. Good speakers also vary the pitch of their voices and rate of speaking to convey emotion and conviction. The most important recommendation for voice quality is to think in terms of friendliness and confidence, and to relax the tension out of your voice. A good speaking voice has the following characteristics:

1. The tone is *pleasant,* conveying a sense of friendliness.

2. It is *natural,* reflecting the true personality and sincerity of the speaker.

3. It has *vitality,* giving the impression of force and strength, even when it isn't especially loud.

4. It has *various shades of meaning,* never sounding monotonous and emotionless.

5. It is *easily heard,* due to both proper volume and clear articulation.[39]

Speaking with Enthusiasm. Effective speakers are enthusiastic and communicate that to the audience. A speaker who looks and sounds enthusiastic will be listened to and the ideas will be remembered.[40] Speaking this way comes from a sincere desire to communicate your ideas to your listeners.

Use Proper Enunciation and Pronunciation. Enunciation and pronunciation refer to the proper articulation of words. Just as standard grammar is important to your presentation of ideas, proper articulation is critical to a successful delivery. The way the majority of educated people talk is the standard against which you should measure your own speaking. Also, your speech patterns should relate to those used in your own circle of associates. You are part of a community that has a particular way of talking, and your speech should sound enough like the other members of that group to avoid distracting your listeners from your message. However, at the same time, your speech should be sufficiently "national" in sound to fit in when you travel beyond your immediate circle of associates.

No matter what dialect you speak, listeners will have difficulty understanding you if you fail to observe proper rules of enunciation. For our purposes, this means to articulate words and phrases distinctly and clearly with your lips, teeth, tongue, and palate. Common errors caused by lazy lips and jaws, or clumsy use of the tongue include:

1. *Omitting sounds.* We all hear (and probably say) such words as "goin'," "comin'," and "s'prise."

2. *Slurring.* When whole syllables and sounds are omitted, the word is slurred, such as "Prob'ly" for "probably" and "d'jeat?" for "did you eat?" A more subtle form of slurring is called "assimilation," where a speech sound is modified by its neighboring sounds for ease of saying it—e.g., making the phonetic transition from *n* to *c* in "include" is not easy, so many speakers slur the word to "include."

3. *Muffling.* This common weakness results from lazy lip, tongue, and jaw action and produces such words as "weat" for "wheat" and "liddle" for "little."

Articulation problems arise from lazy speech patterns, but pronunciation problems are usually born of ignorance. In poor pronunciation, you don't *know* how to say a word correctly. Pay special attention to these common errors, and avoid them:

1. *Adding sounds.* People sometimes insert extra syllables into a word, such as "athalete" for "athlete," "realator" for "realtor," and "fillum" for "film." Sometimes people are misled by the spelling of a word to include silent letters: "mor't'gage," "sa'l'mon." People also add extraneous sounds to words, such as "idear" for "idea," "warsh" for "wash," and "acrosst" for "across."

2. *Transposing.* We have all heard people say "revelant" when they meant "relevant." "Hunderd" for "hundred," and "prespiration" for "perspiration."

3. *Improper Stressing.* This fault of accenting the wrong syllable is so common that the dictionaries have a difficult time keeping up with changing usage. Consult a current dictionary of the English language or a source on American pronunciation to get preferred pronunciations. Also, such words as "rebel" or "digest" can be nouns or verbs, depending on where the stress is placed.

Errors in enunciation and mistakes in pronunciation not only confuse people about your meaning, but leave the impression that you are poorly educated and seriously undermine your personal credibility.

Pause Effectively. Effective use of pauses can be a powerful delivery tool, allowing the audience time to digest your message. Pauses can also add color and feeling to your presentation. Don't underestimate the power of silence: it can underscore important ideas, provide direction, arouse interest, create suspense, and signal appropriate places for applause or laughter.

Eliminate Unnecessary Vocalizations. Such sounds as "ah," "uh," "um," or "er" are distracting to an audience and give the impression that the speaker is unprepared, nervous, or uncertain of the facts being presented. Unnecessary words or phrases should also be avoided. Don't overuse "okay," "see," "like," and "you know." These are often mistakenly used by inexperienced speakers as transitions, but truly effective transitions summarize and forecast.

Much but not all of your message is carried by voice; physical elements also speak quite loudly. Eye contact, facial expression, gestures, and body countenance should further your speaking goal and reinforce the verbal message. They should:

1. convey information and attitudes you want to convey

2. conceal information and attitudes you don't want to convey

3. limit the number of unintended messages you send—the number of sender-associated random factors to which you attribute no conscious meaning, but to which the receiver does ascribe meaning

4. limit, modify, or eliminate factors to which you and the receiver ascribe potentially different meanings

5. minimize factors that send interfering messages—factors with no direct relationship to the issue being considered and that might distract the receiver should be eliminated[41]

Physical messages are an integral part of the totality of public communication. Remember, in the business and professional arena "everybody communicates." The following suggestions can be useful when considering the physical elements for delivery.

Guidelines for Delivery: Physical Elements

Maintain Eye Contact with Your Audience. You must talk to your audience, allowing the focus of your attention to move from one segment of the group to another. This requires that you as a speaker look at the faces before you—not at the ceiling, the back of the room, or the tops of their heads, but *at them.* And learn to do this not as if you were programmed, but as a person with ease and grace, and with the purpose of inclusion. Effective speakers maintain eye contact approximately 85 percent of the time, looking down only to read technical material or to refer briefly to their notes. Speakers who look directly at members of the audience are generally perceived as honest, knowledgeable, and involved with their listeners. Remember that public communication is a mutual exchange, not a soliloquy or personal monologue, and eye contact confirms this exchange.

Be Poised and Confident Behind the Lectern. The lectern should be used to place your notes and perhaps rest your arms or hands. The lectern is an aid, not a crutch, so avoid slouching, leaning on it, or draping your body over it. Effective speakers stand on both feet, observe good posture, and generate confidence. Good posture gives the impression of authority.

Use Facial Expressions to Convey Your Mood. The face is a mirror to the soul, and your facial expressions can communicate sincerity, pleasure, happiness, sadness, certainty, anger, resentment, fear, and concern. Oftentimes inexperienced speakers remain stoically expressionless, or reveal their nervousness and anxiety. Don't be afraid to smile—it breaks down barriers and does not, as many presenters seem to think, suggest that you're not serious about what you're saying. When you smile at someone, he or she feels included and generally smiles back. You want to maintain an accessible, open presence.

Gesture Naturally and Comfortably. A speaker who maintains a white-knuckle grip on the lectern or who stays glued to the overhead projector is terrified, and everyone soon knows it. To project self-confidence and authority use your hands as you speak. Gestures should be as natural and spontaneous as they are during a conversation. Your arms and hands may seem to resist, but don't be afraid to use gestures. They can help your audience follow your outlined ideas and can emphasize your major points. Tailor the gestures to reinforce your message. Avoid pointing, which might seem accusatory and threatening, or making repetitive gestures that become distracting. Rather, gesture with both arms and hands purposefully and with confidence.

Move with Purpose. Your presentation will be enhanced if you make use of bodily movement. If the movement is done at strategic times, such as after the introduction, between main points, or before the conclusion, it can draw appropriate attention to you and add a dynamic dimension to your delivery. Taking a few steps away from the lectern—to the left or right, forward or diagonally—can signal interest or intensity of concern. Movement will make you appear less rigid or statue-like, and more relaxed, confident, and convincing. However, avoid moving about the room randomly or pacing like a caged tiger. To guard against moving too much, stop each time you make a point. The stillness of a complete pause in your movement, like silence, emphasizes the importance of what you are saying. Effective movement is well-timed and meaningful.

Reduce Distracting Mannerisms. Swaying to and fro, clicking a pen, tapping a pencil on the lectern, putting your hands in and out of your pockets, twirling your hair, or jingling change can become distracting to even the most interested audience. These and other idiosyncratic mannerisms may be difficult to eliminate but every effort should be made to reduce them. Videotaping your presentations can greatly assist you in achieving this goal.

Get Up To and Away From the Lectern with Confidence. The audience begins making judgments about you from the moment you rise from your seat to speak, so it's important that you approach the lectern with confidence. Moreover, you should pause a few seconds before speaking to focus the attention of the audience and gain control of the situation. This also permits you a moment to quell any personal anxieties. At the close of your presentation, don't rush back to your seat; instead, pause and maintain eye contact with your audience for a brief moment. Remember: *you* are in control of the speaking situation.

The physical elements of delivery, like the vocal elements, should emphasize meaning and should direct the audience's attention to meaning. Delivery must be adapted to all the demanding elements in the public situation: the occasion, the audience, the material, and the speaker. Effective delivery focuses attention and helps listeners concentrate on what is being communicated; it does not attract attention to itself.

Step Nine: Evaluate Your Performance

Now the analysis begins. Evaluation permits you to review, mull over, and critically consider all aspects of the presentation, letting you identify personal strengths and weaknesses. The question, then, is: how do I rate as a speaker? By examining the following checklist you can determine how good a speaker you really are.

- ♦ I effectively capture the listeners' interest and attention through the appropriate use of questions, quotations, examples, or illustrations.
- ♦ I clearly state and explain the purpose of the presentation, and my purpose statement is a complete statement.

Speaker Traits

A group of Rollins College students conducted interviews with professional people to determine the businessperson's perception of effective and ineffective speaker traits. The results of the interviews are presented here:

Traits of an Effective Speaker

- ◆ Enthusiastic
- ◆ In control of the situation
- ◆ Knowledgeable and credible
- ◆ Keeps strong eye contact
- ◆ Audience-centered
- ◆ Honest
- ◆ Organized/prepared
- ◆ Has a strong voice
- ◆ Direct and open manner
- ◆ Concise

Traits of an Ineffective Speaker

- ◆ Nervous
- ◆ Lacks preparation and organization
- ◆ Has an "I don't care" attitude
- ◆ Uses distracting mannerisms
- ◆ Reads or memorizes materials
- ◆ Bluffs or avoids questions
- ◆ Rambles or wastes time
- ◆ Lacks facts and figures
- ◆ Is sloppy with visuals, grammar, or appearance
- ◆ Apologetic

- ◆ I make the audience aware of why they need the data.
- ◆ I establish a sense of credibility as a speaker, indicating my qualifications as an expert in the area.
- ◆ I suggest the order in which ideas will be developed.
- ◆ The plan of organization is clear, coherent, and easy to follow.
- ◆ The main ideas are clearly distinguishable.
- ◆ The main ideas are well developed and supported by good examples, current statistics, timely testimony, and interesting analogies, comparisons, or stories.
- ◆ I have adequate supporting data to substantiate what is said.
- ◆ The main points of the speech reflect logical reasoning and lead naturally to the conclusion.
- ◆ All the content is meaningful in terms of the topic (the problem and its solution).

- I recognize the importance of transitions and summaries within the message.
- I take time to create the best visual materials to enhance my spoken message.
- I present ideas in a clear, grammatically correct, understandable, and vivid way.
- I carefully choose my words.
- I avoid trite, wordy expressions.
- My language is appropriate for this particular audience and occasion.
- I provide a good summary and synthesis of main ideas.
- I restate the importance of the topic and the value of the findings.
- The conclusion is forceful, challenging, and thought provoking.
- The conclusion leaves the audience in the desired frame of mind with a positive final impression.
- I use a natural, pleasant, conversational style of delivery.
- I work to establish eye contact with all audience members.
- I can be heard easily by everyone; my diction is clear; my rate and pitch of speaking are appropriate and meaningfully varied.
- My voice shows variety in volume and rate.
- I am poised, self-confident, and convincing.
- My facial expression is friendly and sincere.
- I am open and confident in my gestures, posture, and body action.
- Gestures and movement are natural, well-timed, and meaningful.
- I display enthusiasm.
- I practice my presentation sufficiently before giving it.
- The presentation is stimulating, informative, thought provoking, or persuasive.
- The presentation achieves its rhetorical goal(s).
- I have a strong desire to be an effective speaker.

By carefully attending to the outlined stages of preparation, your evaluations will be more positive than that of the young minister invited by the pastor of his home church to give his first sermon. After weeks of preparation, the great day arrived and he delivered the sermon. As the members of the congregation filed past after the service, they told him how nice he looked, how fine his message was, and how they wished him well in his career. When his spunky, no-nonsense grandmother approached, he asked: "Well, how did I do, Granny?" "Sonny," the old woman said, "I only saw three things wrong. First, you read it. Second, you didn't read it well. And third, it wasn't worth reading, anyhow!"

We have been talking about one-speaker-presentations throughout our discussion, largely because we feel team presentations have distinct disadvantages and are very difficult to do well. One critical problem is that the members of the audience may be confused and unable to determine who's in charge. Furthermore, any lapse in the intricate coordination necessary to shift from one presenter to another may result in pathetic silences or comical babble. Finally, the presentations may overlap and be unnecessarily repetitive. When several people are scheduled to present, each should present the material he or she knows best, each should be involved in developing the total program, and all should rehearse together to ensure smooth transitions. If you are part of a group presentation, consider your piece as a presentation in itself, with a beginning, a body, and an end.

Summary

Public presentations play an important role in the modern organization—a primary medium whereby information is processed. Your effectiveness as a public speaker can significantly influence how rapidly you advance with the business and professional environment, so the skills involved in manuscript, impromptu, and extemporaneous speaking are critical. Of particular importance to business and industry are informal internal reports, semiformal and formal reports or speeches, and external public relations speeches.

Public communication is defined as the face-to-face communication in which a speaker has control of the speaking situation and the primary responsibility of presenting a message to one or more people. Although the purposes for public communication have traditionally been to inform, to persuade, or to entertain, the ultimate objective is to influence and impress. As a public speaker, you will to varying degrees offer information, solidify or modify beliefs, move audiences to action, and entertain in every presentation.

The fear of making presentations is common because of the perceived novelty of the speaking situation; the subordinate status, conspicuousness, and dissimilarity felt by many speakers; and a prior history of nervousness. A certain amount of anxiety is considered normal and even desirable, but excessive speaker apprehension can significantly impair your effectiveness. You can control your nervousness by correcting your misperceptions about speaking, by visualizing success, and by practicing thoroughly.

The process of making presentations comprises a number of steps, an understanding of which is necessary if you hope to be effective. Step one: select and narrow your topic, determining what about the topic is both interesting to you and important to your listeners. Step two: define your purpose in terms of the desired audience reaction and behavioral goals. Step three: analyze your audience demographically—by size, age, gender, education, religion, culture, occupation, and knowledge—then focus on their needs and interests. Step four: research your topic, carefully gathering information to support your purpose and provide proof for your arguments. Step five: arrange your information and ideas according to standard chronological, spatial, cause-and-effect, problem-solution, pro-con, or topical patterns. Step six: plan your introduction and conclusion to grab and focus your listeners' attention and to provide a positive closing impact. Step seven: select your visual aids and practice using them. They should create interest, increase understanding, and boost the impact of your speeches and reports. Visual support includes the use of personal demonstration; physical objects; models; text visuals; conceptual visuals; tables, charts, or graphs; pictures or diagrams; maps; and audio/videotapes. Effective visuals are suitable to the medium and the occasion, clear, simple, and large enough to be seen. Step eight: deliver your presentation in an enlarged conversational style with an understanding of both the vocal and physical elements of delivery and an awareness of their powerful influence. Step nine: evaluate your performance with a critical eye toward improvement. Each of these steps is important, but effectiveness and presentational success ultimately depend on practice, practice, practice.

Now you're ready. You're on. You're great!

Questions for Discussion and Skill Development

1. In what ways does presentational speaking make a difference in your corporate life? Is being an effective speaker important to you? To others at your place of work?

2. How would you describe your own speaker apprehension? Specifically, what makes you nervous about making a presentation? Do you agree that it is normal to be somewhat nervous at the start of a presentation? Why? Why not?

3. How does written communication differ from oral communication? Why is this important to understand? Which do you prefer?

4. How do reports and speeches differ? What purposes do they most frequently serve?

5. Why must a speaker be audience-centered? How can you get information about your audience? What are the most important demographic factors of audiences? Why?

6. What are some useful research materials for presentations? Which materials will be most useful in the types of presentations you will deliver at work? Why?

7. Why is it important that presentations be organized clearly? What are the most common organizational patterns? Which patterns do you prefer? Why?

8. Why is the introduction so critical? The conclusion? What are the primary objectives of an introduction? A conclusion? What are common introductory and concluding techniques? Are some more effective than others? Why?

9. In what ways can visual aids support your presentational purposes? Select a chart, graph, or diagram from a newsmagazine and describe how you would adapt it for use in an informative presentation; in a persuasive presentation.

10. Describe the best type of visual aid to use for the following presentations: (a) to inform an audience about the national debt, (b) to inform an audience about the status of drug testing in U.S. corporations, (c) to persuade an audience that computer-generated graphics and presentation programs can significantly enhance a business report. Are visuals more helpful when informing or when persuading an audience? Why?

11. How would you define an effective delivery? What vocal and physical elements are most influential? What is meant by *enlarged conversation?* Which speaking style do you prefer—manuscript speaking, impromptu speaking, extemporaneous speaking? Why do we emphasize practice, practice, practice?

12. Watch a business presentation and critically analyze it. Focus on the speaker's purpose, organization, supporting material, introduction, conclusion, and delivery. How did this presentation compare with other business presentations you have heard? Now, record yourself delivering a short presentation and evaluate the recording. Determine your personal strengths and weaknesses. What presentational skills do you want to improve?

Notes

1. Tom Parker, *In One Day* (Boston: Houghton Mifflin, 1984): 31.

2. E. G. Bormann, W. S. Howell, R. G. Nichols, and G. L. Shapiro, *Interpersonal Communication in the Modern Organization,* 2nd ed. (Englewood Cliffs, NJ: Prentice Hall, 1982): 196.

3. Elizabeth M. Fowler, "Training 21st-Century Executives," *New York Times,* June 20, 1989, D13.

4. Carol Kleinman, "Information Skills Back in Demand," *The Orlando Sentinel,* September 31, 1990, E-21.

5. W. I. Gordon and J. R. Miller, *Speaking Up for Business* (Dubuque, IA: Kendall-Hunt, 1977).

6. Ronald B. Adler, *Communicating at Work: Principles and Practices for Business and the Professions,* 4th ed. (New York: McGraw-Hill, 1992).

7. Frank E. X. Dance, "What Do You Mean by Presentational Speaking," *Management Communication Quarterly* (November, 1987): 260–271.

8. David Wallenchinsky, Irving Wallace, and Amy Wallace, *The Book of Lists* (New York: Morrow, 1977): 469–470.

9. Virginia P. Richmond and James C. McCroskey, *Communication: Apprehension, Avoidance, and Effectiveness,* 2nd ed. (Scottsdale, AZ: Gorsuch Scarisbrick, 1989).

10. James C. McCroskey and Lawrence Wheeless, *Introduction to Human Communication* (Boston: Allyn And Bacon, 1976).

11. Raymond S. Ross, *Speech Communication* (Englewood Cliffs, NJ: Prentice Hall, 1977): 100.

12. James C. McCroskey, *An Introduction to Rhetorical Communication,* 6th ed. (Englewood Cliffs, NJ: Prentice Hall, 1993): 37.

13. Joseph A. DeVito, *Essentials of Human Communication* (New York: Harper Collins, 1993).

14. Judith Martin, "Plain Speech for Carter," *Newsday,* July 13, 1977, 3A.

15. This script reflects visualization scripting principles. See Joseph Ayers and Ted Hoff, "Visualization: A Means for Reducing Speech Anxiety," *Communication Education* 34 (October 1985): 318–323.

16. James C. Humes, *Roles Speakers Play* (New York: Harper and Row, 1976).

17. Robert T. Oliver, *History of Public Speaking in America* (Boston: Allyn and Bacon, 1965): 122.

18. Jo Sprague and Douglas Stuart, *The Speaker's Handbook,* 3rd ed. (New York: Harcourt Brace Jovanovich, 1992): 32.

19. Eliot Asinof, "Dick Gregory Is Not So Funny Now," *New York Times Magazine* (March 17, 1968): 37–45. Copyright © 1968 by The New York Times Company. Reprinted by permission.

20. Kenneth Burke, *A Grammar of Motives* (Englewood Cliffs, NJ: Prentice Hall, 1946): 56.

21. Kenneth Burke, *A Rhetoric of Motives* (Englewood Cliffs, NJ: Prentice Hall, 1950): 23.

22. *The New York Public Library Desk References* (New York: Stonesong-Simon, 1989): xi.

23. G. L. Grice and J. F. Skinner, *Mastering Public Speaking* (Englewood Cliffs, NJ: Prentice Hall, 1993).

24. Thomas Koballa, Jr., "Persuading Teachers to Reexamine the Innovative Elementary Science Programs of Yesterday: The Effect of Anecdotal versus Data-Summary Communications," *Journal of Research in Science Teaching* 23 (1986): 437–449.

25. I. Edmon, ed., *The Works of Plato* (New York: Simon & Schuster, 1928): 309.

26. Ernest C. Thompson, "An Experimental Investigation of the Relative Effectiveness of Organized Structure in Oral Communication," *Southern States Speech Journal* 26 (1960): 59–69.

27. Christopher Spicer and Ronald Bassett, "The Effect of Organization on Learning from an Informative Message," *Southern Speech Communication Journal* 41 (Spring 1976): 290–299.

28. John Greene, "Speech Preparation Processes and Verbal Fluency," *Human Communication Journal* 11 (1984): 61–84.

29. Carolyn R. Planck, President of Communication for Professionals, Winter Park, FL.

30. William J. Seiler, "The Effects of Visual Materials on Attitudes, Credibility, and Retention," *Speech Communication Monographs* 38 (November 1971): 331–334.

31. Grice and Skinner, *Mastering Public Speaking*.

32. Edward R. Tufte, *The Visual Display of Quantitative Information* (Cheshire, CT: Graphics Press, 1983).

33. Patricia Rowell, "Using Storyboards and Visual Imaging to Develop High-Impact Presentations" (Presentation to the Central Florida Chapter of American Society for Training and Development, Orlando, FL, May 26, 1992).

34. Grice and Skinner, *Mastering Public Speaking*, 279.

35. Marya W. Holcombe and Judith K. Stein, *Presentations for Decision Makers* (New York: Van Nostrand Reinhold, 1990).

36. Harold O. Haskitt, Jr., "When Speaking from Manuscript: Say It and Mean It," *Personnel Journal* (February 1972): 109.

37. John Johnson and Nancy Szczupakiewicz, "The Public Speaking Course: Is It Preparing Students with Work-Related Skills?" *Communication Education* 3 (1987): 131–137.

38. Cal Downs, Wil Linkugel, and David M. Berg, *The Organizational Communicator* (New York: Harper and Row, 1977): 223.

39. *Communication and Leadership Program* (Santa Ana, CA: Toastmasters International, 1977): 27.

40. Read G. Williams and John E. Ware, Jr., "Validity of Student Ratings of Instruction Under Different Incentive Conditions: A Further Study of the Dr. Fox Effect," *Journal of Educational Psychology* 68 (February 1976): 50.

41. Wallace V. Schmidt and Jo-Ann Graham, *The Public Forum, A Transactional Approach to Public Communication* (Sherman Oaks, CA: Alfred Publishing, 1979): 97.

◆ ◆ ◆ ◆ ◆ ◆ ◆ ◆ ◆

Excerpts from

Organizational Communication

An Introduction to Communication and Human Relation Strategies

Ken W. White

◆ ◆ ◆ ◆ ◆ ◆ ◆ ◆ ◆

Communicating with
New Technology ◆◆◆◆

More than likely, you have recently been exposed to some new technology in the workplace. Computer-mediated technology and networking are changing the way people work and the way they communicate in organizations. Members of workteams use computer networks to communicate with each other and to access databases and programming tools. Workteams and employees communicate through electronic mail (e-mail), distribution lists, and bulletin boards.

Computer-based communication may even prove to be more significant than the personal computer revolution of a few years ago. Because the technology is used for communication, it affects the most critical process in an organization.

The new technology of communication is about how people communicate; it is about the quality of organizational connections employees have with one another and with managers. It is about performance and success!

We know that you want to succeed in the electronic workplace, and that you now appreciate how that means effective attitudes and communication skills.

This chapter is devoted to tips that can help you communicate effectively with the new technology of computers, specifically e-mail. Ours is a relational and organizational view of computer-based communication. We do not consider the technical details of how information technology (IT) works, but how the technology requires special ways of thinking, relating, and communicating. Our purpose is to help you to see how the changes of new technology can be capitalized on from a communication perspective. If you take these ideas to heart, you may be able to avoid many of the mistakes others have made in the electronic work environment.

We will start with some background information that relates the area of new technology to a general theme of this book: command and relational communication.

Organizational Communication and the New Technology

If you want to stay current in the organization of the nineties and into the next century, you need to learn how to communicate effectively with computer technology. Futurists predict that information and access to it will be the basis for organizational communication in the next century. Whether you want to exchange information with your co-workers or join in a lively departmental meeting, the new technology will be your tool.

> *Computer-based communication will bring employees and information together in a new dimension—an electronic virtual organization where time, space, and communication have different meanings.*

E-mail, or online communication, is a good example. E-mail is electronic mail automatically passed through computer networks and/or via modems over common-carrier lines. (Actually, the word "e-mailed" means "embossed or arranged in a network" but has come to be shorthand for electronic mail.) E-mail is a popular application in organizations today. It is a very powerful organizational tool that is simple to use and easy to understand. It is hard to imagine any other form of computer-based communication that can be so intimate and yet so wide-reaching, so focused, and so expansive. An employee can communicate as easily with someone from another business across 12 time zones as with a co-worker in the same building.

Management researchers Lee Sproull and Sara Kiesler observe that the new technologies, like e-mail, are not just tools. Computer-based communication is extremely fast in comparison with interoffice mail, courier services, or postal mail. A message can be sent down the hall or halfway around the world in seconds. In addition, organizations appreciate the savings that result from reducing telephone tag and mail delays.

Sproull and Kiesler recognize the efficiency effects of a new technology like e-mail, but emphasize that such technologies have both efficiency effects and social effects. We have referred to this distinction as the difference between command and relational communication. Reducing communication costs is not always automatically beneficial to

organizational relationships. Faster and easier command communication is not always better relational communication. Because an electronic message is easier to send, employees may be tempted to "speak"
before they think, and injured relationships may result.

> Changes we make to improve the efficiency of organizational
> communication have offsetting consequences for organizational
> relationships.

Communicating with new technology is not simply a matter of adding hardware to an organization. Communicating with new technology
leads to communicating and relating in new ways, and thereby to fundamental changes in how employees work and relate. In the following
section, we outline some of the command and relational challenges of
computer-based communication.

The Challenges of Online Communication

The challenge of communicating through e-mail or *online* is the inherent
complexity of any human communication and interpretation. Even if
the recipient of face-to-face communication fully understands what our
words mean, misunderstanding can still occur because of faulty *attributions*. What (words) we communicate may be understandable; however,
the *why* (attributions) may be fuzzy. But vague language involving lousy
referents (what is symbolized by a word) also contributes to the formation of inaccurate attributions. Language itself can cause attributions to
widely miss the mark.

Besides language, attributions are influenced by a wide variety of
cultural, social, and contextual factors. In this regard, very clear attributions of other people's communication are often formed from just a
small sample of messages. Essentially, the mind filters observations selectively, subject to recency and order effects. We then form a *prototype*
(our initial metaphor) based on those observations and fill in the gaps of
the prototype where necessary.

People are constantly involved in this type of "cognitive shorthand"
as they strive to make sense of those around them. (While this dynamic
is the basis of stereotyping, it isn't necessarily bad or wrong. We'd get
extremely frustrated if it wasn't for this cognitive shorthand. It isn't necessary or even valid to try to stop the attribution process. Rather, the
idea is to understand pitfalls and to avoid or reduce errors whenever
possible.)

Organizational prototypes formed from attributions reflect organizational biases and information. A wide variety of biases have an important impact on organizational communication. It is inevitable that

personal biases lead to prototype formation, attributions, and subsequent impressions. These impressions then influence subsequent communication in the organization. For example, we may communicate more warmly with a co-worker in the future if we attribute his or her behavior to being unlucky, as opposed to being lazy. We may be more respectful of a manager because we perceive him or her to be bright and lively.

Faulty prototype formation, invalid attributions, and failure to understand communication through the eyes of other parties are all enhanced in online communication where information and feedback are restricted.

E-mail communicators are particularly prone to faulty attributions because online communication excludes rich and significant cues on which people normally rely as information sources. Communication researchers have consistently found that nonverbal cues are the dominant source of meaning in interpersonal communication. One problem is that electronic conversations are missing body language and voice intonations, crucial elements of effective communication. When we take these elements away, people are forced to "fill in the blanks."

Verbal communication (without voice inflection or tonality) is all we have with online communication.

The challenge of communicating with a relative lack of information and immediate feedback in the asynchronous environment of e-mail communication, and the insidious nature of the prototype-building process that is part of attribution formation, quickly leads to anxiety and hostility. Online communicators can "fill in the blanks" with faulty attributions, establish incorrect prototypes, and blow things entirely out of proportion. Online communicators can come out of "left field" with surprising and often insulting language. Onliners refer to this type of communication as *flaming*. (Flaming can be defined as electronic messages or retorts that express startlingly blunt, extreme, and impulsive language because the technology lacks tangible reminders of the audience.)

In this regard, we have all probably been surprised by a hostile, flaming response to what we thought was an innocuous online communication. Faulty attributions usually lie behind every flame. A writer receives a message open to interpretation, lacks the nonverbal and paralinguistic resources to help interpret the ideas appropriately, assigns faulty attributions to the message, and reacts with anger and name-calling. When this happens, everything can go downhill fast!

How do we reduce the likelihood of faulty attributions and flaming in online communication? As a general rule-of-thumb, faulty attributions and flaming mindsets can be reduced by improving the quantity (commands) and quality (relations) of communication. A general implication of this point is that online communicators should check out assumptions more frequently and ask a lot more questions than they normally do in day-to-day, interpersonal communication.

We conclude this section with an outline of other—not necessarily good, not necessarily bad (but definitely different)—aspects of e-mail communication of which you should be aware:

◆ *Individuals and groups communicating in a computer-mediated environment are relatively more uninhibited.* "Flaming" is only one outcome of this dynamic. Online individuals and group members are also more willing to disclose personally sensitive information about themselves relative to face-to-face interaction.

◆ *Status differences play a lesser role in an online environment.* The fact that a person is The Chief Executive or The Boss or Knows What They Are Talking About has a less inhibiting effect on interaction. As a consequence of the low level of social information, individuals lose their fear of social approbation. On the other hand, interaction in online groups tends to be more evenly distributed among group members.

◆ *Online consensus decision making takes significantly longer than when group members interact face-to-face.* It tends to be more difficult for online groups to reach agreement. One difference is that tendencies to be interactive and outspoken in electronic discussions sometimes lead to increased group conflict. Such divergence means that electronic groups have to exert more effort trying to reconcile contradictory opinions than in face-to-face work groups.

The next section will build on our discussion of the nature of communication, online and otherwise, to include techniques for improving the quality of online communication. We will cover techniques—borrowed from traditional training material and adapted for online—intended to improve information and understanding and to lessen faulty attributions among online communicators.

The *Write* Way to Communicate Online

The purpose of this section is to move from a general understanding of principles to the application of ideas in the online environment. To begin with, acronyms are helpful to remember useful concepts. In thinking through what's important in online communication—given problems such as the absence of nonverbal cues, problems with incomplete prototypes, inaccurate attributions, and so forth—friend, teacher, and author Chad Lewis has come up with an acronym that covers the essential skills of online communication. He calls it the *WRITE Way* to communicate online.

The WRITE Way to communicate online involves communicating in a manner that is (W)arm, (R)esponsive, (I)nquisitive, (T)entative, and (E)mpathetic. Here's an explanation of each component of the WRITE Way:

(W)armth

Words on a screen are two-dimensional. Reading these words in isolation of usual communication cues lends itself to "coolness" that can lead directly to overreaction and flaming. Essentially, the goal is to interact with people, not with computers. In addition, online communicators sometimes lose perspective—acting as though messages are going into the relative privacy of a text file saved to the user's hard drive rather than being downloaded and read by perhaps hundreds, even thousands, of people. These people, in turn, read two-dimensional words in isolation and react. Pretty soon it's . . . BOOM! . . . communication that leads to embarrassment, chagrin, guilt, shame, and anger—in short, a whole plethora of potentially counterproductive human emotions.

Increasing warmth of online communication doesn't mean to be "touchy feely"—to give people the electronic equivalent of sloppy hugs and kisses. Rather, increasing warmth means to decrease the psychic distance among communicators. Being warm online is a way of affirming relational communication—it is about communicating with people.

In short, words can be "cold." We need to find effective ways to warm them up when communicating online. Here are ways to increase electronic warmth:

1. *Use the telephone when necessary.* A telephone call to clarify a point or to negotiate a particularly sensitive issue is indicated when text just doesn't cut it. Some onliners think electronic messages should suffice for all communication, but an occasional phone call can be useful. We see this in the common revelation experienced when phoning someone with whom we have been communicating online. Invariably, the confirmation that we are all human and not just words on a screen is the first thing discussed when voice connection is made.

2. *Send sensitive information to private mailboxes.* It's usually much more helpful to offer "constructive feedback" privately. This approach is akin to offering feedback behind closed doors.

3. *Incorporate warmth into the written text.* Professional writers are able to convey a wide range of emotions. It is much tougher for normal mortals to do this. We have found it helpful to occasionally write about our families and interests. Sometimes we tell a bad joke (though the joke needs to be a "sure thing" because humor easily backfires online). Describing the setting from which you are writing, the weather or music to which you're listening, can help readers place you in a human setting.

Playing with language and its symbolism also adds warmth as long as it is not overdone. One way to play with language and symbols online is to use an occasional emoticon in your writing. Emoticons represent a way of bringing so-called "nonverbal" cues into online communication though, technically, they are not "nonverbal" communication in the usual sense of the word. As we mentioned, authentic nonverbal communication is beyond our control. It is not necessarily a conscious effort to communicate a particular meaning and it is readily open to other people's interpretations.

Emoticons are conscious and intend the reader to accept a certain tone or meaning. Emoticons, because they are conscious symbols with intent, cannot be trusted like true nonverbal communication, but they do serve a purpose online. As part of a long-term relationship with established trust, they can warn readers not to misinterpret certain words. Table 15.1 lists some of the more common ones.

TABLE 15.1 Emoticons and Their Meanings

1.	:-)	**User smiling**
2.	:-(	**User sad**
3.	:-<	**User very sad**
4.	:-\	**User undecided**
5.	:-p	**User sticking tongue out**
6.	:-D	**User talks too much**
7.	:-o	**User surprised**
8.	:-O	**User shocked**
9.	:-{	**User has mustache**
10.	:-|	**User has no expression**
11.	:-&	**User tongue-tied**
12.	:-t	**User cross**
13.	:-@	**User screaming**
14.	:-x	**User lips sealed**
15.	:-e	**User disappointed**
16.	::-)	**User wears glasses**
17.	;-)	**User winking**
18.	(-:	**User left-handed**
19.	>:-<	**User mad**
20.	|-)	**User bored**

(R)esponsiveness

"Asynchronous communication" means people sometimes wait several days before getting a response to a message. Not only is there a lack of the usual communication cues, but there is also the need to wait for feedback. As noted previously, this waiting can feed into invalid attributions ("Ken hasn't replied! Hmmm . . . guess he doesn't really think much of my ideas"). A misinterpretation seems to be magnified by the passing of time and can be blown up into a major problem.

A solution is to:

1. *Set deadlines or otherwise be consistent in terms of when you give feedback.* This allays anxiety and creates an expectation on the part of others of when they should hear back from you. Once this expectation is satisfied through timely provision of feedback, trust will be reinforced (a positive contributor to warmth). Generally speaking, try to return messages as soon as possible. Temporal relations or chronemics are a particularly important nonverbal for e-mail communication. Attitudes toward responsiveness are communicated by the ways individuals deal with time online. If they are late with their replies, they send a message of indifference to others.

2. *Remember to provide occasional reminders.* Another aspect of responsiveness is redundancy. Think of issuing reminders as a proactive type of responsiveness. An interesting aspect of online communication is that it is possible to have a perfect memory of what "was said." Unfortunately, it is difficult to access a recollection if it is buried in hundreds of kilobytes of information. Consequently, don't be surprised if people fail to act on an online request, particularly if information is part of a larger message or part of a succession of messages on related topics. The use of short messages and redundancy helps to allay this problem and keeps online communicators on track.

(I)nquisitiveness

Defensiveness is reduced if people ask questions rather than make statements. It is usually more constructive to ask a person "why" than it is to tell them "what." Inquisitiveness serves two important purposes: Besides reducing defensiveness, it often provides information that is useful for solving a problem, resolving an issue, or whatever. Bringing valid information to bear on online communicative exchanges is almost always a good idea.

1. *Be sure to ask questions.* Online defensiveness tends to be reduced when people ask questions rather than make statements.

(T)entativeness

Defensiveness is reduced when people hear or read, "It appears that . . ." as opposed to, "It is. . . ." Inquisitiveness and tentativeness work well together. A question—framed in a tentative manner—reduces defensiveness and can also contribute valuable information (e.g., "Don't you think it'd be better if we . . .).

1. *Use tentative language and posturing, unless the situation dictates otherwise.* The old concept of sending "I" rather than "you" messages works as well in online writing as it does in oral interaction. It is often better to say or to write "I believe . . ." rather than to say or write "You are. . . ."

Sometimes you must make absolute statements. You must occasionally send "you" messages. Communication would otherwise degenerate into a sloppy, gooey, indeterminate mess, not unlike conversations that occur when a bunch of egoists get together to talk out a problem. When to be absolute and when to be tentative is up to you. It is a judgment call.

(E)mpathy

An important aspect of online communication is to:

1. *Put yourself in the shoes of your audience.* Always consider your online audience. There is a wide variety of issues to keep in mind. For example, a person can be a highly effective, intelligent contributor to an online group even if he or she misspells words or doesn't write well.

As noted previously, a wide range of cultural, contextual, and social issues affect the frame of reference people bring to online communication. Empathy also involves inquisitiveness. An idea we have always found to be helpful is to be inquisitive if you need information to better understand your audience. Ask a lot of questions if necessary. This need goes back to the inherent difficulty of invalid attributions and prototype formation in online communication.

To summarize this section, The WRITE Way to online communication involves communicating in a manner that is (W)arm, (R)esponsive, (I)nquisitive, (T)entative, and (E)mpathetic:

(W)armth means to:

◆ Use the telephone when necessary.

◆ Send sensitive information to private mailboxes.

◆ Incorporate warmth into text.

(R)esponsiveness means to:

◆ Set deadlines, or otherwise be consistent, in terms of when you give feedback.

◆ Remember to provide occasional reminders.

(I)nquisitiveness means to:

◆ Be sure to ask questions.

(T)entativeness means to:

◆ Use tentative language and posturing, unless the situation dictates otherwise.

(E)mpathy means to:

◆ Put yourself in the shoes of your audience.

Conclusion—
The Netiquette of Online Communication

Is there such a thing as proper "netiquette"? Yes, and it is a good thing, too! It is easy enough to use e-mail but, as you have seen, there is an art to communicating effectively online. We conclude this chapter with a few additional tips for making friends and influencing people online, and for avoiding unnecessary conflicts, or what we call "flames":

◆ *Keep your messages brief and to the point (unless it is a work assignment where your supervisor or teacher asks for important details and examples).* If you want to make sure people listen to what you have to say, do not bore and confuse them with rambling messages that tend to be skipped in favor of shorter messages that concentrate on one subject. Stick to the subject of that particular discussion.

◆ *If you are responding to a message, quote the relevant and specific passage or summarize it for those who may have missed it.* Do not make people guess about what you are talking about, especially if you are responding to a particular message. Highlight the message that you are responding to right up front (often with a symbol like >) and then follow with your response. One example:

> > What time do you want to meet tomorrow?
>
> Mike—2:00 pm will be fine. See you there! Sue

◆ Don't start a "flame war" unless you are willing to take the heat. Just as you shouldn't drive when you are angry, you should not send e-mail responses when you are mad at someone. Go ahead and type a response, but do not mail it until the next day. Chances are that when you come back later to read your response, you'll be glad that you did not send it.

◆ *Never copy someone else's writing without permission or citation.* Acknowledge your sources. Define the difference between what others have written and what you think. State your own contribution.

◆ *Don't clutter discussions with short "I agree " and "Me too!" messages.* It is very frustrating to find lots of messages with very little substance. Remember that e-mail communication can be "labor-intensive" and that it takes time to read numerous messages.

◆ *Don't type in all caps. (IT'S LIKE SHOUTING!)* You can do it once in a while for strong emphasis, but only for individual words.

◆ *Don't flame people for bad grammar or spelling errors.* Spelling and correct grammar are important, but online communication tends to be informal. Even though sloppy messages that are full of errors stick out, the principle of constructive feedback that says effective feedback is solicited should be followed.

Now go ahead and enjoy your electronic journey!